For a man who was John Calvin's assistant and successor, Theodore Beza is surprisingly little known. This book does us the great service of introducing the man in and through his major works. It is an excellent and much needed introduction to its subject and will be an first class resource for students, pastors and teachers alike.

GERALD BRAY,
Research Professor, Beeson Divinity School,
Samford University, Birmingham, Alabama

Well researched and well written, this is an important book about Beza based on a close reading of Beza. Beza emerges as a pivotal pastor-theologian who, despite his flaws, cared deeply about the Lord's church and from whom we can still learn today. A stellar contribution to Reformation studies and pastoral theology alike.

TIMOTHY GEORGE,
Founding Dean of Beeson Divinity School,
Samford University, Birmingham, Alabama

Shawn Wright is a rare gift of a careful historian with a pastor's heart. In this moving tribute on Beza, Wright captures the true man behind the myth and demonstrates why Beza should be both relevant as well as inspiring to the modern pastor. As I read these pages about this faithful man's life, I was freshly stirred to be a more faithful pastor.

BRIAN CROFT,
Pastor, Auburndale Baptist Church, Louisville, Kentucky
& Founder of Practical Shepherding

Theodore Beza is amazing and Shawn Wright's deep knowledge of the sources, both secondary and primary, is also. Wright knows just when to summarize and just when to quote. His style makes the book a pleasant and lovely reading experience. His thorough knowledge of Beza along with Wright's own instincts of pastoral sympathy help clear away much of the historiographical garbage that has accumulated around the legacy of Beza and made him a feared step-child of the Reformation. The discussion of predestination demonstrates without contradiction that Beza's deepest concern was, first, the glory of God, and, second (and fully concomitant with the first), a full submission to the biblical text. Beza had courage to follow out with detail and precision God's own explanation of the biblical narrative concerning his own just, gracious, holy, and inscrutable purposes. The genuinely pastoral purpose of Beza's doctrine is seen in his discussion of assurance, his attention to prayer, and his analysis of a Christian's stewardship of life and calling during a time of devastation like the plague. Wright gives us an open door to benefit from one of the truly great interpreters of Protestant Christianity, evangelical theology, and pastoral engagement at a doctrinal level. Not only do we have a profoundly helpful description and analysis of Beza's life and doctrine, but Wright's summary makes for a wonderful enchiridion of theology to give pure and unpolluted help in the pastoral task of speaking the truth in love.

Tom J. Nettles,
Senior Professor of Historical Theology,
The Southern Baptist Theological Seminary, Louisville, Kentucky

Theodore Beza
The Man and the Myth

Shawn D. Wright

To Benjamin and Bethany

The Lord bless you and keep you;
the Lord make his face shine upon you and be gracious to you;
the Lord turn his face toward you and give you peace.

(Num. 6:24-26)

Copyright © Shawn D. Wright 2015

paperback ISBN 978-1-78191-684-1
epub ISBN 978-1-78191-706-0
mobi ISBN 978-1-78191-707-7

10 9 8 7 6 5 4 3 2 1

Published in 2015
by
Christian Focus Publications Ltd,
Geanies House, Fearn, Ross-shire,
IV20 1TW, Great Britain.

www.christianfocus.com

Cover design by Daniel Van Straaten

Printed by Bell and Bain, Glasgow

All rights reserved. No part of this publication may be reproduced, stored in a retrieval system, or transmitted, in any form, by any means, electronic, mechanical, photocopying, recording or otherwise without the prior permission of the publisher or a licence permitting restricted copying. In the U.K. such licences are issued by the Copyright Licensing Agency, Saffron House, 6-10 Kirby Street, London, EC1 8TS www.cla.co.uk

CONTENTS

Preface 7

1 Introduction 9

2 Theodore Beza's Life and Context 15

3 Theodore Beza's Theological Vision 39

4 Summarizing the Faith 69
   — Theodore Beza's *Confession of the Christian Faith*

5 Letting God be God 111
   — Theodore Beza's *Tabula Praedestinationis*

6 Trusting God in Life's Difficulties 159
   — Theodore Beza's *Treatize of the Plague*

7 Struggling to Gain Assurance of Salvation 191
   — Theodore Beza's *Treatize of Comforting such as
   are Troubled about their Predestination*

8 Yearning for God 217
   — *Maister Bezaes Houshold Prayers*

9 Conclusion 255

Preface

The Lord has blessed me while I have worked on this project, and I would like to thank the various people He used to help make this book possible. The trustees of The Southern Baptist Theological Seminary granted me a half-sabbatical during which the writing of this book began. I was able to complete it on a subsequent half-sabbatical. It is a joy to serve at an institution which values pastoral scholarship, and I hope that this book represents that goal. My thanks to President R. Albert Mohler Jr and Dean Gregory Wills for supporting and encouraging this project. And my thanks to my students who continue to stoke in me the fire of the love of history, theology, and practical ministry.

At Christian Focus Publications, Willie Mackenzie has been supportive of this project from day one. Stephen Greenhalgh carefully edited the text. It's a joy to write for a publisher who is concerned with the intersection of truth and living.

For the sake of readers who may want to read Theodore Beza's works for themselves (a tremendous idea!), I have chosen to use English translations of the works I discuss. Those texts are noted in the footnotes and the conclusions of the following chapters. Two of the editions I used were from modern English translations. I would like to thank Reformation Heritage Books for permission to use their edition of Beza's *A Brief and Pithy Sum of Christian Faith*, which was published in *Reformed Confessions of the 16th and 17th Centuries in English*

Translation: Volume 2, 1552-1566. My thanks to editor James T. Dennison Jr for his work on this. I would also like to thank Philip C. Holtrop for allowing me to use his translation of Beza's *Tabula* found in his unpublished *The Potter and the Clay: The Main Predestination Writings of Theodore Beza*. I am eager to see the forthcoming publication of Dr Holtrop's multi-volume English translation of several of Beza's works.

Clifton Baptist Church is a wonderful church fellowship in which to see the Lord work. I have been able to experience many of the things Theodore Beza wrote about at Clifton over the years. I especially thank Tom Schreiner and John Kimbell for their faithful preaching of God's word over the years to me and my family. You have given me a big vision of how glorious our Lord is. And thanks as well to Oren Martin who continually provoked me to finish this book.

Of course my family deserves my thanks. I have had the privilege of being married to Gretchen for almost twenty-seven years at the time of the completion of this book. Every one of them has been a blessing I don't deserve. She has exemplified to me time and again what it means to live a life of trust in the Lord through both good times and bad. And she has always seen that Beza was worth spending time with. Thank you, Gretchen. My sons have continually reminded me that theology has to be practical if it is to be biblical. Thank you, Jonathan, Aaron, Nathan, and Stephen.

I have dedicated this book to my oldest son Benjamin and his wife Bethany. From his earliest days (in fact, even before he was born), I would sing Michael Card's rendition of Numbers 6:24-26 to Benjamin every night after praying for him. One of my greatest joys in life has come from seeing Benjamin embrace Christ and grow in love for Him. I thank the Lord for you, Benjamin and Bethany. I pray that more and more you would know and love the God whom Theodore Beza adored.

1
Introduction

'Theodore Beza? Who's he? Why should I care about him?' I can't tell you how many times I've been asked that question over the years. Ever since I first ran across him in my doctoral studies some fifteen years ago and developed some interest in him, that's what I've heard from people time and time again. (Or at least that's the way I've interpreted many a quizzical look when his name comes up.) That's a shame. Everyone knows something about Martin Luther (he nailed up the ninety-five theses and said some mean things about Jews) and John Calvin (he stressed predestination and burned a heretic in Geneva). Beyond that, they know some facts about Augustine of Hippo (he was embarrassed about sex) and Jonathan Edwards (he preached a sermon saying that God holds us over the pit of hell like a spider dangling on a string). And of course they're aware of Billy Graham and his role in evangelicalism in the twentieth century. But, Theodore Beza?, you ask, Who's he?

Well, I'm glad you asked. I'm taking the opportunity in the book to answer that question. In just a short period of time, you should be able to say a few things about this man who in his day was one of the luminaries of the Protestant world, who took the reins of the beleaguered Calvinistic movement after its namesake's death, and who influenced English-speaking Protestantism more than you might imagine. He may not have been a giant like Calvin, but he was certainly bigger than most of us are. He's worth getting to know. I hope you agree as you not only read my interpretation of Beza but also get acquainted with some of his more important works. Let me tell you why I think you will benefit from reading this book. That's another way of telling you why I'm writing it. Here are the three reasons.

In the first place, Theodore Beza's example of loving the Lord Jesus Christ and trusting Him in the midst of tremendous difficulties is worth our investigation. As believers struggle to hold onto the Lord's goodness in the turmoils of life, it is good for us to have the examples of other frail, sinful, weak-faithed believers who persevered. Beza did just this, and he did it in spite of severe hardship. Knowing some of the details of Beza's life story and seeing his attempts to solidify the faith against doctrinal attacks, as well as noting his perseverance in the faith, should inspire Christians to greater faithfulness today. The 1500s were not an easy century in which to live. No electricity or indoor plumbing. Rudimentary medicine and ill-conceived notions of hygiene. Add to that military attacks and resurgent Catholicism which was out to gain back souls and territory from the Protestants. Beza struggled through tumultuous times.

Additionally, for over a century now Beza has been regularly maligned by both historians and theologians. The usual tack has been to identify him as the change agent from John Calvin's biblical orientation to a philosophical and scholastic trajectory that led to 'Calvinism'. Calvin was good, or at least we appreciate the fact that he was trying to be biblical. But we know that Beza (even though we probably haven't even read one word of him!) was bad, or so it is claimed. He morphed Calvin's thought into a rigid, philosophical, non-biblical system. In the process of this gross over-generalization, however, Beza's theological and pastoral contributions have almost always been overlooked. The result has been a portrait of Beza that may make sense to his interpreters but which, in reality, is foreign to the man himself. His ideas and his actual words are almost never considered when making this assessment. In this book I hope to introduce you to the real Beza, not a figment of other people's imaginations.

Introduction

There is also the reality, in the third place, that we live in a time of a revival of interest in Calvinistic theology and history. What better way could there be to enter into the discussion of Calvinism than by reading about 'the Calvinist' himself? Given Beza's prominent role in the historical and theological rise of Calvinism, and given the fact that Beza has almost never been evaluated carefully enough in these discussions, this book should serve those wanting to better understand what Calvinism is all about. The answer might surprise you!

Before we jump into trying to understand Theodore Beza, let me lay out our plan. Chapter two will briefly place Beza in his historical context. He lived and breathed, prayed and preached in a particular setting. It will help us both to understand him better and to appreciate him more if we understand the times in which he lived and ministered. Following this historical introduction, chapter three will attempt to get into the mind and heart of Beza. Here I will try and lay out what I think Beza saw as the reason for all of his work, the thing that drove him to labor as he did. Chapter three will thus serve as a kind of theological introduction to Beza.

Next will follow the five main chapters of the book, each one dealing with a work of Theodore Beza that explains an important facet of his thinking. Chapter four will summarize Beza's *Confession*, a comprehensive treatise covering all of Christian theology. More importantly, we will see here that, according to Beza, the purpose of theology is to glorify God and to save sinners. The gospel is at the heart of Beza's theology. This is also true of the Bezan theology of predestination, to which we turn in the fifth chapter. Here we will interact with misconceptions of his thought and look in detail at a major apology for the doctrine of double predestination. As we'll notice, even here Beza doesn't move far away from the gospel, although he doesn't shy away from some of the harder truths for us to comprehend from Scripture. In this defense of predestination, Beza shows himself to be a pastor whose concern is for his readers. He eagerly helps them to apply this doctrine to their lives, especially trying to show them where they can find hope if they're worried about the reality of their salvation.

The sixth chapter follows logically from the fifth. It also has to do with facets of Beza's understanding of God's sovereignty and its interplay with true human responsibility. Here we will look at a unique treatise by Beza on the plague, known as the Black Death, which first appeared in Europe in the fourteenth century. The treatise specifically addresses the questions of whether or not the plague was contagious and whether or not Christians should flee when the plague struck. Beza pastorally, and masterfully, here deals with the intersection of God's providence and human choice. Chapter seven addresses a different issue that arose from consideration of Beza's doctrine of God's sovereignty. Could Christians have certainty of their salvation if God had chosen people for salvation and damnation before the creation of the world? Unwilling to leave people with no hope, Beza here pastorally and sensitively helped hurting Christians to gain assurance of salvation. Chapter eight completes our study of Beza's thought by listening in on him while he prayed. Beza composed a little book of prayers for his own use, and we will look at both his doctrine of prayer expressed here and some of his selected prayers. In hearing him pray, we will come to a fuller understanding of who Theodore Beza was. A short concluding chapter will help us to synthesize what we have seen in the book up to this point. Like Beza would want us to do, we will conclude especially by asking some questions of application.

There is certainly more that could be said about Beza. The endnotes will guide you to other works should you desire further interaction with this fascinating reformer. For a compilation of most of Beza's writings, you can consult a bibliography of most of his works put together by Frédéric Gardy and Alain Dufour.[1] In another book I have arranged a bibliography of most of Beza's

---

1. Frédéric Gardy and Alain Dufour, *Bibliographie des Oeuvres Théologiques, Littéraires, Historiques et Juridiques de Théodore de Bèze* (Geneva: Librairie Droz, 1960).

Introduction

works (including English translations alongside the original Latin and French versions) as well as a chronological listing of Beza's writings where I also tried to categorize them according to five different types (humanistic, polemical, doctrinal, biblical, and pastoral).[2]

Now, though, let's try to understand a little bit about who Theodore Beza was. Hopefully after reading this book you'll be able to differentiate the man from the myth.

---

2. Shawn D. Wright, *Our Sovereign Refuge: The Pastoral Theology of Theodore Beza* (Carlisle: Paternoster, 2004), pp. 235-9, 279-83.

2
Theodore Beza's
Life and Context

Before we launch into our examination of some significant works of Theodore Beza, we must attempt to understand something about him as a man. Several important advantages will flow out of this historical excursus. We will grasp the richness of his thought much better when we know the times in which he lived, who influenced him, what his theological training was, and the varied roles he had and the variety of works he wrote. It's a maxim of proper biblical exegesis that 'context is king'. The same can be said for historical study. Only when we understand something of Beza's context will we be freed from our prior presuppositions about him, presuppositions we blindly adopt from our culture and context. Understanding Beza's life and times will allow us to understand his thought more perceptively.

Another reason for this historical introduction is that it reminds us of a simple fact: Theodore Beza was a real human being who lived a real life in a really difficult time. Difficult, that is, if you like indoor plumbing and electricity, if you've come to appreciate antibiotics and aspirin, or if you relish not being attacked by armies and mobs for your faith. Like Calvin before him (Calvin was ten years older than Beza but died in 1564, forty-one years before Beza), Beza led an exciting life. He had a mistress, almost died from sickness, was burned in effigy, and knew kings and queens. Those are certainly out-of-the-ordinary occurrences, if not all things we'd want to emulate! Beza, like Calvin, had to flee France because of his new-found Protestant faith. He, like Calvin, suffered the encroachment of Catholics on the beleaguered city-state of Geneva. But he was different from Calvin as well. Beza was in Geneva when it was almost overrun by the Catholic Savoyards, for instance. Not only was he from a different socio-economic class than Calvin, but he played a different role than had his mentor. Calvin in a sense solidified the Reformed faith for his time with his *Institutes of the Christian Religion* (the final edition was published in 1559). To Beza, then, was left the almost herculean task of shoring up the Reformed churches after Calvin's death in the midst of revived Catholic apologetic efforts to win Protestants back to the 'true Church'. He bore the weight of keeping the Academy afloat and teaching students from throughout Europe, sometimes with little support from the city or other teachers. He traveled extensively to defend the Reformed faith (especially against Lutheran opponents) and worked tirelessly for the cause of the Reformed churches in France. France, in fact, was very near to his heart, as it always was to Calvin's. Unlike Calvin, Beza lived through the worst of the 'Wars of Religion' between Catholics and Protestants in France. He tried to influence the political climate so that Protestants would be treated more favorably than they had been, he experienced the repercussions of the St Bartholomew's Day massacre in 1572 that saw the slaughter of thousands of Protestants, and he served as the 'Father' to one of the rulers of France. And all the while Beza sought to love God, lead the church of Geneva, preach, teach, write, love his wife (in fact, he was married twice, as we shall see), shepherd the citizens of Geneva, and be a friend and mentor to his fellow pastors. If nothing else, we see in this short resumé of his life his true humanity. Warts and all, he was a real man. But his true humanity also makes his achievements that much more astounding. He is someone we can learn many lessons from.

Theodore Beza's Life and Context

Good biographies of Beza already exist, some more comprehensive than others.[1] Without trying to be comprehensive, then, we shall notice several aspects of his life that will help us to orient our study. We will see, first of all, his early life up until his exodus from France in 1548. Much is worthy of notice here—his social class and family, his education, his relationship to Wolmar and his mistress, his dissolute life, and his near death. Second, we shall see his growing relationship with Calvin while he served in Lausanne. Not only did Beza begin to teach theological students and write theology during this time, but he also fought some doctrinal struggles that showed his affinity to the thought of Calvin, who became a mentor to him during this time. In the third place, we will notice how Beza served alongside Calvin in Geneva in the final years of Calvin's life—both in the church and in the Geneva Academy—and the manner in which he upheld his mentor's legacy in the years to come. We will conclude by looking at Beza's resumé of interaction with France during the emergency of the wars of religion and also examine the whole scope of his literary output.

---

1. Complete biographical accounts include Henry Martyn Baird, *Theodore Beza: The Counsellor of the French Reformation, 1519-1605* (n.p., 1899; reprint, New York: Burt Franklin, 1970) and Paul-F. Geisendorf, *Théodore de Bèze* (Geneva: Alexandre Jullien, 1967). I have also consulted these shorter studies: John L. Farthing, 'Beza, Theodore (1519-1605),' in *Historical Handbook of Major Biblical Interpreters*, ed. Donald K. McKim (Downers Grove, IL: InterVarsity Press, 1998), pp. 153-7; Scott M. Manetsch, *Calvin's Company of Pastors: Pastoral Care and the Emerging Reformed Church, 1536-1609* (Oxford: Oxford University Press, 2013); Richard A. Muller, 'Theodore Beza (1519-1605),' in *The Reformation Theologians: An Introduction to Theology in the Early Modern Period*, ed. Carter Lindberg (Oxford: Blackwell, 2002), pp. 213-24; Jill Raitt, 'Theodore Beza, 1519-1605,' in *Shapers of Religious Traditions in Germany, Switzerland, and Poland, 1560-1600*, ed. Jill Raitt (New Haven and London: Yale University Press, 1981), pp. 89-104; Jill Raitt, 'Bèze, Théodore de,' in *Oxford Encyclopedia of the Reformation*, ed. Hans J. Hillerbrand (Oxford: Oxford University Press, 1996), vol. 1, pp. 149-51.

Theodore Beza

All of this will remind us that Theodore Beza was a sixteenth-century, hard-working, French nobleman who did yeoman's work in stabilizing the Reformed faith in the later part of the century against attacks both internal and external. Was he perfect? Absolutely not! Is he someone worth getting to know? Yes!

'Baptized Dieudonné de Besze, Theodorus Beza Vezellii, as he often signed his Latin works, was born on June 24, 1519, at Vézelay, France.'[2] Dieudonné, and its Greek equivalent, Theodore, means 'gift of God'. Perhaps his parents felt that described their seventh, and last child, upon his baptism as an infant in the Catholic church. Whatever the case, he grew to be a true divine gift not only for the church of Geneva but for many who looked to him for guidance and encouragement throughout Protestant Europe in the tumultuous second half of the sixteenth century. Born in a time of intense socio-economic stratification in Europe, Theodore was privileged to be born to a family of the lower nobility in France. He had well-to-do relatives who used their influence to seek his betterment. His father, Pierre de Bèze, was the king's bailiff in the district of Vézelay, in Burgundy, a district about 140 miles southeast of Paris. His uncles also occupied prominent positions. One, Nicholas, was a member of the Parlement in Paris and another, Claude, was an abbot of a Cistercian monastery. Theodore was a sickly boy and was taken as a child to Paris where Nicholas helped him to receive a fine education. The boy never saw his mother again as she died soon after his departure.

Not much is known of Beza's early childhood. His privileged status continued when, in December of 1528, as a nine-year-old, he was sent to Orléans, where he studied under the tutelage of a German humanist scholar named Melchior Wolmar. One can only imagine the kind of damage that could be done to a little boy were he to be placed under the care of an evil man. In God's good providence, however, Wolmar was a good man.

---

2. Raitt, 'Theodore Beza, 1519-1605,' p. 89.

In fact, he was one of the few men in France at that time who embraced the Protestant faith.

Wolmar, who had been a student of such French humanist luminaries as William Budé and Jacques Lefèvre d'Etaples, taught the boy well. Beza mastered Latin and learned Greek under his instruction, so much so in fact, that he became one of the greatest Latinists of Europe during his lifetime.[3] 'Humanism' should not be misconstrued to be secular—as opposed to religious—in its orientation. It was, rather, an intellectual movement of the last hundred or so years that was intent on going back to the ancient literary sources of Greece and Rome in order to promote virtuous individuals and sane societies. For this reason there were Catholic humanists such as Desiderius Erasmus just as there were Protestants like John Calvin and Theodore Beza who subscribed to this form of education.[4] Beza's love for languages would manifest itself in numerous ways in the following years, most evidently in his New Testament translation and *Annotations*. Wolmar impacted this young man greatly.

Were it not for Wolmar's influence on Beza in another way, though, you would probably not be reading this book. Wolmar influenced his student to think about and embrace the Protestant faith. Wolmar, in fact, had already led another of his students, John Calvin, to abandon Rome for the evangelical faith. At some time during his long stay with Wolmar, Beza

---

3. John S. Bray, *Theodore Beza's Doctrine of Predestination* (Nieuwkoop: B. De Graaf, 1975), p. 30.

4. When he became an educator, Beza still thought that a humanistic curriculum centered on the ancient Greek and Latin authors in their original works was the best means of educating young men, even those who were preparing for Christian ministry. See, for example, his address to the Academy on the occasion of his assuming the post of Rector of the Geneva Academy. 'Beza's Address at the Solemn Opening at the Academy of Geneva,' trans. Lewis W. Spitz, in *Transition and Revolution: Problems and Issues of European Renaissance and Reformation History*, ed. Robert M. Kingdon (Minneapolis: Burgess, 1974), pp. 175-9.

embraced the gospel. Later, Beza noted that it was his reading of a little treatise by the Zurich reformer Heinrich Bullinger, *De origine erroris*, while he was in Wolmar's charge that convinced him of Protestantism. This work showed Rome's errors in its doctrines of the saints and the Mass. Beza considered Wolmar his father in the faith, referring to December 9, 1528, as his 'second birthday' because that was the day he went to live with Wolmar in Orléans. Beza was tutored by Wolmar for over six years. Certainly Beza was influenced even more in this direction when, in 1530, he moved with Wolmar to the University of Bourges, where several scholars who were attracted to the French Reformation cause congregated. There they were under the protection of Marguerite d'Angoulême.

In a dedication to Wolmar in a 1558 treatise Beza explained the tremendous spiritual impact that Wolmar had on him. Beza celebrated his going to live with Wolmar because 'that day was in my case the beginning of all the good things which I have received from that time forward and which I trust to receive hereafter in my future life.'[5] Further recounting the manner in which Wolmar led him to faith in Christ, Beza heaped praise on his German tutor: 'It was, however, by far the greatest of the benefits I received at your hands, that you so imbued me with the knowledge of true piety sought in the knowledge of the Word of God, as in the most limpid fountain, that I should be the most ungrateful and churlish of men did I not cherish and honour you, I say not as an instructor but as a parent.'[6]

In 1535, when Beza was fifteen years old, Wolmar left France for the more religiously-comfortable post of teaching in Tübingen, Germany. At his father's request, Beza entered the University of Orléans to study law. Unlike twentieth-century law students, Beza was not required to memorize vast amounts of case law. Legal studies in the sixteenth century were

---

5. Theodore Beza, 'Autobiographical Letter of Beza to Wolmar,' trans. Baird, *Theodore Beza*, p. 359.
6. Beza, 'Autobiographical Letter,' p. 360.

more about learning to read old texts and to express oneself persuasively in print and in speaking. Just like Calvin before him, Beza's study of law would eventually serve him well in his role as a reformer, teacher, and pastor.

By 1539 Beza completed his law degree and moved to Paris where he began practicing civil law. This was to be his stepping stone to a future role in politics, his father hoped. But his heart was not in it. Rather, Beza was enamored with the life of the literary elite in Paris. Receiving his father's permission to abandon the practice of law, Beza devoted himself to the reading and writing, especially, of poetry. His father probably allowed this because of the belief that Beza could become a member of parliament in the near future. Out of this time came his collection of Latin love poems, *Poemata*, which would later be fuel for no little ridicule by Beza's Catholic detractors. Later, when Beza edited them for re-publication, he removed the more scandalous poems of his youth.

Beza was only able to live during this period of no employment due to his family's connections. He received the income of at least one benefice—money given to a local parish church. Beza, in effect, served as a type of absentee priest. When his brother Audebert died in 1542, Beza added at least a second benefice, that of Saint-Eloi-lès-Longjumeau. The money that he received from the Catholic church, as well as the dissolute life he was leading as a proto-Parisian bohemian, served as a temptation to him and the Protestant faith he had embraced under Wolmar. He also struggled with marital desires, desires that were not consonant with his Catholic income. So he did something scandalous. He took as a mistress, or at least entered into a clandestine marital contract with, Claudine Denosse. 'In order not to be vanquished by evil desires,' he wrote, 'I married, but secretly, telling only two or three friends who shared my convictions. I married secretly both to avoid scandal and in order not to lose that cursed money which I received from my benefices. But I did it with the formal promise that as soon as I could, having rejected all obstacles, I would take my wife into the Church of God and there confirm my marriage openly. Meanwhile I would not take any of the sacred orders of the papists.'[7] We come face to face here with the humanity, and the frailty, of Theodore Beza. Theodore and Claudine would live happily together for forty years of encouraging life, she preceding him in death childless.

Beyond these few facts, we know little about Beza's early life. Some have spoken of the years 1539-1548, which correspond to Beza's time in Paris after obtaining his law degree, as a kind of 'parenthesis' in his life. But the Lord was not through with him.

The year 1548 was not only significant for Beza as the year his *Poemata* were published. This year he also almost died from a sickness that had him bedridden for some time. This shook Beza up and brought him back to his senses, reminding him of the eternal realities he had embraced previously, under the influence of Wolmar. As Richard Muller remarks, the change was quite drastic: 'Quite abruptly, Beza gave up his ecclesiastical income and left for Geneva. Once there, he identified with the Protestant cause, married Claudine (who had been living with him as his mistress), and turned his literary skills toward the task of reform.'[8] Beza's life would never be the same.

The French government looked askance at the Protestant cause, presaging the trials that would come for evangelicals there in the decades to come. Jill Raitt points out that 'France, however, would not let her promising young humanist go so lightly. On April 3, 1549, parlement decreed Beza an outlaw and confiscated his goods, and on May 31, 1550, it ordered him burned in effigy and confiscated his goods, the latter sentence lifted only in 1564 when he had become a diplomat of considerable importance.'[9] Beza would have many dealings

---

7. Quoted in Geisendorf, *Théodore de Bèze*, pp. 26-7; trans. in Raitt, 'Theodore Beza, 1519-1605,' p. 90.
8. Muller, 'Theodore Beza (1519-1605),' p. 215.
9. Raitt, 'Theodore Beza, 1519-1605,' pp. 90-1.

with France in the future, but he never went there or negotiated with them as a citizen of France. He was a Genevan, not a Frenchman; a Huguenot, not a Catholic.

Therefore, in 1548 Theodore Beza found himself in Geneva, Switzerland. The Protestant reform there had been going on for more than a decade, first under the leadership of Guillaume Farel and now guided by John Calvin. Calvin was the bright light of the French Protestant movement, having made his mark as the author of the *Institutes of the Christian Religion*. By 1548 he had already revised and lengthened it twice (1539 and 1543) from the first edition of 1536. He had also made his mark as a commentator, a preacher, and a polemicist of no mean account. Beza knew of him and wanted to work with him. There was, however, no work available for Beza in Geneva. So he waited until, finally, a position opened up in Lausanne, a Protestant city on the north shore of Lake Geneva (Lac Léman in French). In this Swiss city, under the authority of Berne, resided Pierre Viret, a friend of Calvin. Viret asked Beza to come and aid the reform efforts in Lausanne, especially taking a role as instructor in the Academy there. Beza eagerly consented.

So, in November of 1550, a new phase in the life of Theodore Beza began. Arriving in Lausanne, he began teaching Greek and the New Testament in the Academy (eventually serving as its rector), aided Viret in leading the church, and (as a self-identified Protestant) started producing treatises that would strengthen the Reformation cause. In fact, his literary output was quite significant in the 1550s.

Before we look at some of his most important works from this decade we should pause to note an important fact. Up to this point, Theodore Beza had no formal theological training. Like Calvin, his training was in the language-heavy, text-saturated humanist tradition. He read books in Latin and Greek and wrote well. He hadn't studied the intricate theological and philosophical differences between two of the most prominent medieval Catholic theologians, Thomas Aquinas and Duns Scotus, for example, at the University of Paris which was the great center of Catholic theological training. Others have noted that Calvin may have only had a year or so of formal theological training. Beza had even less—none. This should make us wary of quickly labeling his work 'scholastic' and discounting his conclusions as somehow obviously unbiblical. He possessed an agile mind, one that was eager to understand and express ideas lucidly. But whatever 'scholastic' tendencies he had were not ingrained in his educational training. His dearth of formal theological training should also make us ponder the fact that he became one of the great Reformed theologians of the sixteenth century. The Lord uses people like Beza who know how to read and understand the Scripture. He used Theodore Beza for this reason.

Some of Beza's early works deserve comment, for they show that he definitely had a humanist's bent towards the proficient understanding and use of language. They also display the humanist's bent to persuasive polemics. Before moving to Lausanne, Beza published *Abraham sacrifiant*, a drama about Abraham's near-sacrifice of his son Isaac. Here he highlighted the differences between Catholic works-righteousness and the biblical teaching that Christians are justified by faith alone. The year 1554 saw the publication of *Concerning the Punishment of Heretics by the Civil Magistrate*, a defense of Geneva's execution of Michael Servetus for heresy in 1553, an event that was gaining much attention (a lot of it negative) for Calvin and the Protestant cause. That year he also saw to the press his Greek handbook, *Alphabetum Graecum*. The year 1555 saw the publication of a work that would gain a great deal of attention, the *Tabula praedestinationis*, his defense of double predestination.[10] The following year there appeared the first edition of what many consider Beza's most important work, the *Annotations of the New Testament*. This linguistic masterpiece included, in columns, the Greek text, the Latin Vulgate, and Beza's own Latin translation. To the main text he

---

10. We will notice Beza's treatment of double predestination in chapter 5.

appended textual footnotes and his own explanations of the meaning of the text. Beza re-worked this volume several times over the course of his life, and it influenced not only future translations of the New Testament but also the way in which the text was understood. For instance, scholars see the influence of the *Annotations* in the 1560 English *Geneva Bible* (which had a tremendous impact on the English Puritan movement) and the 1611 *Authorized Version*, the King James Bible which continues to aid English-speaking Christians in their biblical insight.[11] The year 1558 marked the publication of another very important work for the young scholar, his *Confession of Faith*, a short comprehensive account of the Christian faith written to persuade his father of the Protestant faith.

We already have a vision, then, of the greatness of Theodore Beza. Just to write one of these works might have been enough to mark him out as a significant French Protestant leader of the later Reformation. But to have written three very different, and extremely influential, works (the *Tabula*, the *Annotations*, and the *Confession*) within three years of each other is nothing less than extraordinary. Each different from the others, they show us that Beza was a multifaceted thinker and writer. No wonder that John Calvin took positive notice of his young friend.

Before Beza went to work with Calvin in Geneva, though, he took part in several trips in order to serve different persecuted groups. The year 1557 was a full year of this activity. He embarked, for example, on a trip with Farel to organize help for Waldensians who were suffering in France. Other excursions took him to Berne, Zurich, Basel, Schaffhausen, Strasbourg, Montbéliard, Baden, and Göppingen. Towards the end of the year he visited Strasbourg and Worms to convince the German Lutherans to join the Swiss in protesting French persecution of the Huguenots.

---

11. See Farthing, 'Beza,' pp. 153-4; Irena Doruta Backus, *The Reformed Roots of the English New Testament: The Influence of Theodore Beza on the English New Testament* (Pittsburgh: Pickwick, 1980).

Furthermore, 1558 was a year of transition for Beza. The situation in Lausanne had always been tense because the Bernese exercised political control there. And the Bernese (who were Protestant) did not approve of some of Calvin's theology, especially his stance on double predestination. Beza had already come out in print defending specifically this doctrine of Calvin in the *Tabula* against Jérome Bolsec, who, after fleeing Geneva, found protection in Berne! It seemed like a good time to leave Berne. So, when Calvin invited him to Geneva, he went immediately. As Raitt comments, 'both Beza and Viret were suffering at Lausanne under the heavy hand of Bern, which did not appreciate their outspoken advocacy of Calvin and the Genevan church.'[12]

Because Calvin approved of Beza's work and appreciated the friendship the two of them had developed over the last decade, the Genevan reformer invited his younger friend to become professor of Greek at the new Geneva Academy, soon to be followed by the position of rector there. As Muller notes, 'The appointment marks not only Beza's transfer of residence to Geneva but also the beginning of his work as the primary assistant and, ultimately, the successor of Calvin.'[13] Surely Calvin would not have done this had he not been convinced of Beza's like-mindedness theologically, a fact that will influence how we read the *Tabula* below, since that treatise was published three years prior to Beza's move to Geneva.

Thus began a fast friendship that would grow over the next five years until Calvin's death on May 27, 1564, at the age of fifty-five. Calvin loved Beza, and the younger man adored his mentor in the faith. 'I would be very cold-hearted,' Calvin once wrote, 'if I did not care deeply for Beza, who loves me more than a brother and honors me more than a father.'[14]

---

12. Raitt, 'Theodore Beza, 1519-1605,' p. 92.

13. Muller, 'Theodore Beza (1519-1605),' p. 215.

14. In Manetsch, *Calvin's Company of Pastors*, p. 38.

Theodore Beza's Life and Context

In Geneva, during Calvin's life, Beza had several roles. He continued, of course, publishing. His two most significant works in this time were his *Response* to Sebastian Castellio, a long-time opponent of Calvin, and his completed work of the French Psalter in 1561. The French metrical translation of the Psalms had begun in 1533 by Clément Marot who labored on it for the next decade. Calvin tried his hand at it, but he was no poet. Beza was, and he completed what would become a powerful tool in the hands of Reformed Protestants at worship as well as of the French Huguenots marching to battle against Catholic armies. According to John Farthing, for example, 'Beza's rendering of Psalm 68 became "the Huguenot battle song"'.[15] Huguenots fought while singing the psalms. And the Calvinists of Geneva and France were known as great singers, largely due to Beza's work in finishing this book which came out in more than sixty editions by 1565.

The transition from the leadership of Calvin to Beza brought many new responsibilities to the younger man, who assumed the mantle of responsibility at the age of forty-five. According to Muller, 'After Calvin's death, Beza assumed Calvin's role as the primary teacher of theology in the Geneva Academy, leader and moderator of the Company of Pastors, and advisor to the Huguenots in France. He continued to defend the Genevan position in polemics, responding to the last of Calvin's Eucharistic adversaries, Tilemann Hesshusius and Joachim Westphal, and continuing the debate with Johannes Brenz, Nicolaus Selnecker, and Jakob Andreä.'[16]

On his deathbed, Calvin made Beza his successor in leadership. Beza became the 'Moderator of the Venerable Company of Pastors of Geneva' until 1580. Much of Beza's time, then, was spent in coordinating the pastoral ministry in

---

15. Farthing, 'Beza,' p. 153. Also see W. Stanford Reid, 'The Battle Hymns of the Lord: Calvinist Psalmody of the Sixteenth Century,' *Sixteenth Century Journal* 2 (1971), pp. 36-54.

16. Muller, 'Theodore Beza (1519-1605),' p. 216.

the growing city of Geneva, which was often being flooded with refugees from the wars of religion in France. He also preached regularly, leading him to publish several treatises in his final decades that flowed out of his teaching and preaching ministries in the church.[17] Unlike Calvin, who confessed on his deathbed that he had always struggled with anger and pride, Beza was known for his humility.[18] Of course, this was a boon for his ministry and for his relationships with fellow pastors and parishioners. Unfortunately for the church in Geneva, though, Beza's character did not result in greater influence for the church in the city's politics over the course of Beza's life. Rather, the opposite was true.

The relation between the church and the government in Geneva had never been easy. Calvin had to fight against what he thought were ungodly political intrusions into the moral life of the city until finally he saw allies elected to the city's council in 1555. The last decade or so of his life, then, was the only period of his life when his friends exercised control over the city's politics.[19] Beza was not the same man as Calvin, and the church's influence in Geneva eroded during his later life. At times he felt like the local politicians were overstepping their authority in matters of morals so much that he threatened to resign from his position within the church. He felt it was only the church—not the city council—that should speak to issues of dress, behavior at parties, Sunday recreations, the prices of grain when food was stretched, and interest rates, among other issues. Raitt notes that 'after Calvin's death, the magistrates began the slow alteration of that balance in their favor, and Beza did not wish to dominate Geneva as had Calvin.' Beza refused to serve as moderator of the Company of Pastors for life (as Calvin

---

17. See Jill Raitt, 'Beza, Guide for the Faithful Life,' *Scottish Journal of Theology* 39 (1986), pp. 83-107.
18. See Manetsch, *Calvin's Company of Pastors*, pp. 63-5, 303.
19. E. William Monter, *Calvin's Geneva* (New York: John Wiley and Sons, 1967; reprint, Huntington, NY: Robert E. Kreiger, 1975).

had done). He made the moderator's position one that was filled annually by election of the pastors. Indeed, 'Beza made no objection to being given a lower seat on the council than Calvin had had, nor did he object to the reversal of precedence on civic occasions when the magistrates walked ahead of the pastors.' Again, Raitt helpfully notes that 'the Ordinances of Geneva bound the pastors to obey the magistrates, who, in turn, vowed to obey the Gospel. The interpreters of the gospel were the pastors, who believed they had the duty of correcting the moral behavior of all residents of Geneva. Here the conflict began.'[20] Beza and the other pastors felt obligated to denounce ungodly behavior from the pulpit, even if it meant stepping on council members' toes. They, of course, were not eager to be reprimanded. The last decades of Beza's life saw the church's power decrease while the magistrates' authority grew. For most of his life, a balance of sorts was maintained, but as Beza advanced in age and became more tired, the city magistrates exercised more and more control over the pastors.[21] By 1600 it had swung in favor of the magistrates.[22]

Perhaps one of the reasons that Calvin was initially drawn to Beza was because of their common French heritage. They were also united in their on-going concern for their countrymen. Towards the end of his life, Calvin had urged the Genevans to send French-speaking church planters to France to bring the gospel there and to pastor Protestants who had fled the Roman church, even though there was a high likelihood of persecution if they were discovered. The success of these zealous young men was monumental. Robert Kingdon recounts the manner in which Calvin's Geneva sent out men, starting to be recorded in the records of the pastors in 1555. 'Between 1555 and 1563,' he notes, 'the "Register of the Company of Pastors" records

---

20. Raitt, 'Theodore Beza, 1519-1605,' p. 102.
21. Manetsch, *Calvin's Company of Pastors*, p. 179.
22. Raitt, 'Theodore Beza, 1519-1605,' p. 102.

some 88 missionaries sent, but this is only a partial number for the registers are incomplete.'[23] The growth of Protestantism in France due to this influx of church planters was phenomenal. Pierre Courthial charts the course of the growth of Calvinism during this period: 'In 1555 there were five organized Reformed churches in France; in 1559, the year the first national synod assembled in Paris, there were nearly 100; and by 1562 they numbered 2,150.'[24] The explosive growth was done at the behest of the Genevan church leaders, first Calvin and then Beza.[25] Beza had a heart for his homeland.[26]

Not only did Beza have a heart for his homeland, but he was actively involved in promoting the cause of Protestantism there by journeying to France several times and seeking to influence its leaders to make decisions that would benefit the Protestants.[27] Unlike Calvin, Beza lived to see the intense heat

---

23. Robert M. Kingdon, *Geneva and the Coming of the Wars of Religion in France 1555-1563* (Geneva: Librairie Droz, 1956), p. 14.

24. Pierre Courthial, 'The Golden Age of Calvinism in France,' in *John Calvin: His Influence in the Western World*, ed. W. Stanford Reid (Grand Rapids: Zondervan, 1982), p. 77.

25. This should put to rest the erroneous view that 'Calvinism' doesn't do missions and evangelism. It does, and it certainly did. See also Philip Benedict, *Christ's Churches Purely Reformed: A Social History of Calvinism* (New Haven: Yale University Press, 2002), pp. 127-48; Michael A. G. Haykin and C. Jeffrey Robinson Sr., *To The Ends of the Earth: Calvin's Missional Vision and Legacy* (Wheaton, IL: Crossway, 2014).

26. Robert M. Kingdon, *Geneva and the Consolidation of the French Protestant Movement 1564-1572: A Contribution to the History of Congregationalism, Presbyterianism, and Calvinist Resistance Theory* (Madison: University of Wisconsin Press, 1967), and Scott M. Manetsch, *Theodore Beza and the Quest for Peace in France, 1572-1598* (Leiden: Brill, 2000).

27. Short but helpful overviews of the French Wars of Religion are found in J. H. M. Salmon, 'Wars of Religion,' *The Oxford Encyclopedia of the Reformation*, ed. Hans J. Hillerbrand (New York: Oxford University Press, 1996), 3:258-63; and Jeannine Olson, 'The Cradle of Reformed Theology: The Reformed Churches from Calvin's Geneva through Henry IV and the Edict of Nantes,' in *The Theology of the French Reformed*

of persecution decimate the French Protestants, and, in many ways, he served as their counselor during this difficult time. His diplomatic–theological ministry there started when he went to the colloquy held at Poissy in 1561 to represent the French and Swiss Reformed. This gathering of Catholic and Protestant leaders was called to figure out if there might be a way for the two groups to come to some rapprochement. All seemed to be going well until they got to the topic of the Lord's Supper, which was one of the most debated topics of the sixteenth century. There was no way around the differences between the two approaches to the eucharist. No reconciliation happened. At Catherine de Medici's request, Beza stayed in France after the end of the colloquy in the hope that he might help to effect an agreement between the two sides. When the 'Wars of Religion' between Catholics and Protestants in France began, Beza was there. He encouraged and sought to influence Protestant nobility who were leading the war efforts, represented the Reformed at the Colloquy of Saint-Germain in 1562, and finally returned to Geneva after a truce was negotiated at the Peace of Amboise in 1563. For over a year and a half Beza had served the Protestant cause in France, demonstrating his love for his homeland and making his literary accomplishments during this period that much more impressive.

Two other incidents having to do with France are worth noting, both of which occurred after Calvin's death. This reminds us that even though Beza was similar to his mentor in many ways, they were unique men living in unique times. After having presided over the French Reformed church's national synods at La Rochelle in 1571 (where he was able to lead the church to adopt Calvinistic language about the eucharist in the 'Gallican Confession' that the assembly ratified), Beza lived through one of the most difficult times French Protestants

---

Churches: From Henri IV to the Revocation of the Edict of Nantes, ed. Martin I. Klauber (Grand Rapids: Reformation Heritage, 2014), pp. 9-23.

had ever endured, the Saint Bartholomew's Day Massacre of August 1572.

This horrific event deserves our attention because of Beza's heightened response to it.[28] Beza lamented the mob violence because of its destruction of those he loved, out of fear that it would boil over into Geneva, and because it dashed all hopes of Protestant success in his beloved France. Until that time, Protestants' hopes for their fortunes in France were bright. Robert Kingdon wrote that 'the two years stretching from the Peace of St Germain, signed in August of 1570, to the massacres of St Bartholomew's, perpetrated in August of 1572, were probably the most halcyon in all of history for those French Protestants who looked to Geneva for guidance.'[29]

Beza's influence in France, in particular, was great. He traveled to La Rochelle in 1571, where he acted as the chairman of the Reformed churches' synod there. He also attended the synod at Nîmes the following year, though as a regular delegate this time.[30] The French Protestants were growing in number and influence, with Geneva functioning as their spiritual leader.[31] After the St Bartholomew's Day slaughter of thousands of Protestants, including several leading Protestant noblemen, by Catholic mobs throughout France, Protestantism never regained its footing in the country. Although the tragedy began as an organized action in Paris on 23 August, it evolved into mob outbursts against the Huguenots throughout much of France and lasted for several days. The Protestant cause in France suffered a debilitating blow.[32]

---

28. My discussion of the Saint Bartholomew's Day Massacre is adapted from Wright, *Our Sovereign Refuge*, pp. 9-10, 136-7.
29. Kingdon, *Geneva and Consolidation*, p. 193.
30. Kingdon, *Geneva and Consolidation*, pp. 194, 197.
31. Scott M. Manetsch, 'Theodore Beza and the Quest for Peace in France, 1572-1598,' (Ph.D. diss., University of Arizona, 1997), pp. 62-3.
32. Mark Greengrass, *The French Reformation* (Oxford: Basil Blackwell, 1987), p. 79.

Beza was distraught at the death and destruction.³³ He 'struggled between hope and despair,' according to Scott Manetsch, 'clinging anxiously to the reports delivered by the hundreds of refugees filling Geneva's streets. "Daily I receive news from the farthest corners of France that those whom I thought safe have been killed; by contrast, I have been overjoyed to learn that some—but so very few—have survived whom I had given up for dead. O, how happy we would be if very soon we might be numbered among so many blessed martyrs!"'³⁴ Writing to German Protestants on 4 September 1572, Beza said, 'One thing only consoles me, the hope that my future life will be but brief, so that I may soon draw nearer to my God.'³⁵ Kingdon observed about Beza that 'if his correspondence provides any index, he was never, in his entire tumultuous life, so near to real despair as in the first days after news of the massacres reached Geneva.'³⁶

Not only did Beza lament the deaths of his brethren, but he also thought the massacre was part of a Catholic plot to stamp out Protestantism in French-speaking lands, a plot that would sweep into Geneva. Beza saw behind the massacre an organized, and evil, Catholic plan. At that time he wrote to Heinrich Bullinger in Zurich: 'This is perhaps the last letter I will ever write to you. For it is abundantly clear that these massacres are the unfolding of a universal conspiracy. Assassins are seeking to kill me, and I contemplate death more

---

33. For a helpful summary of Beza's attitude at this time, along with excerpts from his letters, see Geisendorf, *Théodore de Bèze*, pp. 306-8.

34. Theodore Beza, *Correspondance de Théodore de Bèze, 1572*, eds H. Aubert, A. Dufour, F. Aubert, H. Meylan, and C. Chimelli (Geneva: Librairie Droz, 1988), 13:190; translated in Manetsch, 'Theodore Beza,' p. 58.

35. Alastair Duke, Gillian Lewis, and Andrew Pettegree, eds and trans, *Calvinism in Europe 1540-1610: A Collection of Documents* (Manchester: Manchester University Press, 1992), p. 113.

36. Kingdon, *Geneva and Consolidation*, p. 200; also see Geisendorf, *Théodore de Bèze*, pp. 306-9.

than life.'[37] The Catholic triumph over the Huguenots filled Beza with a bleak outlook for the viability of Protestantism in France. For the rest of the decade and into the 1580s, he did not think that the Huguenots had any future in his homeland.[38] Even though the Edict of Nantes (1598) provided some relief, Protestantism would never flourish in France again.

The events surrounding the St Bartholomew's Day Massacre led Beza to write one of his most influential treatises. He published *The Right of Magistrates* in 1574. The question of the right of the populace to rebel against an evil ruler had long plagued Christian Europe. The almost universal belief was the 'divine right' of monarchy, the belief that a monarch reigned at God's behest and was therefore subject to divine authority alone. No earthly person or persons could oppose his rule. After the events of 1572, though, Beza questioned the legitimacy of this long-held view in *The Right of Magistrates*. The book's claim was so scandalous at the time that the Genevan authorities wouldn't allow it to be published in their city. Beza published it anonymously in Lyons, France. According to Raitt:

> [The treatise's] thesis was that all authority, including the authority of the French king, comes from God through election by the people. Kings remain responsible to the people, and if they abuse their authority by playing the tyrant, the people may rise up under the leadership of their elected magistrates. Calvin had counseled passive resistance; most political theory of the time required that a justified revolt must nevertheless be led by princes of the blood royal. Bèze removed both of those requirements for justified rebellion.[39]

---

37. Beza, *Correspondance*, 13:179; translated in Manetsch, *Theodore Beza*, p. 34.
38. Manetsch, *Theodore Beza*, p. 116.
39. Raitt, 'Bèze, Théodore de,' p. 150.

Beza's ideas of rightful rebellion would impact not only Europe but the colonies of England in America.

As we saw above, after 1572 Protestant hopes in France were dashed. Beza, however, still had some influence there in the person of Henry of Navarre, who became King Henry IV of France in 1594. Henry famously converted from Protestantism to Catholicism, saying 'Paris is worth a mass', in order to be able to take the throne. A Protestant would never reign in France. But Henry held Beza in high regard due to Beza's friendship of him and his mother, Jeanne of Navarre, when he was a boy. For instance, in 1600 Henry led his troops in a campaign against Savoy. He camped close to Geneva and sent word that he would like Beza to visit him. Even though the eighty-one-year-old Genevan reformer was sick in bed, he got up and rode out on horseback to greet the French king. On seeing him, Henry called Beza 'Father' as he had since his childhood at Nérac.[40]

In the decades following the St Bartholomew's Day Massacre Beza continued his writing ministry at a frantic pace. For posterity he edited his major theological works, which were released as the *Tractationes theologicae* in three volumes between 1570 and 1582. The 1570s also saw the publication of his *Little Book of Christian Questions and Responses*, a fascinating in-depth catechism of the Christian faith, which became one of Beza's most popular works.[41] In 1575 Beza's *Little Catechism* was printed. In this book, as he had almost twenty years earlier with his *Confession*, Beza showed both his dependence on Calvin and his willingness to chart new paths. He felt that

---

40. Raitt, 'Theodore Beza, 1519-1605,' p. 93. Manetsch masterfully traces Beza's involvement in the French Wars of Religion in Scott M. Manetsch, 'Theodore Beza (1519-1605) and the Crisis of Reformed Protestantism in France,' in *The Theology of the French Reformed Churches: From Henri IV to the Revocation of the Edict of Nantes*, ed. Martin I. Klauber (Grand Rapids: Reformation Heritage, 2014), pp. 24-56; a full-length study is Mack P. Holt, *The French Wars of Religion, 1562-1629* (Cambridge: Cambridge University Press, 1995).

41. See Wright, *Our Sovereign Refuge*, pp. 126-30.

Calvin's lengthy catechism was too long to be useful, so he composed his smaller one for the use of the Genevan church.[42] Beza also came back to his hugely influential New Testament work, the *Annotations*. Originally published in 1556, the book was released in new, expanded editions in 1582, 1589, and 1598. Muller notes the influence of this book: 'Given the wide use of the *Annotationes* both in Beza's own time and in the seventeenth century, together with the use of Beza's Greek text both by Stephanus in Geneva and by Elzevir in Leiden (in what became known as the *Textus receptus*), this was certainly Beza's most influential work.'[43]

This period of his life also saw the publication of several works Beza devoted to Scripture. His publications included those on Job, the Psalms, Ecclesiastes, and the Song of Songs. The first of these, his work on Job, is especially noteworthy because of the historical situation that called it forth. Beza began lecturing on Job (which would become the published work) in January of 1587. Raitt explains why this was an important time for Beza and the Geneva populace:

> In January of 1587, Geneva had been blockaded for two years by Savoy, long jealous of the tiny republic and eager to possess its fine hilltop command of Lake Leman. Savoy had succeeded in closing the port and inadequate supplies trickled too slowly into the heavily walled city. Students could not return to the Academy nor could Geneva pay its professors. Beza kept the Academy going almost singlehandedly and led the Company of Pastors in appealing for lower grain prices and collections for the poor. To comment on Job in such a time of affliction seemed most appropriate, for Job provided on the one hand a model of fidelity in spite of anguish, and on the other a source for preaching on the providence and fidelity of God.[44]

---

42. See Wright, *Our Sovereign Refuge*, pp. 130-2.
43. Muller, 'Theodore Beza (1519-1605),' p. 217.
44. Raitt, 'Beza, Guide for the Faithful Life,' p. 85.

Savoy, indeed, continued to be a thorn in the Genevans' side. Its leader, the Catholic Charles Emmanuel (with the Pope's blessing and with Spanish troops helping), amassed some 2,000 troops and attacked Geneva on the night of December 11 and 12, 1602, a surprise engagement called l'Escalade. The Genevans were able to repel the attack, and Theodore Beza, though eighty-three years old, led the victors in giving thanks to God for His protection.[45]

The 1580s saw several other significant events in the life of the aging church leader. In 1586 he made the journey to the Colloquy of Montbéliard to combat Lutheran ideas. This event, which we will discuss in some depth in chapter seven, is remarkable for several reasons, including that it reminds us of one of the realities of Protestantism in the second half of the sixteenth century. The divide was not just Protestants vs. Catholics. In fact it was Reformed vs. Lutherans vs. Catholics, and all too often (at least from the Reformed perspective) it seemed like the Lutherans were more closely allied with the Catholics against the Calvinists. The unfortunate events after Montbéliard confirmed this. Towards the end of his life, Beza knew that the Reformed churches he was part of leading were playing third fiddle to the ecclesiastical power houses of Europe.

In 1588, Beza's wife of forty years, Claudine, died. The couple had had no children, but had apparently had a wonderful relationship over the decades. Their home was filled with visitors, boarders, and much affection and friendship. Beza was devastated when she suddenly died. He wrote to a friend, pouring out his heart in grief for his lost loved one:

> She was a woman endowed with all the virtues of a wife, with whom I spent 39 years, 5 months, and 28 days in complete harmony. She never undertook formal studies, but she possessed so many remarkable virtues that I found it easy to

---

45. Baird, *Theodore Beza*, pp. 346-8.

endure this lack. Nothing more bitter in this life could have happened to me, and I have never craved the comfort of friends more. Just when I am in need of help—soon to be 70 years old, if the Lord wills it—I have lost an incredibly devoted wife. Yet blessed be the name of the Lord.[46]

At his friends' urging Beza remarried four months later. His new bride was Catherine del Piano, a widow twenty-seven years younger than he. The short time elapsed between marriages, and perhaps the age difference between Theodore and Catherine might shock modern sensitivities, but it was not uncommon in a world where marriages tended to last only fifteen or twenty years due to the multiple hardships of life.[47] In this way, as many others, the sixteenth century was distinctly unlike the twenty-first.

Financial hardships and declining health marked Beza's last years. In 1594 he noted that his hands were trembling so much that he was having difficulty writing. The next year, he asked the city council to add a second chair in theology at the Academy to relieve his teaching responsibilities. In 1597 his decreasing wealth forced him to sell his substantial library, which included many of Calvin's personal books. By 1599 his health had diminished to the point that he could no longer teach, and two years after that he began attending the Company of Pastors meetings infrequently. Geneva was losing its leader. Finally, he died at 8 a.m. on October 13, 1605.

---

46. Beza to Constantine Fabricius, April 30/May 10, 1588; translated in Manetsch, *Calvin's Company of Pastors*, p. 111.

47. Manetsch, *Calvin's Company of Pastors*, p. 102.

3

Theodore Beza's
THEOLOGICAL VISION

We have encountered some of the life and labors of Theodore Beza. From what we've discovered so far, we might conclude that he led a remarkable, event-filled life, that he sought to lead the Reformation cause for French-speaking Protestants in Switzerland and France, and that he ministered to non-Catholics more generally through his Latin writings. Additionally, we would surmise that Beza's intention was to continue the theological trajectory of his mentor, John Calvin, as he took over the leadership of the Genevan Reformation. In fact, these conclusions are correct. Numerous scholars beginning in the nineteenth century, however, have disagreed with the final point. Beza, they have urged, was not faithful to the theology of Calvin.

A host of scholars have argued that Calvin's theology is different from later 'Calvinism'. The progenitor of this newly-minted 'Calvinism' is usually identified as Theodore Beza. The problem, it is usually claimed, is that Calvin was more circumspect and explicitly evangelical in his theology than were his later followers. Calvin was biblical; they were philosophical. Since he wanted to be tied to Scripture, Calvin was willing to allow for mystery and imprecision in his doctrine; Calvinists were unwilling to allow for the possibility of mystery, desiring above all else to be logically precise. Calvin didn't tie all the loose ends together regarding the extent of the atonement

Theodore Beza

and the doctrine of predestination; not so his followers who absolutely limited the atonement, made predestination double, and, indeed, made predestination the central doctrine of their entire system. The person who started this slide away from Calvin's biblical orientation into a rigid system (usually called 'scholasticism') was Theodore Beza.

It is not hard to find this negative evaluation of Beza. The Reformation historian, David Steinmetz, was scathing in his criticism of the Genevan reformer: 'Predestination is clearly the nerve center of Beza's theology. For many years it was believed to be the center of Calvin's theology as well, partly because Calvin's theology was read by later generations with the spectacles of Beza.' He continued by arguing:

> The leitmotif of Beza's theology is the doctrine of the sovereign will of God. God has willed everything which comes to pass in human history, including man's fall into sin (a position which is called supralapsarianism and which runs counter to even the radically Augustinian theology of many medieval Augustinians). Because predestination is no longer treated in the context of justification and the church, election and reprobation become of equal weight in all respects and not merely in some. Since God is glorified by the reprobation of some men as well as by the election of others, it becomes almost a matter of indifference to God which fate befalls a man. Divorced from the context of faith and of the surprise of the elect, predestination begins to live a life of its own and is no longer a partial doctrine. Indeed, one sees in the theology of Beza the worst fears of Melanchthon come to pass. Predestination becomes in the hands of this speculative theologian a form of philosophical determinism, scarcely distinguishable from the Stoic doctrine of fate. It is Beza, therefore, and not Calvin, who becomes the father of the hyper-Calvinism of Reformed Orthodoxy.[1]

---

1. David C. Steinmetz, *Reformers in the Wings* (Philadelphia: Fortress, 1971; reprint, Grand Rapids: Baker, 1981), pp. 168-70. Happily, Steinmetz was influenced by his former student, Richard A. Muller, to

Brian Armstrong, an historian of the French Reformation, critiques Beza specifically for his theological method because he abandoned Calvin's careful biblical method. In its place Beza erected speculation. Beza's scholastic theological method, according to Armstrong, 'represents a profound divergence from the humanistically oriented religion of John Calvin and most of the early reformers. The strongly biblically and experientially based theology of Calvin and Luther had, it is fair to say, been overcome by the metaphysics and deductive logic of a restored Aristotelianism.'[2]

Armstrong codified for academics what it meant to say that Beza and others were 'scholastic'. He summarized scholasticism by four characteristics. Protestant Scholasticism was:

> (1) that ideological approach which asserts religious truth on the basis of deductive ratiocination from given assumptions or principles, thus producing a logically coherent and defensible system of belief. Generally this takes the form of syllogistic reasoning. It is ... invariably based upon an Aristotelian philosophical commitment and so relates to medieval scholasticism.

> (2) the employment of reason in religious matters, so that reason assumes at least equal standing with faith in theology, thus jettisoning some of the authority of revelation.

> (3) the sentiment that the scriptural record contains a unified, rationally comprehensible account and thus may be formed

---

abandon his harsh critique of Beza in the second edition of this work. See Raymond A. Blacketer, 'The Man in the Black Hat: Theodore Beza and the Reorientation of Early Reformed Historiography,' in *Church and School in Early Modern Protestantism: Essays in Honor of Richard A. Muller on the Maturation of a Theological Tradition*, eds Jordan J. Ballor, David S. Sytsma, and Jason Zuidema (Leiden: Brill, 2013), p. 227, n. 2.

2. Brian G. Armstrong, *Calvinism and the Amyraut Heresy: Protestant Scholasticism and Humanism in Seventeenth-Century France* (Madison: University of Wisconsin Press, 1969), p. 32.

into a definitive statement which may be used as a measuring stick to determine one's orthodoxy.

(4) a pronounced interest in metaphysical matters, in abstract, speculative thought, particularly with reference to the doctrine of God. The distinctive scholastic Protestant position is made to rest on a speculative formulation of the will of God.[3]

Beza was a chief proponent of this anti-biblical and anti-Calvin methodology, according to Armstrong.

Armstrong's negative view of Beza and Protestant Scholasticism became so accepted that it has been adopted as the 'correct' view in several textbooks, thus enshrining it in the minds of a generation of students. Alister McGrath, for example, has followed Armstrong's lead in claiming: 'It seems to be a general rule of history that periods of enormous creativity are followed by eras of stagnation. The Reformation is no exception.'. Beza's work is representative of this stagnation, presenting 'a rationally coherent account of the main elements of Reformed theology, using Aristotelian logic.'[4]

Perhaps no person in the English-speaking world has done more to advance the 'Calvin vs. the Calvinists' idea than R. T. Kendall. Maybe it's due to the title of his book, which encapsulates his thesis, *Calvin and English Calvinism to 1649*.[5] Or maybe it's because of the memorable way in which he stated his views:

> This matter of going beyond Calvin is actually what became known as Calvinism, at least in England. ... The one man

---

3. Armstrong, *Calvinism and the Amyraut Heresy*, p. 32.
4. Alister E. McGrath, *Historical Theology: An Introduction to the History of Christian Thought* (Oxford: Blackwell, 1998), pp. 169, 172.
5. R. T. Kendall, *Calvin and English Calvinism to 1649* (New York: Oxford University Press, 1979; reprint, Carlisle, UK: Paternoster, 1997). For a shorter statement of his thesis, see R. T. Kendall, 'The Puritan Modification of Calvin's Theology,' in *John Calvin: His Influence in the Western World*, ed. W. Stanford Reid (Grand Rapids: Zondervan, 1982), pp. 199-214.

more than any other who was the architectural mind for English Calvinism was Calvin's successor at Geneva, Theodore Beza (1519-1605). Beza perhaps would not have wanted his theology to be known as Calvinism, but his systematizing and logicalizing theology had the effect of perpetuating a phenomenon that bore Calvin's name but was hardly Calvin's purest thought.[6]

Kendall especially critiques Beza for moving beyond 'Calvin's purest thought' on election, reprobation, and the extent of the atonement. In doing this, though, Kendall was guilty of a selective reading of Beza. He makes Beza into the nefarious transformer of Calvin's thought by making passing reference to only six of Beza's works and showing careful attention to none of them! His is anything but a model of careful historical work.[7]

No one has done as much as Richard Muller to respond to the charges of critics like Armstrong and Kendall. Muller is so prominent in this regard that his views are known as 'the Muller Thesis' with little else needed by way of explanation.[8] Muller has done yeoman's work in pointing out that to ask an 'either or' question of the relationship of later 'Calvinists' to Calvin is a fallacious effort from the start. There is both continuity and discontinuity from Calvin to his later followers, just as there was both continuity and discontinuity from later medieval thought to that of Calvin himself. The discontinuities, especially in the earliest phase of post-Calvin scholasticism (he calls this phase 'early orthodoxy', from about 1565 to 1630 or 1640), were not due to substantial theological reorientation

---

6. Kendall, *Calvin and English Calvinism*, p. 201.
7. See my criticisms of Kendall's misrepresentation of Beza in Wright, *Our Sovereign Refuge*, pp. 63-5.
8. For example, see Martin I. Klauber, 'Continuity and Discontinuity in Post-Reformation Reformed Theology: An Examination of the Muller Thesis,' *Journal of the Evangelical Theological Society* 33/4 (1990), pp. 467-75.

but were rather driven by external realities.[9] Largely, Protestant scholastics (and Beza's mature career following Calvin's death fits right into Muller's chronological scheme) were dealing with two needs. They needed, first of all, to codify their doctrinal views so that they could teach early generation Protestants their faith. Related to this, they needed to both bolster their own doctrinal positions and respond to those critical of their faith, such as the revived Catholicism in the era following the Council of Trent (1545-63) and other perceived deviations from the faith. Their means of doing this was 'scholasticism', which merely means 'school theology'. This was partly because of the historical situation in which they found themselves (they had the freedom to start schools, for example; Calvin didn't found the Geneva Academy until late in his life, in 1558). It did not foreshadow any deviation from Calvin's theology.[10]

According to Muller, although the theologians of the post-Reformation period such as Theodore Beza used a scholastic methodology to clarify the Reformed theological system, they remained in essential agreement with the first generation of Reformed thought in content. Muller's definition of 'Reformed Scholasticism' is significant, for it shows that pastors and theologians may change their methodology to meet changing needs. But this does not necessarily mean that they have morphed the received theology. Protestant Scholasticism, he avers, is:

> a highly technical and logical approach to theological system, according to which each theological topic or *locus* was divided

---

9. Richard A. Muller, *Post-Reformation Dogmatics: Rise and Development of Reformed Orthodoxy, ca. 1520 to ca. 1725*, Vol. 1, *Prolegomena to Theology* (Grand Rapids: Baker, 2003), pp. 31-2.

10. Muller has also been adamant in showing that we must not assume that John Calvin was the only prominent theologian in the Reformed tradition during the middle and late sixteenth century. There were numerous others who influenced later 'Calvinism'. See Richard A. Muller, *After Calvin: Studies in the Development of a Theological Tradition* (New York: Oxford University Press, 2003).

into its component parts, the parts analyzed and then defined in careful propositional form. In addition, this highly technical approach sought to achieve precise definition by debate with adversaries and by use of the Christian tradition as a whole in arguing its doctrines. The form of theological system was adapted to a didactic and polemical model that could move from biblical definition to traditional development of doctrine, to debate with doctrinal adversaries past and present, to theological resolution of the problem. This method is rightly called scholastic both in view of its roots in medieval scholasticism and in view of its intention to provide an adequate technical theology for schools—seminaries and universities. The goal of this method, the dogmatic or doctrinal intention of this theology was to provide the church with 'right teaching,' literally, 'orthodoxy'.[11]

We must realize that 'scholasticism' should not bear any negative connotations. It was merely the way in which theology was taught from the late twelfth through the seventeenth century. Muller thus concludes: 'Since scholasticism is primarily a method or approach to academic disciplines it is not necessarily allied to any particular philosophical perspective nor does it represent a systematic attachment to or concentration upon any particular doctrine or concept as a key to theological system.'[12]

We have strayed a bit from Theodore Beza's theology. Don't worry; we're coming back! This bit of a technical interlude was important, I think, to allow us to see some of the mis-characterizations of Beza that have been put forth, as well as a recent move to correct some of these mis-steps. Now, let's go to Beza himself and see what he thought the aim of the Christian life and of Christian theology was all about. It should come as no surprise that Beza was remarkably like Calvin in the way

---

11. Richard A. Muller, *Dictionary of Latin and Greek Theological Terms: Drawn Principally from Protestant Scholastic Theology* (Grand Rapids: Baker, 1985), p. 8.

12. Muller, *Post-Reformation Dogmatics*, vol. 1, p. 37.

in which he oriented theology. We will proceed in two steps. First, we will briefly look at Beza's orientation towards 'piety'. Second, and more fully, we will examine Beza's vision of reality, a vision that informed all that he did as a Christian, a pastor, and a teacher.

Beza and Piety

'*pietas*: piety, the personal confidence in, reverence for, and fear of God that conduces to true worship of and devotion to God. Thus, piety together with devotion constitutes true religion.'[13] In this brief definition, Richard Muller gets us a good bit of the way to the heart of the Protestant Reformation. It was certainly at the very center of the labors of both John Calvin and Theodore Beza. For both of them, true religion was knowing God personally.

Before examining Beza's thought on this aspect of piety, let us briefly note the contours of Calvin's doctrine of the knowledge of God. In 1542 Calvin published his *Geneva Catechism* to be used as a teaching device among the students in Geneva. The opening question is 'What is the principal end of human life?' to which the answer to be given was 'It is to know God.'[14] We can see quite plainly that Calvin's primary emphasis in the Christian life was that believers know God. This is similar to his starting point in the *Institutes*, his *magnum opus* of Christian theology and piety. The first words Calvin writes there were 'Nearly all the wisdom we possess, that is to say, true and sound wisdom, consists of two parts: the knowledge of God and of ourselves.'[15] This *duplex cognitio Dei*, i.e., 'two-fold knowledge of God', became the outline for the rest of the *Institutes*. One of Calvin's points in referring to the

---

13. Muller, *Dictionary*, p. 228.
14. Timothy George, *Theology of the Reformers* (Nashville: Broadman, 1988), p. 163.
15. John Calvin, *Institutes of the Christian Religion*, ed. John T. McNeill, trans. Ford Lewis Battles (Philadelphia: Westminster, 1960), 1.1.1.

knowledge of God is certainly that a Christian, by definition, knows God.[16] This point is even clearer when we are aware of Calvin's equally strong insistence, at the beginning of the *Institutes*, that the essence of the Christian life is *pietas*, 'piety'. This quality, which Calvin says he desires for all Christians, is not nebulous but is rather very definite. He defines 'piety' in this way:

> That reverence joined with love of God which the knowledge of his benefits induces. For until men recognize that they owe everything to God, that they are nourished by his fatherly care, that he is the Author of their every good, that they should seek nothing beyond him—they will never yield him willing service. Nay, unless they establish their complete happiness in him, they will never give themselves truly and sincerely to him.[17]

Knowledge of God, piety, and affection for God are used almost interchangeably by Calvin.[18] Thus, he goes on to show that true knowledge of God is relational, not merely intellectual. He says that correct knowledge of God should first of all 'teach us fear and reverence' of the Lord; second, with this knowledge of God 'as our guide and teacher, we should learn to seek every good from him, and, having received it, to credit it to his account.'[19] Wrapping up his discussion of the centrality of

---

16. On Calvin's doctrine of the knowledge of God, see Benjamin B. Warfield, 'Calvin's Doctrine of the Knowledge of God,' in *Calvin and Calvinism* (New York: Oxford University Press, 1931), pp. 29-130; J. I. Packer, 'Calvin the Theologian,' in *Honouring the People of God: The Collected Shorter Writings of J. I. Packer*, Vol. 4 (Carlisle: Paternoster, 1999), pp. 46-52; and George, *Theology of the Reformers*, pp. 189-91.

17. Calvin, *Institutes*, 1.2.1.

18. Calvin says that 'we shall not say that, properly speaking, God is known where there is no religion or piety' (Calvin, *Institutes* 1.2.1). Note the relationship, then, between true knowledge of God and piety.

19. Calvin, *Institutes*, 1.2.2.

piety, Calvin says that 'pure and real religion' is this: 'faith so joined with an earnest fear of God that this fear also embraces willing reverence, and carries with it such legitimate worship as is prescribed in the law.'[20] The Christian life for John Calvin, then, is fundamentally a life lived in relation to God, which willingly loves and submits to Him, and seeks to honor Him in all spheres of one's life.

Beza agreed with Calvin about the centrality of the relational component in the Christian faith. According to him, the heartbeat of Christian piety is to know God. Like Calvin, he believed that Jesus' words in John 17:3 ('And this is eternal life, that they know you the only true God, and Jesus Christ whom you have sent') were central to the Christian faith. The central aspect of piety, then, is a relationship. We must point this out, since scholars often portray Beza as a rationalist who was concerned only with right knowledge *about* God. On the contrary, Beza was primarily concerned with knowledge *of* God. Of course, Christians should endeavor to understand the truth God has revealed about Himself in His word. But that is secondary to, and only follows, the Christian's prior relationship with God. We will observe this in two places. First, we will note the manner in which Beza framed his catechism around the knowledge of God. Second, we will note the emphasis in his most systematic treatise of theology. For Beza, the purpose of theology was to know God.

Beza also agreed with his friend and mentor on this central definition of the Christian life. We can see this in at least two ways. First, when Beza wrote his catechism he began in a fashion remarkably similar to Calvin's catechism. Beza published his *Little Catechism* in 1575. His rationale for publishing the catechism need not concern us here.[21] We see, though, that Beza's primary concern in this basic tool of

---

20. Calvin, *Institutes*, 1.2.2.
21. See Wright, *Our Sovereign Refuge*, pp. 130-2, 223-5, on Beza's purpose in composing his *Catechism*.

Christian instruction was that a believer should know God. His first question asked, 'Why has God placed us in the world?' The expected answer was 'so that we might know and serve him.'[22] The fundamental *raison d'être* of the Christian life is to know God.

In the second place, Beza's most fundamental concern throughout his writings was that persons reading his treatises and biblical commentaries and sermons should be Christians. That is, Beza desired that they would be those who are saved by the sacrifice of Christ and have a lively faith in Him.[23] More simply said, he wanted them to know Christ. We see this clearly in Beza's most systematic treatise of theology, his *Confession of the Christian Faith* of 1559.[24] Beza's thrust in this systematic compendium of the Christian faith is that people need to be Christians.

Beza's Pastoral Vision

From the little we've seen in Beza's thought already, we can say with certainty that there is a great deal more to him and his thought than just a passion for rationally-constructed doctrines of double predestination fueled by an insistence on limited atonement. He was both more biblical and more pietistic (in the sixteenth-century sense of that word) than that. We can further delineate the contours of Beza's thought by attempting to answer the question, What was it that drove Theodore Beza

---

22. Theodore Beza, *Petit Catéchisme, C'est à dire, Sommaire Instruction de la Religion Chrestienne. Latin-François, par Theodore de Beze* (n.p.: n.d.), p. 237. See also the English translation, *A Little Catechisme, That is to Say, A Short Instruction Touching Christian Religion* (London: Hugh Singleton, 1579), A.1.

23. This is an important point to make to contrast those who label Beza a scholastic logician who was fundamentally concerned with philosophical speculations. I have shown, on the contrary, that Beza's fundamental concern, even in his very technical treatises, was that his readers would be Christians. See Wright, *Our Sovereign Refuge*, pp. 115-32.

24. For a full discussion of Beza's *Confession*, see chapter 4.

to do the many things he did? What fueled all his efforts at the helm of the Genevan, and in many ways, the European church for so many decades? The answer, I propose, is what I call Theodore Beza's 'pastoral vision' or his 'eschatological vision'. The meaning of this foundational belief of Beza will become clear as we discern it from several of his writings.[25]

Beza's pastoral, or eschatological, vision—his 'worldview' we might call it—is evident throughout his writings. It permeated all that he did, including his historical, devotional, pastoral, and doctrinal treatises. This pastoral view of reality drove what Beza did as a Christian, as a pastor, and as a professor. It undergirded and fueled everything that Beza accomplished. Understanding Beza's pastoral vision is essential to comprehending the utility of God's sovereignty in his thought. For Beza, God's sovereignty was vital for believers. The realities of Satan, of a raging spiritual battle, of hell, and of heaven necessitated an omnipotent hand to preserve and guide Christians through their earthly pilgrimage.

Life of Calvin

Beza's *Life of Calvin* offers a fitting introduction to his pastoral vision because in it God and Satan, along with Calvin, were the key actors. Beza initially wrote this in the year of Calvin's death, to commemorate the life of 'my father in Christ'.[26] Although it contains the requisite references to dates, places, and events, there is much more. The most surprising fact about the eulogy is the heightened spiritual activity that Beza

---

25. Much of the following is borrowed from Shawn D. Wright, 'The Reformation Piety of Theodore Beza,' *The Southern Baptist Journal of Theology* 10/4 (2006), pp. 38-53.

26. Theodore Beza, *Correspondance de Théodore de Bèze*, ed. H. Meylan, A. Dufour, C. Chimelli, and B. Nicollier, 21 vols. (Geneva: Librairie Droz, 1960-1999), vol. 6, p. 266. Frédéric Gardy noted the three editions of this work during Beza's life and its translation from French into Latin, German, English, Dutch, and Hungarian, which suggest its popularity (Gardy and Dufour, *Bibliographie des Oeuvres*, pp. 104-26).

noted around the life and labors of his beloved Calvin. Beza punctuated his prose with numerous evaluative judgments and assertions of divine or demonic causation of events in Geneva, showing that for him the fact of spiritual activity was a given. In fact, besides Calvin, God (the one providentially guiding all that went on, including the schemes of Satan) and Satan (opposing Calvin and the truth at every turn) are the two key actors in this spiritual drama.

Beza held that the conflict between God and Satan affected civic and ecclesiastical affairs in Geneva. He wrote that Satan was 'exasperated (but in vain)' when Geneva adopted the Reformation in 1537, for 'the Lord had anticipated Satan'.[27] God's hand even stood behind Calvin's forced departure from Geneva to Strasbourg, for 'the event showed that the purpose of Divine Providence was partly, by employing the labors of his faithful servant elsewhere, to train him, by various trials, for greater achievements' when he returned to Geneva.[28] With Satan opposing the Lord at every turn, God guided Calvin back to Geneva in 1541 and used his return to bring about Geneva's adoption of Calvin's ecclesiastical discipline. Beza commented that 'these laws Satan afterwards made many extraordinary attempts to abolish, but without success.'[29] Satan afterward promoted dissension and controversy to derail Calvin's efforts at reform. The devil would stop at nothing; thus Beza charged that Satan did an 'almost incredible' thing, 'making use especially of the very persons who were most desirous of suppressing [the devil's work]; I mean Farel and Viret.'[30] The spiritual conflict raged throughout Calvin's career.

---

27. Theodore Beza, *The Life of John Calvin*, in *Selected Works of John Calvin: Tracts and Letters*, vol. 1, ed. and trans. Henry Beveridge (1844; reprint, Grand Rapids: Baker, 1983), p. xxx.

28. Beza, *Life of Calvin*, p. xxxiii.

29. Beza, *Life of Calvin*, p. xxxviii.

30. Beza, *Life of Calvin*, p. lii.

According to Beza, God and Satan were primarily battling over the truth because truth was the tool that bent the soul. Although he recounted the rise of factions and the ousting of persons, Beza's central theme in the *Life* was the antagonism between truth and error. God empowered Calvin to adhere to the Scriptures and teach the truth; Satan vigorously opposed this teaching, raising up heretics who tried to expunge the truth of God. Thus Beza lauded the almost superhuman efforts of Calvin, empowered as he was by divine aid: 'The thing to be wondered at rather is, that a single man [Calvin], as if he had been a kind of Christian Hercules, should have been able to subdue so many monsters, and this by that mightiest of all clubs, the Word of God. Wherefore, as many adverseries as Satan stirred up against him, (for his enemies were always those who had declared war against piety and honesty), so many trophies did the Lord bestow upon his servant.'[31] In Beza's estimation, then, Geneva was central to the Lord's purpose since it was the place where, 'by the singular providence of God', the Lord had over and over again caused 'the purest light to arise out of the thickest darkness.'[32] Through Calvin's exposition of the truth, 'the arch-enemy', Satan, 'was most powerfully opposed'.[33] Calvin's experience in Geneva proved that the spiritual battle for souls would be decided in the struggle for the truth.

This spiritual battle for the truth produced numerous deadly skirmishes in Geneva, according to Beza. For instance, Jérome Bolsec's heretical opinions about predestination indicated spiritual attack. The Lord won this encounter, for 'all that Satan gained by these dissensions was, that this article of the Christian religion, which was formerly most obscure, became clear and transparent to all not disposed to be contentious.' Yet, 'as if Satan himself had blown the trumpet', the opponents

---

31. Beza, *Life of Calvin*, p. xcix.
32. Beza, *Life of Calvin*, p. lxxvii.
33. Beza, *Life of Calvin*, p. xlvi.

of the truth were roused from their slumber to oppose God through Bolsec's boldness.[34] Likewise, Beza blamed the devil for the controversy surrounding Michael Servetus who was 'a monstrous compound of mere impiety and horrid blasphemy'.[35] To Beza, then, God and the devil were engaged in martial combat, wielding the weapons of truth and heresy. Calvin manifested God's power because 'in defending his doctrine,' he 'trusted solely to the power of truth.'[36]

Beza's *Life* delineates the contours of his pastoral vision. A spiritual battle was raging whose main combatants were God and Satan. The battle concerned the truth and therefore was waged with the weapons of correct doctrine and heresy. The outcome of each engagement meant the salvation or damnation of souls. For that reason the main locus of activity in the battle was the church, for God appointed it to preserve the truth. The stakes in this combat were eternal. For those who persevered under God's providence, the reward was heaven; hence the time of Calvin's death, though 'to us of the greatest and best founded grief', 'was to him the commencement of perpetual felicity.'[37]

This vision of reality was the basis of Beza's insistence that God had to be completely sovereign in order to protect His children in the battle. The components of his pastoral vision previously noted in his *Life* permeated Beza's writings, of all genres, as the following overview will demonstrate.

The Fact of the Spiritual Battle

Beza depicted Satan as active in the world, indefatigably trying to harm Christians.[38] So he indicted Satan as the foremost of

---

34. Beza, *Life of Calvin*, pp. lvii, lix.
35. Beza, *Life of Calvin*, p. lxv.
36. Beza, *Life of Calvin*, p. lx.
37. Beza, *Life of Calvin*, p. lxxxii.
38. Compare Manetsch's opinion that when Beza referred to Protestants' opponents as 'Satan' his 'use of biblical images like these often served as a barometer of his angst and anger. When the reformer wished to express

'my enemies' in his meditation on Psalm 102. The devil was 'that great devouring lion, who has spoiled, torn, and swallowed so many' Christians 'from the beginning of the world'.[39] Satan was the deadly aggressor in the spiritual battle.

Satan's schemes took many forms. In the first place, he was incessant in troubling Christians, and in tempting them to sin. 'Satan, the prince of darkness, lays always in wait to hurt us, seeking principally to make a breach into our hearts when we stand least upon our guard,' Beza warned. 'Give us grace,' he therefore prayed, 'to be delivered from the temptations of the devil, from uncleanness … into which our infirmity leads us.'[40] The devil also troubled Christians when they attempted to pray, 'for besides that the devil at all times lies in wait, to seduce us, so does he, especially, at such times, seek to creep into our minds, to divert our thoughts elsewhere, that they may be polluted with many blemishes.'[41] One of the prerequisites of fervent prayer was thus to abandon 'Satan with all his baits'.[42]

Only God could make Christians strong for the combat. They could not rely on their own efforts in the spiritual battle. Indeed, one of the devil's favorite schemes involved making believers think they could stand against him in their own strength: 'We have to learn how Satan,' Beza urged his listeners, 'is never more ready for us to surrender, than when we think we have won the upper hand.'[43] Rather, the omnipotent God

---

his deepest pain, frustration, or indignation, he frequently appealed to scriptural characters and concepts, interpreting the data of his experience in light of the biblical drama of God's chosen people struggling against Satan and his minions' (Manetsch, *Theodore Beza*, pp. 53-4).

39. Theodore Beza, *Christian Meditations upon Eight Psalmes of the Prophet David* (London: Christopher Barker, 1582).

40. Theodore Beza, *Maister Bezaes Houshold Prayers*, trans. John Barnes (London: n.p., 1603), P3r-P3v.

41. Beza, *Houshold Prayers*, B6r.

42. Beza, *Houshold Prayers*, B5v.

43. Theodore Beza, *Sermons sur l'Histoire de la Passion et Sepulture de nostre*

would protect His children. 'Does Satan amaze you?' Beza asked his listeners when the Genevans feared a Catholic attack in 1587.[44] If so, believers need not worry, for their Lord

> has vanquished him for you. Does the corruption of your nature astonish you? The Son of God making himself man has fully sanctified it for you. Do your sins make you afraid, which be fruits of this corruption? He has borne them all upon the tree, and has paid for your discharge. Which more is, his righteousness is yours, if he himself is yours. Are you afraid of men, if God is for you? Does death make you afraid? It is vanquished and turned into an entry of life. Behold then all your enemies scattered, behold quite under foot, all such as afflicted you within and without, because the Lord allows you for one of his servants and household.[45]

The battle was real, but God would protect His children and bring them safely to Himself. Although Satan's schemes were evil and troubling, 'it is not in the power of any to trouble us, except when and how far it pleases God they shall do it.'[46] Thus, Beza urged his listeners to forgo trusting in their 'imaginary powers' by partaking of the 'real remedy' Christ modeled for them, namely, 'to know prayer, provided that it is lifted up' to almighty God.[47]

Seigneur Jesus Christ, descrite par les quatre Evangelistes (Geneva: Jean le Preux, 1592), p. 197.

44. Raitt, 'Beza, Guide for the Faithful Life,' pp. 97-8.
45. Beza, *Christian Meditations*, on Ps. 143:12.
46. Theodore Beza, *Master Bezaes Sermons Upon the Three First Chapters of the Canticle of Canticles*, trans. John Harmar (Oxford: Joseph Barnes, 1587), p. 236.
47. Beza, *Sermons sur la Passion*, p. 29. Based on the devil's heightened activity against believers, in another place Beza chided Christians: 'Let us be ashamed hereof, that Satan is more diligent in doing mischief, daily laboring to bring us to destruction, than we are careful in the whole course of our life, to perform the duties of our vocation, and to keep

The Battle for the Truth

Satan especially sought to destroy the church because God cared for it and appointed it the guardian of the truth. The devil attacked the church by trying to foster heretical beliefs in her midst. So Beza warned his listeners to be on 'guard here of a great ruse of Satan, pushing us if he can, from one extreme to the other, which are so many precipices. Therefore let us know that those are grandly self-deceived who want to subjugate the word of God to their own natural sense.' Instead believers must lean 'on the word of God understood, and not at all on our imaginations, whether they are old or new.'[48] Satan moved in those 'deceived who seek for the true religion in the crowd, in custom ... as if there had not already been more fools than wise men.' But, he went on to warn his listeners, 'Let us defend ourselves here from Satan's ambushes, and let us remember this, which the true Jesus Christ admonished us (Matt. 24:24) to know, that false christs and false prophets' would come.[49]

The conflict between orthodoxy and heresy heightened the importance of schools, for these were charged with instructing students in the truth. Again, Beza highlighted Satan's malicious schemes in the schools, especially 'the school of divinity' because here 'Satan has served his turn with sugar to turn it into most bitter and deadly poison.' The devil 'banished out of the school of divinity that which was the only subject thereof, I mean the reading and expounding of the text of holy Scripture, to thrust thereunto an abominable confusion of dreaming sophistications, some as vain as curious, others absurd, others full of impiety.'[50] In another place, Beza identified a principal 'craft' of Satan as 'these human traditions and this glorious theology

---

ourselves out of the danger of so deadly an enemy.' (Theodore Beza, *Job Expounded by Theodore Beza, Partly in Manner of a Commentary, Partly in Manner of a Paraphrase* [Cambridge: n.p., 1589], on Job 1:13).

48. Beza, *Sermons sur la Passion*, p. 437.

49. Beza, *Sermons sur la Passion*, pp. 325-6.

50. Beza, *Canticles*, p. 135.

called "scholastic'" which consisted of 'so many buckets and stamps to oppose what is this truth of God.'[51] Schools must teach the truth because of the on-going spiritual battle.

Satan not only drew people away from the Bible to human traditions; he also introduced outright heresy. Remarkably, when writing to the French Protestant leaders in 1565 exhorting them not to turn away from the Protestant cause in the face of persecution, Beza's chief concern was Satan. The evil one, he said, had been responsible for fomenting heresy throughout the history of the church. Satan, Beza averred, 'still forges other secret mysteries, against which it is necessary that you resist and stand steadfast, by the sincerity and pure simplicity of Christian doctrine.'[52] Advisors who promoted compromise were in league with the devil for 'their words have a great show and a beautiful [one], but it proceeds from the spirit of Satan.'[53]

Biblical truth was essential. If one did not believe certain truths, one would be damned eternally. That is why Beza prayed that the church would 'be my whole desire, and the sole subject of my delights, that I may never depart from there, notwithstanding whatsoever assaults and temptations I am to endure.' He yearned to remain in the church in the midst of the spiritual battle because 'there is not any such mishap, or so much to be feared, as to be out of this holy temple, wherein only abides all light, truth, salvation, and life.'[54] The church, Beza prayed to God, was 'where your truth is lodged.'[55] As such, it was the locus of salvation and life. Although the truth was being assailed by the schemes of the devil, it would prevail: from

---

51. Theodore Beza, *Sermons sur l'Histoire de la Resurrection de nostre Seigneur Jesus Christ* (Geneva: Jean le Preux, 1593), pp. 188-9.
52. Theodore Beza, 'An Exhortation to the Reformation of the Church' in *A Confession of Faith Made By Common Consent of Divers Reformed Churches Beyond the Seas* (London: n.p., n.d.), n.p.
53. Beza, 'Exhortation to the Reformation,' n.p.
54. Beza, *Houshold Prayers*, G2v-G3r.
55. Beza, *Houshold Prayers*, G1r.

true doctrine 'proceeds the stability of the Church, which the endeavors of Satan cannot shake, because the foundation of her faith and doctrine is grounded upon the true, and immoveable rock, even the pure confession of the name of Christ.'[56] Though Satan endeavored to destroy the church, the confession of the truth protected her in the midst of the spiritual battle.

Satan's Schemes in Human History
The spiritual battle also raged outside the confines of the church. Satan connived in secular affairs, trying through these mechanisms to oppose God and His truth. In the preface to his *Histoire ecclésiastique*, Beza noted two ways of reading history, one seeing God's providential hand behind events and the other seeing only material causes.[57] 'A very great mistake,' he averred, was committed when one merely looked at 'the boundary marks of this frail and transitory life.' This was merely the secondary arena of history. The principal arena of history was God's 'spiritual government, in which shines sovereignly and in a particular way the providence, wisdom, power, and infinite mercy of God. Persons were principally created and formed for the contemplation' of this providence.[58] Beza had two overriding purposes in composing this martyrology. In the first place, he wanted people 'to return the honor to [God] that belongs to him' when they had seen 'the great works that he has done in our time.' But, secondly, Beza thought his history would be a means of helping Christians to persevere in the midst of the spiritual battle. He wrote it 'to put before the eyes of those God opened, that which can and must infinitely

---

56. Beza, *Houshold Prayers*, G1r.
57. Although the compiler of *Histoire ecclésiastique* is not named, Beza probably oversaw its composition. See Manetsch, *Theodore Beza*, p. 39 n. 80, and Beza, *Correspondance*, 21:vii-xi.
58. Theodore Beza, *Histoire ecclésiastique des églises réformées au royaume de France,* ed. G. Baum and E. Cunitz (Paris: 1883; reprint, Nieuwkoop: B. de Graaf, 1974), 1:i.

encourage them not to grow weary, on account of any difficulty, of following the good path which they entered' when they were reminded of God's providential care in the midst of intense hardship.[59]

The Eternal Stakes of the Battle

Theodore Beza's pastoral vision was eternal in its scope. He had his eyes fixed on eternity as he lived and ministered in this life. He wanted himself and those under his care to go to heaven and not to have to suffer the perpetual torments of hell.

Beza acknowledged that eternity was an awesome experience to contemplate in this life. In the prayer 'upon temporal death', which we will examine in chapter eight, he exhorted people to dwell upon the inevitability of eternity so that they might escape God's judgment and resort to Christ for salvation. 'O Lord,' he prayed,

> your indignation against sinners is manifest, and there is none righteous, your vengeance is ready against rebellion, whereof we be all guilty, which does also cause, that death is unto us, not only as a temporal ending as concerning the flesh, whereat nature is moved and abashed, but also an interior feeling of the curse fallen upon sin, yea even an entry into eternal death, unless there be for us with you, our Father, redemption in our Lord Jesus Christ.[60]

So those who did not receive redemption must certainly go to 'the tribunal seat of [God's] sovereign justice' and experience God's 'indignation against sinners' and His 'vengeance [which] is ready against rebellion.'[61]

So hell should be abhorred and avoided at all costs. Conversely, Beza encouraged believers to desire and seek after

---

59. Beza, *Histoire ecclésiastique*, 1:x.
60. Beza, *Houshold Prayers*, in the prayer 'Upon temporal death'.
61. Beza, *Houshold Prayers*, in the prayer 'Upon temporal death'.

heaven with their most diligent effort. Heaven was a wonderful and joyful place, where a Christian would be freed from the trials of his or her earthly pilgrimage. In heaven Christians 'may once for all, wholly be set free from so miserable bondage of sin' and 'they may behold [God] as it were face to face, yea and more rightly serve and honor him, whom all their lifetime they have most earnestly sought.'[62] Thus Beza prayed that the Lord would allow a believer who was near death 'with the eyes of his faith, to behold the eternal blessings you reserve for him in your paradise, to live happy for ever.' Such a person could endure death since he knew he would soon 'enjoy your presence in heaven.'[63]

Having an eternal perspective fortified believers in the present spiritual battle, according to Beza. It empowered Christians to withstand the temptations of the world. 'To the children of darkness,' he commented, 'the uncleanness of the flesh is a pleasant habitation. But to the children of light, to the immortal spirits, to the regenerate hearts, heaven is much more desirable.' He thus prayed: 'Grant therefore, my God, that as I daily grow towards my end, so I may live the more cheerfully, learning in your school, to prefer your eternal life, before the light of the Sun, the glory of heaven, before the vanity of the earth, the glorious habitation in paradise, before the painful tumults of the world, the society of angels, before the fellowship of mortal men, the only blessed and permanent life, before the passing shadow of this life.' He continued asking that he would 'know how to prepare myself by continual meditation in these excellent Christian consolations, that happy are they that die in the Lord.'[64] Similarly, in his prayer 'For heavenly life', Beza asked the Lord 'to give me grace, that withdrawing my affection more and more from the dark cloisters of the earth, sprinkled

---

62. Beza, *Job*, on Job 3.

63. Beza, *Houshold Prayers*, in the prayer 'At the visitation of the sick'.

64. Beza, *Houshold Prayers*, in the prayer 'Upon temporal death'.

with tears, I may lift up my desires to the lightsome habitation of thy deity, where the treasures and incomparable joys of your paradise do remain in an eternal life.' He prayed that he might comfort 'myself incessantly night and day, in that the promise is made unto me through my savior Jesus Christ, to the end, that in my last hour—come out of my misery and entered into my felicity—I may with a happy flight go take my rest above in your peace, O my God, which surmounts all understanding, and for to sing psalms of thanksgiving unto you without end.'[65]

God's Sovereignty: Solace in the Battle

Beza's eschatological vision—his belief in believers' pilgrimage through a spiritual battle on their way to the eternal joy and happiness of heaven—informed his pastoral view of reality. The times were precarious. The plague threatened and Catholic armies besieged the city; Lutheran antagonists repeatedly attacked the Reformed doctrine of the eucharist and predestination; fellow believers in his beloved France suffered death under Catholic rule; the future of the Geneva Academy appeared bleak. But above and behind all these concerns, Beza perceived a battle between God and Satan, a war which inevitably involved Christians. How could believers have confidence in such dangerous times? Their assurance of salvation and the certainty that they would persevere all the way to heaven, their survival in times of political turmoil, their strength in the midst of Satan's attacks, their very salvation—all these things depended on God's absolute sovereignty, according to Beza. God's sovereignty at its heart was a pastoral doctrine for Theodore Beza.

Beza's writings are replete with applications of the truth of God's sovereignty to his listeners and readers. He did not, to be sure, shy away from very technical discussions about predestination and providence in his teaching or his polemics. But his overriding concern remained the comfort and assurance

---

65. Beza, *Houshold Prayers*, in the prayer 'For heavenly life'.

of believers. The following survey of the pastoral uses Beza made of this doctrine will demonstrate that he taught that God's sovereignty was the ultimate source of joy, assurance, and salvation for Christians in the midst of the spiritual battle raging around them.

Beza produced a litany of pastoral applications of God's sovereignty. All of them were based upon his firm belief that the present life of Christians would be hard but that the eternal glory which awaited them in heaven was stunning and filled with eternal joy. The vehicle God employed to uphold His servants in the midst of their sufferings consisted of His promises to them in the Bible, all of which stood firmly on the solid foundation of God's goodness, wisdom, and omnipotence. God's sovereign ability to keep these promises was thus the anchor for His hurting people.

So Beza urged Huguenot leader Gaspard de Coligny to trust in the Lord as he led the Protestants during precarious times in France. Beza exhorted his friend to be 'assured of the faithful guidance of such a Guide, who will lead you through the right path, whatever difficulty there is of unknown and inaccessible places.' He counseled him to rely 'upon that faithful Leader, who can lead you through a sure path in the midst of impassable and inaccessible places.'[66] And in the midst of evil, indeed sometimes inexplicable evil, Beza insisted that even when they did not understand God's ways, Christians must seek to trust in Him and His providential control over all things. 'If you see in a country oppression of the poor, and defrauding of right and equity, think not too much upon this manner of doing whatsoever men list. For he that is higher than the highest works these things,' he wrote. Rather, he cautioned his listeners not

> to begin to doubt of that providence of God. For however these things seem to be tossed up and down, as if the world had no governor, yet be sure there is one above all these, that

---

66. Beza, *Correspondance*, 6:19.

abuse the honor whereunto they are advanced, who has also standing by him innumerable and most mighty ministers, whom in due time he may set a work to execute his decrees upon these proud men.[67]

In another place, Beza wrote that 'it pleases God to temper the life of man by giving sometimes prosperity, sometimes adversity,' but that persons 'are not able to attain to his wisdom' in these matters. The only proper course, and the only avenue open to prospering in adversity, was to rest wholly in God's wisdom: 'The only means to escape out of all these straights' is 'neither profanely inquiring into God himself' nor 'wickedly scorning at that, which he cannot conceive, but falling down before the majesty of God, which we cannot comprehend.' Such persons 'rest wholly in his will.'[68] God would take care of His people, even when they did not understand His ways.

The schemes of Satan were especially vexing to God's people. The devil tried to keep Christians apart from Christ and incited heinous evil against believers through those who opposed the Protestants. But God in His sovereignty would prevail over Satan and judge the wicked. In 1586 Beza described the two sorts of 'mountains' that might tend to separate believers from the Lord, whom Beza identified with the 'bridegroom' in his exposition of Canticles:

> For first of all Satan and his accomplices do what lies in them to hinder that this bridegroom and this spouse should never see each the other, leaving no kind of cruelty unpracticed, nor any kind of subtle and crafty sly means unattempted to work this division and divorce, which is verified throughout the whole sacred history. But to go no farther for proof hereof,

---

67. Theodore Beza, *Ecclesiastes, or the Preacher. Solomons Sermon Made to the people, teaching every man howe to order his life, so as they may come to true and everlasting happines. With a Paraphrase, or short exposition thereof, made by Theodore Beza* (Cambridge: n.p., n.d.), on Eccles. 5:8.
68. Beza, *Ecclesiastes*, C4-C5.

what has been done in this behalf in our time by kings and emperors enchanted and bewitched by that whore of Rome, and by her slaves? And what does the world still every day? Read we over all the histories of the ancient persecutions, no one excepted, shall we find the like unto that which has been practiced in our time? For there is neither fire, nor water, nor air, nor earth, which have not all of them been employed to suck the life of our poor brethren: there is no kind of cruel death through which they have not passed, neither have the hands of the hangmen only been wearied with their slaughter, but the people also have been employed to imbrue themselves with the blood of the poor, meek and innocent, without distinction of age or difference of sex, or any privilege of nature whatsoever. And this licentiousness has been permitted, to any that would dye his hands red with innocent blood, not in time of war and hostility, but in the greatest appearance and confidence that might be of peace and friendship.[69]

In the midst of this calamity Beza encouraged his listeners to trust their Lord: 'Let us therefore know and hold this for an irrefragable point and undeniable, and altogether resolved upon ... that the Lord is never late or slack in coming, that is to say, fails not to come at the point, yea and that leaping over all that which might seem to slack and stay his coming.'[70]

God's control, Beza asserted, reached right down to ordering the deeds the devil should do. Rather than causing consternation among believers, though, Beza argued that this truth should comfort them: 'This doctrine is full of excellent comfort. For thereby we understand, that by the power of our God, the rage of that hungry lion is abated and bridled, and that God will never suffer him to do anything against his children, which shall not be to their good and profit, as the apostle tells us (Rom. 8:28) and also teaches us by his own example (2 Cor. 12:7).'[71]

---

69. Beza, *Canticles*, pp. 246-7.
70. Beza, *Canticles*, p. 247.
71. Beza, *Job*, on Job 1:6.

Beza argued that God's sovereignty assured Christians of their salvation. Their Sovereign was the author of salvation from its very beginning until the time He brought His children to be with Him in heaven. As believers held on to this promise, Beza argued, it would produce comfort and joy, even during times of earthly conflict. Thus Beza offered a prayer 'To obtain the gift of faith':

> So great is the vanity, ignorance, and infirmity of our nature, that if you, O most merciful God, work not that in us, which you command us to do, if you do not teach us that we may know, if you do not convert us, that we may cleave to your word, if you do not give us to your Son, that he may keep us yours, if he bring us not clothed in his righteousness to the throne of your grace, and if your spirit leads us not in the paths of your kingdom, holding us fast in the effects of his gifts, upon the way of your truth, we cannot hearken to this voice of the shepherd of our souls, neither in our hearts conceive such and so lively a faith, that all uncertainty might be banished, and the same sealed with his own efficacy: much less can we feel the peace and joy that true faith brings with it.[72]

It was absolutely essential, Theodore Beza argued, that God be sovereign in salvation. Beza took great pains to controvert those who 'utterly take away the supernatural grace of God, which is the first ground and foundation of our salvation.' These false teachers who had been 'rightly condemned and detested,' charged that the Genevan ministers 'transform men into blocks and stones, depriving them utterly of understanding and will.'[73] They failed to notice why God must be absolutely sovereign in salvation, Beza argued.

> For, on the contrary, there is in our nature nothing but most desperate and most obstinate rebellion, until the spirit of God

---

72. Beza, *Houshold Prayers*, in the prayer 'To obtain the gift of faith'.
73. Beza, *Canticles*, p. 57.

do drive away, first, the darkness of our understanding, which cannot, nor will not of itself, so much as think upon the things of God (2 Cor. 3:5) and that secondly it correct the forwardness of our will, which is an enemy of God, and of whatsoever is truly good (Rom. 5:10 and 8:7). And this is the cause why the apostle (Eph. 2:1) says not simply, that we are wounded, but that we are naturally dead in our sins and offences.[74]

Christians' hopes, then, rested in the Lord who had sovereignly saved them in love.

As He had saved them, so God would grant His children the grace to persevere, Beza argued. Believers could take great comfort in their Lord's continuing sovereign grace in their lives. 'He who has obtained the gift of true faith and has trusted in that same goodness of God,' Beza urged, 'must also be concerned about his perseverance. Yet he should not doubt, but should rather call on God in every kind of temptation and affliction, with the sure hope of attaining what he asks, at least as far as it is expedient, since he knows himself a child of God, who cannot fail him.'[75] They would persevere because God who required holiness in His people would sanctify them sovereignly as well. So Beza urged his listeners when they were troubled about their standing to call upon the Lord:

> Have recourse unto him which has made us, and who alone can make us anew, by the same power, which is his holy spirit, enlightening the eyes of our understanding (Eph. 1:18, Acts 26:18), framing a clean heart within us (Ps. 51:10), creating in us both to will and to do (Phil. 2:13), in a word, making us from the head to the feet new creatures (2 Cor. 5:17), that is to say, such as this spouse is set before us here to be, which is at large described unto us by Ezekiel.[76]

---

74. Beza, *Canticles*, p. 56.
75. Theodore Beza, *Tabula Praedestinationis*, in *The Potter and the Clay: The Main Predestination Writings of Theodore Beza*, trans. Philip C. Holtrop (Grand Rapids: Calvin College, 1982), p. 58.
76. Beza, *Canticles*, pp. 36-7.

The grand result of God's sovereignty for a believer in this life was assurance of salvation, Beza argued. In the troubles of life, believers could trust that God, in His power, would uphold them, and they could hope that God would grant them a sense of His love:

> It may please the Lord who has drawn us out of darkness into this light of his truth, and has placed and preserved us most miraculously here in this holy rest and peace of conscience, waiting for the full accomplishment of his promises, to settle and engrave in our minds this holy assurance of his mighty power in good will towards us, that we be never astounded by the assaults of Satan, and of such his adherents as he employs and uses against us: but that contrariwise we persevere and continue in this holy profession of his truth, as well by mouth, as also by an holy and Christian life, until we come unto the real enjoying of all that, which he has made us to believe and hope for, according to his most holy and most assured promises. Conformably unto which doctrine acknowledging our over great negligence here and laziness in our duty, with other infinite faults and offences of ours, we will crave mercy at his hands.[77]

Ultimately, though, Beza looked forward to heaven as the answer to the vicissitudes of the earthly pilgrimage. The prospect of eternal felicity might seem remote during one's earthly life, but it was certain because of God's sovereign action on behalf of His people. So while he was praying 'That we may well use afflictions,' Beza exuded confidence in God's eternal goal for His people:

> Especially grant, O Lord, that I may attain to this reason of true wisdom, always to be content with your will, the sovereign and just cause of all things; namely, in that it pleases you, that the livery of your household should consist in carrying their cross after your Son, to the end, that I should never but be seasoned to drink the wholesome myrrh which purges the soul

---

77. Beza, *Canticles*, p. 358.

from the lusts of the flesh, and replenishes the same with the desires of eternal life. Also that I learn in whatsoever my estate, cheerfully to submit myself to the conduct of your providence, as being well assured, that whatsoever I suffer, all the crosses of my life shall be unto me so many blessings and helps from you my Father, to make me go the right way into your kingdom, and increase unto me the price of glory in the same.[78]

The wise, powerful, and loving Father would certainly bring His children to Himself for eternity. The complete sovereignty of God was the foundation of Beza's pastoral vision.

Conclusion

Theodore Beza was not John Calvin's clone. But neither was he Calvin's arch-nemesis. Rather, living in different times than Calvin, Beza stressed the same big view of the sovereign God of the Bible as the only hope for troubled Christians. God's complete sovereignty over all aspects of a Christian's life—from his spiritual birth to his resurrection to eternal joy with Christ—was the one certainty that a believer could rely on in troubled times.

It was this vision of reality that drove all that Theodore Beza did. It defined him as a human being, and as a Christian. It is to five of his treatises where he displays this vision that we now turn.

---

78. Beza, *Houshold Prayers*, K3v-K4v. We will look at this prayer in some depth in chapter 8.

4

Summarizing the Faith—
Theodore Beza's *Confession of the Christian Faith*

The Setting

Theodore Beza, then, was a Christian with a remarkably spiritually-sensitive view of the world. He was a pastor who cared deeply for those under his care. And he was a man who had great affection for the life and labors of John Calvin. We move on now to a subject that demonstrates Beza's familiarity with Calvin, as well as his willingness at times to chart a new course—his distillation of the essence of the Christian faith. Beza summed up Christian doctrine with eternity in view and as a seasoned Christian and pastor.

He especially condensed biblical doctrine in his *Confession of the Christian Faith* of 1559, initially containing six chapters. Not only did he revise and lengthen the French edition in 1560, but that year he also translated it into Latin for a wider reading audience. This brief work became one of the most popular in the entire Bezan corpus. The Latin edition was reprinted eleven times during Beza's life, the last just ten years before his death, in 1595. It was also popular in the English-speaking world, having been translated in 1563 and going through four reprintings, the final one in 1589.[1] His

---

1. For accounts of the publication of this work in the sixteenth century, see Gardy and Dufour, *Bibliographie des Oeuvres*, pp. 60-80. Also see Wright, *Our Sovereign Refuge*, pp. 116, 236.

Confession proves Beza's acumen at expressing the substance of Christian doctrine in short form, and it also highlights his acute pastoral orientation.

Beza was part of a long line of Protestants who felt the need to compose doctrinal introductions. This makes sense due to the fact that these Protestant pastors and teachers judged that the church had been in error for centuries; the grave heresies of Catholicism needed to be overturned. More than that, even, they felt that Protestant laypeople and students would benefit from introductions to the Christian faith so that they would be personally buoyed up against the onslaughts of errors prevalent in their day. Some of the many such doctrinal précis included those of Philipp Melanchthon and Martin Luther of Wittenberg, Huldrich Zwingli and Heinrich Bullinger of Zurich, and, of course, John Calvin of Geneva. Melanchthon was the first to enter into the systematizing role with his *Loci communes* in 1521.[2] Luther also felt the need to summarize doctrine, especially for laypeople, in his *Small Catechism* in 1529, along with his *Smalcald Articles* in 1537.[3] On the Reformed side of the Reformation, just a year before his untimely death fighting against an invading Catholic army, Zwingli wrote his *An Exposition of the Faith* in 1530.[4] Bullinger succeeded Zwingli at the helm of the important German-speaking Protestant center of Zurich and became, along with Calvin and Peter Martyr Vermigli, one of the most important second-generation leaders of the Reformed tradition in Protestantism. He presented a summary of his faith in his *Second Helvetic*

---

2. Melanchthon revised and lengthened it three times up to 1559. See Diarmaid MacCulloch, *The Reformation: A History* (New York: Viking, 2003), p. 140.

3. Both of these works are found in Timothy F. Lull and William R. Russell, eds, *Martin Luther's Basic Theological Writings* (Minneapolis: Fortress, 2012), pp. 322-62.

4. G. W. Bromiley, ed., *Zwingli and Bullinger* (Philadelphia: Westminster, 1953), pp. 245-82.

Confession, published in 1566.⁵ Calvin's magnum opus, of course, was his *Institutes of the Christian Religion*, first published in 1536 and going through several editions until he was satisfied with the final 1559 edition.

Given the recognized brilliance of the *Institutes*, one might wonder why Calvin's friend would publish another summary of the Christian faith in the same year that his mentor's final edition went public, 1559. Beza's *Confession* rings with the pastoral bent of its author who composed it for both family and pastoral reasons. In the first place, Beza tells us that he initially wrote the work for his father in order to win him over to the Protestant faith. Beza's father remained in France, and people there had almost convinced him that his son was a heretic. Beza, then, first of all published this treatise in 1559 to defend his Protestant faith to his father and hopefully to win him to it. 'I wrote', Beza recounted, 'at first in the French language, for the purpose of satisfying my own father, whom the calumnies of certain persons had alienated from [me], as though I had been an impious man and a heretic, and with the further view of winning him, if possible, to Christ in his extreme old age.'⁶

However, the *Confession* was more than merely an apologetic letter to Beza's father. When he had it published for a wider audience, Beza had two sets of persons in mind, as he clarifies in the preface to the work. First, he wanted the book to serve laypeople who needed to 'understand and learn what [pastors] teach them to be edified and comforted by it. Also, they must take heed and beware of false prophets and wolves.'⁷ Believers

---

5. Philip Schaff, ed., *The Creeds of Christendom, with a History and Critical Notes* (1876; Grand Rapids: Baker, 1990), 1:396-420.
6. Theodore Beza, 'Autobiographical Letter of Beza to Wolmar,' in Baird, *Theodore Beza*, p. 366.
7. Theodore Beza, *A Brief and Pithy Sum of Christian Faith*, in *Reformed Confessions of the 16th and 17th Centuries in English Translation: Volume 2, 1552-1566*, ed., James T. Dennison Jr (Grand Rapids: Reformation Heritage, 2010), p. 239.

needed to read the Bible on their own, but without a handbook helping them to put the parts of the Bible together they might draw wrong conclusions. 'Until they are put to the reading of the texts of the Scriptures, they have some brief instruction which may open the matter plainly to them and accustom them with the manner of speech of the Holy Ghost to gather the true sense and meaning, and refer the whole to the right use and end.'[8] So, laypeople were at the forefront of Beza's mind. But Beza also had others in mind as he wrote his *Confession*. He had it published for pastors so that they would know how to 'feed their flock with the Word of life' in a more biblically-faithful manner.[9]

In the preface Beza also clued his readers into his method. He had read and researched a great deal before writing this little Christian handbook. He tried to arrange the parts of the *Confession* according to 'the best order' following the thought 'of those things which I have learned in the Christian religion by reading the Bible with the conference of the most faithful expositors.'[10] His goal was that the *Confession* aid Bible readers, but not that it supplant the authority which resided in the Bible alone. He wished 'that all those that will see this confession will compare it diligently with the Scriptures which are the only true touchstone by which to prove true doctrine.'[11] He elaborated on this goal in the preface to the Latin edition. There he lauded those 'who compose short and perspicuous summaries' of biblical truth—indeed that was his goal in writing the *Confession*[12]—so that those who 'apply themselves to the reading of the sacred Scriptures may have certain heads ready to hand, to each of which they may afterwards refer

---

8. Beza, *Brief and Pithy Sum*, p. 239.
9. Beza, *Brief and Pithy Sum*, p. 239.
10. Beza, *Brief and Pithy Sum*, p. 239.
11. Beza, *Brief and Pithy Sum*, p. 241.
12. Beza, 'Autobiographical Letter,' p. 367.

and accommodate what they read.' Beza claimed faithfully to adhere to the doctrine of Calvin's *Institutes* in the *Confession*. Calvin had treated the same subject matter 'very copiously' in his *Institutes* and 'very briefly but very accurately' in his 1542 Catechism. But Beza noted that 'nothing forbids that the same feast be repeated with a slight change in the arrangement, to the great enjoyment of those who partake.'

The preface Beza wrote for this *Confession* ably demonstrates what the essence of being Protestant meant to Beza. He did not care fundamentally about winning debates with the Catholics for the sake of forensic bragging rights. Protestantism mattered because eternity was in the balance. People needed to believe the truth in order to experience salvation. Rome taught people to believe the church, and that the church's faith would protect them. This sort of ignorance, though, could be damning. Faith is essential, and as we'll see when we examine the contents of the *Confession* below, faith requires knowledge. It was this concern for people's salvation (first for his father, then for others) that fundamentally moved Beza to write this treatise. We must remember this. If we forget that Beza's overwhelming pastoral concern for people's eternal well-being was at the heart of this work, we are in danger of losing the forest for the trees in the midst of our discussion of his *Confession*.

It's not unrealistic to suppose that Beza followed the contours of Calvin's *Institutes* while composing his *Confession*. One historian has suggested that Beza's intention may have been to summarize the doctrine of Calvin in a more manageable size. Michel Réveillaud believes that the four main theological works of the French Reformation are Calvin's *Institutes*, Calvin's *Catechism*, the *Confession of Faith* adopted by the French Reformed church at La Rochelle in 1559, and Beza's *Confession*. Each of these works, he suggests, had different audiences which account for the different levels of detail in each of them. The *Institutes* expounded in detail the important matters of the Christian faith, acting as a theological resource for the French church. The *Catechism* and the La Rochelle *Confession of Faith*, on the other hand, served as shorter summary statements, a kind of quick reference guide for new Protestants struggling to maintain their faith. Beza's *Confession* served an intermediate role. It is fuller than Calvin's *Catechism* and the French church's *Confession of Faith*, but not nearly as extensive as Calvin's *Institutes*. It served, in fact, as a popularization of Calvin's masterpiece. The fact that it was written to those who were struggling with believing the faith, or who were being tempted to abandon the faith, accounts for some of the *Confession*'s emphases. Beza is relatively quick to cover those doctrines agreed on by both Protestants and Catholics (such tenets as the Trinity and the person of Christ) while he labors over those doctrines that separated the two communions. This may account for the lengthy seventh section on the errors of Roman Catholicism, which are more polemical than most of the book.[13]

The Content

Reading the *Confession* is certainly a different experience than perusing the developed and poetic language of Calvin in his *Institutes*. Beza's work is shorter and punchier. More than that, though, it's more utilitarian, trying to convey as much weighty theological definition in short order as is possible. To be sure, there are moments of literary elegance. For the most part, however, in this short piece Beza is content to go directly to the meat of Christian doctrine for the sake of clarity and the spiritual good of his readers. What makes the work read less like an elegant treatise and more like a scholastic disputation are the multiple numbered articles that Beza includes in each chapter. The advantage of these articles is that one can trace his argument throughout as he moves from article to article with logical precision, orderly presenting the faith for new believers.

---

13. Michel Réveillaud, ed. '*La Confession de Foi du Chretien* par Theodore de Beza' (*La Revue Réformée* 6 [1955]), pp. 1-7; Wright, *Our Sovereign Refuge*, pp. 15-16.

Summarizing the Faith

Beza divides the book into seven chapters. They deal with the Trinity, God the Father, Jesus the Son of God, the Holy Spirit, the church, final judgment, and the differences between the Reformed church and the doctrine of Rome. Beza never tells us why he organized the book as he did. The trinitarian structure of the first four chapters is apparent, so he may have intentionally presented the material so as to mirror the arrangement of the Apostles' Creed, which would have been familiar to all of his readers. Even though the final polemical chapter was absent in early editions of the *Confession*, Beza had it included in subsequent publications of the work, so we will deal with it in our summary.

Chapter 1: Of the Trinity

Chapter one, 'Of the Trinity', comprises only three short articles. But here Beza lays the groundwork for all the biblical theology to follow. There is only one God. We see this in nature, but we believe this 'much rather because the Holy Scripture witnesses and declares it unto us.' Yet this one divine essence eternally is three distinct Persons who are 'consubstantial and coeternal, without confusion of property and relationship.' Heretics deny this, but their errors are evident. What is essential to know of this one, undivided, trinitarian God is that He controls everything. So, in the last article of chapter one, Beza speaks of God's eternal providence:

> Nothing is done at adventure or by chance or without the most just ordinance and appointment of God, although God is in no way author nor culpable of any evil which is committed. For His goodness and mighty power is such and so incomprehensible that He ordains and does well and justly even what the devil and man do evil and unjustly.[14]

---

14. Beza, *Brief and Pithy Sum*, p. 242. I will refer to a section by chapter and then article number (e.g., 1.1) when not directly quoting it. For the sake of reading ease, I am not including the biblical prooftexts that Beza included.

Chapter one, then, lays the foundation for all the doctrine to come. God is one and also a personal trinitarian being. We know this primarily from Scripture. And Scripture teaches us most fundamentally that God is supremely sovereign, ruling over all the affairs of men according to His righteous decree.

Chapter 2: Of God the Father
Almost as short as the first one, chapter two, 'Of God the Father', highlights the role of the Father in creation. First, Beza teaches that the Father is a distinct person from both the Son and the Holy Spirit. To the Father, especially, is the oversight of creation to be assigned; 'when it seemed good to Him,' He sent forth His eternal Word and both together sent the Spirit. The Father not only created the visible world, but He also created all spiritual beings. Some of these, 'by the singular grace of God', are the angels who minister to the elect. Others, 'the devils', fell by their own malice and face eternal condemnation. Yet, even though there are distinct personal properties in the persons, we should not 'separate from the Father, either the Son, or yet the Holy Ghost, either in the creation or in the government of all things, or yet in anything which pertains to the substance of God.' As the third article's title asserts, 'the works of the Trinity are inseparable.'[15]

Beza has summarized centuries of Christian discussion and debate in this short chapter. He adheres to the trinitarian doctrine as found in the pronouncements of the Council of Nicaea (A.D. 325). He is Augustinian in his providential prescription. Supremely he is biblical in his presentation of potentially difficult ideas from Scripture.

Chapter 3: Of Jesus Christ, the Only Son of God
Chapter three, 'Of Jesus Christ, the Only Son of God', is much more extensive than the previous two chapters, comprising twenty-six articles. The chapter title might suggest that the

---

15. Beza, *Brief and Pithy Sum*, p. 243.

Summarizing the Faith

discussion will all be about who Jesus is. Indeed, Beza spends some time speaking of Jesus' person and His qualities. But much more space is devoted to Jesus' work in saving His people. Even prior to that, though, Beza details the state of humankind in sin, which necessitates that there must be a mediator between them and God in order for them to be saved. We will notice these three facets of Beza's discussion—Jesus' person, the state of humanity in sin, and Jesus' saving work.

First of all, then, in language reminiscent of the early councils of Nicaea (A.D. 325) and Chalcedon (A.D. 451), Beza asserts that Jesus, according to His divine nature, 'is the only Son of God, begotten from everlasting and not made, one with the Father in substance, co-eternal and consubstantial, equal to God His Father in all things and everywhere.' Rather than considering the person of Christ in more detail, Beza next teaches that this eternal Son took on flesh in order to save, according to the Father's decree: 'This is He alone whom the Father has ordained from everlasting to unite to man's nature, in order to save His elect, chosen by Him.'[16]

God's supreme desire is to portray His character to men. He is both just and merciful, as His decree concerning the work of Christ shows. The saving work of the Son manifested the eternal love of God for His elect, as Beza notes in the following four articles. This saving work had to proceed according to justice, for 'God is perfectly righteous' and unable 'to leave any injustice to go unpunished.' But it also proceeds from God's kindness for He is 'also perfectly merciful' so that when He acts to save men He does it 'of His full and sole grace'. All that occurs with humanity happens according to God's eternal decree which is immutable, but this does not negate the fact that God employs 'second causes'. This is so because God 'in ordaining what ought to come, ordains also the measures by which it pleases Him that such things should come to pass.' In this way, evil occurs but God is not the one responsible for it.

---

16. Beza, *Brief and Pithy Sum*, p. 244.

In conclusion, God created humanity according to His eternal decree to show He was both just and merciful:

> There will be some saved and some damned, and all for the glory of God as the whole Scripture declares. It follows then that since nothing happens or comes to pass at a venture or by chance, and that God never changes His purpose or mind, and God not only has foreseen, but has also eternally ordained to create man to spread forth and declare His glory, He saves those whom it pleases Him (forgetting nothing pertaining to His justice without which He cannot be God) and condemning others by His judgment.[17]

Jesus' person, then, is best understood in relation to God's desire that His character would be shown in relationship to sinful people, either to save them or to damn them.

Second, God is merciful towards His elect and we learn about the Son only in His response to sinful creatures who deserve His judgment. Beza delineates the contours of humanity in sin in the following nine articles (3.7-15). To accomplish His goal of manifesting His manifold character, first of all, God created humanity good (3.7). Humanity's goodness, however, needed to be mutable in order for the Lord to accomplish the revelation of His character. So, man fell from his state of goodness, to show God's character: 'For if sin had not so entered the world, God would not have found such a cause to magnify His mercy in saving those whom He has ordained to salvation; nor matter to declare His justice in condemning those whom He has ordained to His wrath, to the end that He may punish them for their demerits.'

Therefore, in order to accomplish His will, God created Adam and Eve in a state of 'righteousness and true holiness', in His image. But man, 'willingly and without any constraint, [did] join and knit himself to the devil.' He made himself liable to both physical and eternal death. Not only he, but all his

---

17. Beza, *Brief and Pithy Sum*, p. 244.

posterity, die and face impending eternal judgment for their sin (3.10). Physical death awaits us all (3.11-12).[18]

Because of Adam's 'original sin' every part of us—'the whole man, no part excepted'—is corrupt. Due to this corruption, 'every man, even from the very first beginning of his conception, [is] a child of wrath.' This corruption 'makes us altogether unprofitable, yes, contrary to all goodness and wholly subject to sin.' Augustine corroborates this view that humans are in bondage to sin, saying that 'men labor to find what good there is in their own will, but do not know how a man should find any.'[19]

Having asserted the bondage of the will in sin, though, Beza is quick to deflect criticisms of fatalism. Humans still have freedom, but it is limited. To be sure, men are not 'stocks or blocks'. They have enough light to render them inexcusable. They have faculties such as 'reason, judgment, will, and such others' which have been 'corrupted, not removed.' The outcome of this is that men still have 'free will', but it must be defined according to Scripture, not the vagaries of human reasoning:

> By this free will is not understood a natural power to think, will, or do good or evil, but a will not constrained, which notwithstanding cannot nor will not anything but altogether evil as long as the nature of man not being regenerated (that is to say, not healed and restored by grace) is not only wounded or hurt, but utterly and altogether corrupted and also willingly becomes the servant of sin.

Referring to Augustine as an authority at this point—perhaps as an authority palatable to his Catholic father?—Beza asserts that 'free will as it is bound and in thrall, is worth nothing but to sin and fall.'[20]

---

18. Beza, *Brief and Pithy Sum*, pp. 244-5.
19. Beza, *Brief and Pithy Sum*, p. 246.
20. Beza, *Brief and Pithy Sum*, p. 246.

That, then, is the ability humanity has in its sin. Original sin leaves us spiritually destitute, affecting as it does 'the whole nature of man'. Three types of sins flow out of this first sin and the corruption that follows: first, 'every inward motion and thought in man's understanding'; second, another sin occurs 'when the will and affection consent to it'; third, they sin when they 'force themselves to execute what inwardly they have conceived and willed.'[21]

Third, only after laying this groundwork of humanity in a bleak quagmire of sin does Beza address how Jesus is the only possible savior for a damned race. God chooses to show mercy to some of this race and to manifest 'the declaration of His power and wrath by the just judgment and condemnation of the vessels of wrath prepared for destruction.' The salvation of God's people was accomplished by the incarnation and death of God's Son, whose ministry was foretold throughout the Old Testament so that 'man might be saved by faith in Jesus Christ to come.' The reason that all persons were saved similarly by Christ is that God has decreed 'but one covenant of salvation' between Himself and men. The 'substance' of this covenant is Jesus Christ even though circumstantially there are 'two testaments or covenants'. The second one, the New Covenant, 'is the better, abolishing the Old since the Old did not propound and set forth Jesus Christ but afar off and hidden under shadows and figures which were abolished by His coming.'[22]

In order for Jesus to be the mediator of God's gracious covenant it was necessary that He be fully human and truly God as well. First of all, He had to be 'true man and without any spot of original sin or any other' sin for several reasons. There had to be 'a true man in whom this ruin and decay should be thoroughly and perfectly repaired to please God.' There had to be a man who would perfectly fulfill all the

---

21. Beza, *Brief and Pithy Sum*, pp. 246-7.
22. Beza, *Brief and Pithy Sum*, p. 247.

Lord's commands for righteousness. There had to be a man to 'accomplish perfectly all righteousness to please God' since all other men 'are covered with an infinite number of sins.' There had to be a perfect man, because every other human would first need a savior from his sin before he could save others. 'It was necessary, therefore, that the Redeemer and Mediator of man should be a true man in body and soul and yet nevertheless perfectly and altogether pure and clean from all sin.'[23]

In the second place, Jesus had to be fully divine. Had He not been God, He would first of all have needed a savior Himself. God demands infinite payment for sin since 'the offense or fault is infinite against whose majesty it is committed'; only an infinite person can provide an infinite satisfaction. So no created being could bear the infinite wrath due to our sin. Finally, 'to better declare His incomprehensible goodness, God would make His grace not only equal with our offense, but [would make it] exceed and surmount the trespass.' Since Jesus is God, we have certainty that His sacrifice more than atones for our sins.

To accomplish our salvation, the eternal Son of God took on human flesh, except for sin (3.21). In terms reminiscent of the Council of Chalcedon's definition of Jesus Christ, Beza carefully explains what occurred at the incarnation:

> We confess that from the first instant of this conception, the person of the Son was inseparably united with the nature of man, in such a way that there are not two sons of God, not two Jesus Christs, but only one Son of God, Jesus Christ, very God and very man. Yet nevertheless both these natures abide and remain in their several properties. For the divinity separated from the humanity or the humanity divided or plucked from the divinity, or the one confused with the other would serve no purpose.

Jesus Christ is therefore true God and true man. He took on human flesh in order to save people from their sin. From

---

23. Beza, *Brief and Pithy Sum*, p. 248.

the moment of His conception until His resurrection, 'He has fulfilled perfectly all righteousness in order to cover our unrighteousness.' And He did this by uniting us together with Him in His glorious work of salvation. Beza waxes eloquent in painting the picture of this glorious union:

> For the whole and full satisfaction for our sins which He took upon Himself, He was bound to unbind us; condemned to deliver us, He suffered great and infinite shame to deliver us from all confusion; He was nailed on the cross to fasten our sins there; He died and sustained the curse and malediction which was due to us to appease the wrath of God forever, which He made by solitary oblation; He was buried to approve and verify His death, and to vanquish death, even to the house thereof, i.e., even to the grave (in which He felt no corruption) to declare that even in dying, He had overcome and vanquished death. He was raised again in triumph as conqueror to the end that all our corruption being dead and buried, we would be renewed into a spiritual and everlasting life; and that by this, the first death should no more be a punishment to us due to sin, and as it were an entrance into the second death, but on the contrary a finishing and end of the death of our corruption and an entrance into eternal life. Finally, being raised afterwards, He was conversant here on earth for forty days to confirm and approve His resurrection. He ascended visibly and verily into heaven where He sits on the right hand of God His Father, and has taken possession of His eternal kingdom for us and for our good; for whose sake also He is the only Mediator and Advocate, governing His church by His Holy Spirit, until the number of the elect of God His Father is accomplished and fulfilled.[24]

Jesus' accomplishments thus are ours, even though He is bodily in heaven 'until the time He will come to judge the quick and the dead.' His benefits come to us via His Spirit, by whom He promises to be with us until the end. In conclusion, God has

---

24. Beza, *Brief and Pithy Sum*, pp. 249-50.

Summarizing the Faith

revealed Himself to be true God in our redemption, because He has shown Himself to be both just and merciful at the cross. We should hold to this truth tenaciously. 'But on the contrary, all religion which opposes the wrath of God, anything other than the sole innocence, righteousness, and satisfaction of Jesus Christ, apprehended by faith, spoils God of His perfect righteousness and mercy.'[25] In the conclusion to the third chapter, therefore, Beza comes around to the grand theme of the Christian faith: our sin demanded satisfaction, and God showed Himself supremely just and merciful in the satisfaction procured by Jesus Christ—true God and true man—on the cross. Only in His work there can we find hope.

The third chapter shows us Beza's ultimate concern, and it demonstrates the essence of Protestantism to him. Theology matters. But it is significant not just for academic precision's sake. It matters because it deals with what concerns us most. How can a holy God forgive sinners who have rebelled against Him? How can He reconcile us to Himself and still remain just? In this chapter we have seen that Beza was concerned with salvation more than with anything else. This is the essence of his disagreements with Catholicism. And it is also the essence of what he yearns for his readers to embrace.

Chapter 4: Of the Holy Ghost

Chapter four, 'Of the Holy Ghost', is the longest in the *Confession*, comprising fifty-one articles. Given the length of the chapter, however, it has remarkable cohesion. Beza follows the contours of the New Testament in not speaking at length of the Spirit's person, although he touches on that. Instead, he elaborates on the manner in which the Spirit gives faith to the elect and discusses what that faith is. In the process, Beza fills the bulk of the chapter with pastoral counsel telling whether or not one has true faith in Jesus and helping believers to discern the proper role of good works in their lives. He concludes the

---

25. Beza, *Brief and Pithy Sum*, pp. 251-2.

chapter by discussing the Spirit's activity in the two sacraments of the church.

Only the first two paragraphs deal with the Holy Spirit Himself. Beza writes that 'We believe in the Holy Ghost,' reminiscent of the wording of the Apostles' Creed. He is the power of the Father and the Son, co-eternal and consubstantial with them, proceeding from them. He is 'one God with them and nevertheless distinct in person.' Although the Spirit creates and preserves His creation, Beza is especially interested in demonstrating the way in which the Spirit applies the work of Christ to believers.

> [The Holy Ghost] principally will be considered by us in this present treatise according to the effects which He brings forth in the children of God, in beginning with His grace, to make them feel the efficacy and virtue thereof; and briefly to bring them from degree to degree to the right end and mark to which they are predestined before the foundation of the world.[26]

In the next seven articles (4.3-9) Beza discusses what faith is and how the Spirit works in the elect to grant them faith. The Spirit is absolutely essential because He is 'the same by whom the Father puts and keeps His elect in possession of Jesus Christ His Son, and consequently of all the graces which are necessary to salvation.' The 'only instrument' the Spirit uses to save Christians is faith, by which we take 'hold of Jesus Christ when He is offered to us, and the only vessel to receive Him.' To create faith, the Spirit uses two means: the preaching of the word and the sacraments (4.4). Beza will return to preaching and the sacraments, but first he discusses what faith is and how we should discern its effects. The Spirit creates the faith God requires of us. Beza delineates this faith at length, and so we should pay careful attention to his summary:

---

26. Beza, *Brief and Pithy Sum*, p. 252.

Summarizing the Faith

> Now the faith of which we speak is not to believe only that God is God and that the contents of His Word are true (for the devils have this faith and cannot but tremble at it), but we call faith a certain knowledge which the Holy Ghost by His grace alone and goodness engraves more and more in the hearts of the elect of God, by which each one of them being assured in his heart of his election, applies and appropriates to himself the promise of his salvation in Jesus Christ. Faith, I say, believes not only that Jesus Christ is dead and risen for sinners, but proceeds to embrace Jesus Christ in whom alone he trusts and so assures himself of his salvation that he doubts not. For that reason St Bernard said, according to all the Scriptures that follow, 'If you believe that your sins may not be put away, but by Him whom you have offended, and also who is not subject to sin, you do well; but yet join thereunto another point, that is to say that you believe also that by Him your sins are forgiven.'[27]

In a manner certainly drawing on the work of his mentor, John Calvin, Beza stresses here that faith is more than intellectual knowledge. It includes a 'certain knowledge' that a person is saved. True belief manifests itself in a Christian's experience so that he is assured of salvation and no longer doubts it. As we will see, though, Beza follows Calvin in dealing with instances where a believer has doubts. The ideal of faith, then, is constantly being assailed.

'Since Jesus Christ is the mark of our faith', 'the one that has Jesus Christ by faith has all.' When believers have 'Jesus Christ by faith,' they 'have all things in Him.' The power of faith is not faith per se. Rather, faith is merely the instrument by which we receive Christ. Faith 'embraces Him who justifies us, i.e., Jesus Christ, in such a way that it unites and knits us together with Him to be partakers of all the goodness which He has.' To believe this is not to succumb to pride; rather it 'is the only means for taking all pride from ourselves and to

---

27. Beza, *Brief and Pithy Sum*, pp. 252-3.

give all glory to God. For faith alone teaches us to go out of our own selves and to know that in us there is nothing but the matter of damnation, and sends us to one alone—Jesus Christ, by whose righteousness alone it teaches and assures us that we will find salvation before God.' Faith in Jesus Christ, then, is absolutely central. With it we have everything. Without it we have nothing but damnation.[28]

For this reason Beza is going to discuss at length how we may have true and abiding faith (4.9). He recounts several temptations against faith that Satan and our consciences use to attack us. First, he reminds us of God's infinite perfection and our infinite sins. What shall we do? We certainly at this point have no recourse to the saints, who themselves looked to someone else to save them. Here, then, is how we defeat the tempter, by saying,

> You say, Satan, that God is perfectly righteous and avenges all iniquity. I do confess it, but I will join to that another property of righteousness which you have left out, i.e., since God is righteous, He is content with one payment. You will say then that there is infinite iniquity in me which deserves eternal death. I grant it, but I add more to it which you have maliciously omitted, i.e., that the iniquities which are in me were most sufficiently avenged and punished in Jesus Christ who has borne the judgment of God in my stead. So upon this I make my conclusion contrary to yours, i.e., since God is righteous and will not be paid double, and Jesus Christ, God and man, has by one infinite obedience made satisfaction to the infinite majesty of God, it follows that my iniquities can no more distress or trouble me, my accounts and debts being assuredly razed and wiped out by the precious blood of Jesus Christ, who was made accursed for me, being righteous for the unrighteous.

In the same vein Satan assaults us, claiming that we must be completely righteous to stand before a holy God. We must put

---

28. Beza, *Brief and Pithy Sum*, pp. 254-5.

Summarizing the Faith

Jesus Christ up in response to this assault, for 'here is declared a perfect obedience according to the Law, which was never found but in Jesus Christ alone.' And by faith we are clothed with Christ's perfect righteousness; by faith Christ is now 'proper to us'.

Satan is not done, though. He claims that as true as all this is, God is still angry with us on account of our corrupt nature. Surely God cannot accept us since we are not holy. Against this we need again to appropriate Christ. 'Since the sanctification of Jesus Christ is imputed to us as our own, then the natural corruption which rests partly yet in us cannot come into account, since it is covered and clothed with the holiness of Jesus Christ, who is much more able to sanctify and cleanse us before God than the natural corruption is to defile and corrupt us.'[29] These, then, are the responses to Satan's first temptation, the accusation that we are not worthy to stand before the holy God.

The evil one's second temptation is to make us doubt that we possess true faith. Beza avers that it is essential for us to know for certain that Christ is ours, not to be satisfied with a general belief about Jesus. The way to do this is 'ascend by the effects to the knowledge of the cause which works them.' If Jesus Christ has truly taken hold of us, He will produce two effects: first, 'the testimony which the Holy Spirit brings to our spirits that we are the children of God'; second, a real change in us, called in Scripture 'regeneration' and 'sanctification', which 'make us new creatures with regard to qualities we may have.' The regeneration of a person consists of distinct parts: the putting to death of the old man, whereby Jesus 'quenches and subdues little by little this cursed corruption of our nature'; and the Lord also gives us 'new strength and power.' The Spirit's testimony and a change of our nature, then, are the two effects 'which, if we feel them working in us, the conclusion is

---

29. Beza, *Brief and Pithy Sum*, pp. 257-9.

infallible—that we have faith and consequently Jesus Christ in us unto eternal life.'[30]

It is thus absurd for opponents to claim that Beza does not stress the importance of good works (4.14). So Beza spends five lengthy articles (4.15-19) discussing good works. In the first place, we must let God's word and not our faulty reason determine what works are good or bad (4.15). Scripture teaches us that there are two great works God requires of us—prayer and love for our neighbor. Prayer, 'calling on the name of God through Jesus Christ', pleases God more than any other thing we do. Prayer should be offered with the expectation that God will answer, according to Scripture's teaching, only because of Jesus Christ our mediator. We must remember that 'our requests are not grounded on any worthiness that is in us, but only upon the excellence and dignity of Jesus Christ alone (who is promised and communicated to us by faith with all His benefits),' as both John Chrysostom and Ambrose teach. Prayer pleases God because it recognizes who He is and who we are in light of Him. Secondly, God requires of us 'works of charity toward our neighbors,' as long as they are performed in recognition of the reality that Jesus has saved us. Other works are indifferent but please God if they flow from faith. We must also recognize that any good works we do flow not from our fallen and feeble free will but only from the will of God who has to draw us to Himself in the first place. 'So then since grace must make us good trees before we can bear good fruit, it follows that there is no meeting together of grace and free will.' We must also know that our works are not good relative to God's holiness; they don't deserve or merit anything good from the Lord. 'Good works come from Jesus Christ dwelling in us.' The conclusion is encouraging for Christians: 'In this lies all our consolation—that we have our only refuge in the special grace and mercy which is presented to us in Jesus

---

30. Beza, *Brief and Pithy Sum*, pp. 260-1.

Summarizing the Faith

Christ alone, who is not our Savior and Redeemer in part, but altogether.'[31]

Having admitted that our works do nothing to save us, however, does not mean that they are not useful. In fact they have several benefits. First, they serve our neighbors and also 'provoke unbelievers to give glory to God.' Second, they 'assure us more and more of our salvation.' Third, our loving Father views our works through the blood of Jesus; instead of looking at our sinfulness His eye is turned to the purity of Christ. He considers His children in Christ, 'regarding the fruits of His grace, not as they are polluted by their infirmities and weaknesses, but because they have as it were proceeded or issued from Him.' Fourth, they prove to us that we are elect, 'for faith is necessarily joined to election…faith is no other than an assurance which we have that the promises of eternal life pertain to us because we were predestined and elected to it.' So 'when Satan puts us in doubt of our election, we may not first search the resolution in the eternal counsel of God, whose majesty we cannot comprehend.' Rather, look to see if you are being sanctified, for sanctification 'is a certain effect of faith; or rather of Jesus Christ dwelling in us by faith.'[32]

The last and most dangerous temptation of Satan is to ask a Christian if he truly is elect. The problem is exasperated by the reality that even 'the most perfect and holy persons fall into this extremity, sorrowing and lamenting because they do not feel these good motions; rather it seems that it is utterly quenched in them.' Beza addresses this problem in the lengthy twentieth article. He gives his readers several ways to combat this demonic attack. First, the effects of good works and the testimony of the Holy Spirit to our consciences work like 'two anchors to hold us fast'. So when one is lacking, we should look to the other. Second, we need to realize we're saved by Christ

---

31. Beza, *Brief and Pithy Sum*, pp. 263-7.
32. Beza, *Brief and Pithy Sum*, pp. 267-9.

whether or not the two effects of faith are present. Beza's pastoral counsel is insightful:

> although both these operations and effects are very feeble and weak, yet there is no reason to be discouraged. For it is not required of us to believe fully and perfectly, but to believe only in such a way as that one little spark, and so following one little motion of it in us (for it is true and unfeigned, i.e., coming from the true root of faith), it is sufficient to assure us of our salvation. The reason is that our salvation is not only established on our faith (although without faith none can be saved), but upon him whom we apprehend by faith, i.e., Jesus Christ. And faith is of such virtue that according to the promises of God, one little spark thereof, however little it is, apprehends Jesus Christ fully and perfectly.

Third, when we are frustrated with our lack of good works, we should take heart from the examples of believers of old who struggled with the same thing. Fourth, we should turn to 'the surer and more perfect remedy, which is the certainty of our election, established on the immutable purpose of God.' We need to remember that 'God never changes His purpose,' so He will keep us in the way. Also, we need to recollect that 'what He has once purposed must come to pass, whatever hindrances come.' Especially, we should remember that faith is a gift given to the elect alone, and this gift is always connected with God's gift of perseverance, even if it experiences obstacles along the way. Because of God's election, a Christian may be certain of his salvation even if the good works are lacking at times: 'Whoever has a certain testimony of his faith once in all his life, may be assured that it is there still and will be until the end, although for a time they may not feel it, nor perceive it.' Such a doctrine doesn't lead to licentiousness, but rather it's an incentive for us to do works that please the Lord.[33]

---

33. Beza, *Brief and Pithy Sum*, pp. 269-72.

Summarizing the Faith

To this point, Beza has argued that the Holy Spirit is the one who creates faith. Now, he shows how the Spirit does this creative work: through the word and the sacraments (4.21). In 4.22-30 Beza begins by discussing the word of God. The first thing to note about Scripture is that it's comprised of two parts, the law and the gospel. In the law, God 'sets out for us the obedience and perfect righteousness which we owe to His majesty and our neighbor.' On the other hand, in the gospel, 'God declares to us that He will save us freely by His only Son, so that we embrace and accept Him by faith as our only wisdom, righteousness, sanctification, and redemption.'[34] Beza urges his readers to pay attention to these two different parts of the Bible, for confusion of them is one of the chief causes of religious difficulties.

He identifies four differences between the law and the gospel. First, the law is natural to humans, whereas the 'gospel is a supernatural doctrine, which our nature could never attain nor allow without the special grace and gift of God.' Second, the law subjects us to God and His wrath, whereas the gospel pacifies Him. Third, the law tells us to save ourselves, whereas the gospel sends us to Christ for salvation. Fourth, the law has no power to save us, whereas 'the gospel, over and above the declaration of the remedy and medicine against malediction of the Law, then immediately being joined and accompanied with the virtue and power of the Holy Ghost, regenerates us … creating in us the instrument and means to appropriate this medicine.' The law has its place, and therefore it must be preached. It makes our faults known, leading us to feel guilty, and then confess our sin to the Lord. But the law alone can never save a sinner.[35]

For salvation, we need the gospel, which was written by the apostles and the evangelists. It follows that nothing is to be added to God's written word and that it needs to be translated

---

34. Beza, *Brief and Pithy Sum*, p. 273.
35. Beza, *Brief and Pithy Sum*, pp. 274-5.

into the common language so that people have access to the gospel. Since the gospel is 'the only means by which God from the beginning of the world has always saved His elect,' it includes the Old Testament revelation of God. The gospel is 'those happy tidings which God by His grace and mercy alone has declared to His church from the beginning of the world', i.e., 'whosoever believes in Jesus Christ shall be saved.' For this reason, it must be translated into vernacular languages. For 'how will they understand what is sung or read in an unknown tongue, or not sincerely and truly expounded?' Indeed, people are responsible to read the Bible themselves in order 'to be confirmed in what has been expounded' by the pastors in the preaching of the church.[36]

The Bible, then, is central because it is what the Holy Spirit uses to change people, both in conversion and in sanctification. The Spirit

> uses this outward preaching as a pipe or conduit which enters and pierces the very depth of the spirit, as the apostle says, to make, by His grace and goodness alone, the understanding of the children of God capable and fit to conceive and understand this high mystery of their salvation through Jesus Christ. Moreover He uses it to reform and renew their judgments by which they may approve that to be the wisdom of God which our sense and reason esteem to be folly. Moreover He uses it to correct and change their will so that with an ardent affection they may embrace and appropriate for themselves the remedy which is given to them and show forth Jesus Christ against despair, into which without the same they would fall perhaps headlong through the preaching of the Law.

Indeed, after Christians are converted the Holy Spirit makes the law 'easy and light' to us. So 'instead of making us afraid, [the law] comforts us.'[37]

---

36. Beza, *Brief and Pithy Sum*, pp. 279-80.
37. Beza, *Brief and Pithy Sum*, pp. 280-1.

Summarizing the Faith

After his discussion of the word of God, Beza moves to the sacraments as the second means that God uses to support His people. The sacraments flow from the kindness of God to us: 'In order to heap on us a number of His infinite mercies and goodnesses, He joins to the preaching of His Word certain things to do which should come to move' and stir us up to love Him more. In the Old Testament these actions included things like circumcision and sacrifices to show God's gentleness to His people and to give them hope.[38]

Thus we arrive at Beza's definition of sacraments. They are 'added and joined by Himself to the Word of His gospel ... to represent to our outward senses those things which He permits us to understand by His Word.'[39] In addition, the sacraments remind us of our obligations to our neighbors. Since they are intimately connected with faith, sacraments should never be received apart from the word of God preached (4.32). As in receiving the word preached, so we must exercise faith when we receive the sacraments or they will only result in our damnation (4.33). In sum, the sacraments are useful because they reach more of our senses than the Word does: 'Since the simple Word preached touches only one of the senses, the sacraments touch more (such as sight and other bodily senses).'[40]

For this reason, there are only two sacraments—baptism and the Lord's Supper—which Beza now discusses under four headings. First, sacraments are 'signs', meaning that they 'represent to us the greatest and most excellent things, declared effectually in the lively Word of God.' These sacraments undergo no change in their substance; rather, it's only by the power of the Holy Spirit, 'according to the ordinance of the good will of God which is testified to us by that promise to which the sign is joined' so that 'the water, the bread and wine become

---

38. Beza, *Brief and Pithy Sum*, p. 283.
39. Beza, *Brief and Pithy Sum*, p. 284.
40. Beza, *Brief and Pithy Sum*, p. 287.

sacraments, i.e., true signs of these things which the Word promises and which are truly represented by them.' Second, Jesus Christ alone 'is declared to us and represented with all His goodness and treasures by the signs of the sacrifices.' We receive this reality only by faith, which the Spirit stirs up both by the word and the sacraments. Third, the reality of Jesus Christ is joined to the signs not by magical incantations but by the Holy Spirit alone. Fourth, the Holy Spirit communicates the reality of the signs to us, but this reality is only received by faith.[41]

Beza then applies these four points to the two sacraments. His discussion of baptism is noteworthy. After discussing the meaning of baptism, he argues that infants should be baptized both because baptism has replaced circumcision and because Scripture has special regard for the children of believers: 'We justly presume to be the children of God all those who are the issue and descended from believing parents according to the promise.' And baptism—even if performed by heretics or Catholics—is not to be repeated because God's mercy is great. Beza concludes his discussion of the sacraments by applying all he has said to believers for the strengthening of their faith: 'The sacraments are not only ordained to offer to God a giving of thanks (which is also called a sacrifice and acceptable offering), but rather that we should receive His grace and liberality, which is more precious than heaven and earth (i.e., the confirmation of our faith) and so to be the more nearly united and joined to Jesus Christ unto eternal life.'[42]

This lengthy chapter is, once again, all about salvation. Not only being concerned that his readers know how salvation is accomplished (what he spoke of in chapter three), in this chapter Beza applies this truth pastorally to them. The Holy Spirit creates faith, and they can know if they possess real saving faith. Their response shouldn't be morbid introspection

---

41. Beza, *Brief and Pithy Sum*, pp. 288-90.

42. Beza, *Brief and Pithy Sum*, pp. 294, 298.

but thanksgiving to their Father for giving the means that creates faith and the means of sustaining their faith through all the days of their earthly pilgrimages.

Chapter 5: Of the Church

Moving from the first four chapters to chapter five, 'Of the Church', is like moving from a warm pastoral encouragement to a polemical tract with the Catholic church largely in its sights. Beza is pastoral in this section on occasion. For the most part, though, this section reads like a workbook on Protestant church government.

Beza begins with a wonderful description of the church which is worth noting in full since it sets the paradigm for all the discussion to follow. Here is his rationale for why the church is important:

> All those things of which we have spoken as established and performed by the goodness of God are in vain if there are not certain people who feel and taste the fruit and abundance of it. But since Jesus Christ has an eternal kingdom, He can never be without subjects. It was appropriate, then, from the beginning of the world, that there should be a church, i.e., a congregation and assembly of people whom it has pleased God to choose by His grace, which have acknowledged and served the true God according to His will by means of Jesus Christ alone attained by faith, as it has been amply declared. And we must confess moreover that by the same means His church and assembly will last forever, whatever assaults all the devils in hell gather or prepare against them. Finally, it must be confessed necessarily that without Jesus Christ there is no salvation. And whoever dies not being a member of this congregation and assembly is excluded and locked out from Jesus Christ and from His salvation. For the power to save which is in Jesus Christ pertains to none but those who acknowledge Him for their God and only Savior.[43]

---

43. Beza, *Brief and Pithy Sum*, pp. 298-9.

God's plan had always been to display His glory among a people. These people have submitted to Him as their King and have received salvation by faith in Jesus. Only in the church is there hope of salvation.

Having laid out this paradigm, in the next eight sections (5.2-9) Beza discusses the points of his lengthy description of the church. In the first place, since there's only one God, one faith, and one Mediator, there is only one true church (5.2). This church, composed of all believers who are dispersed over all the earth, is called 'Catholic' or 'universal' since its members are dispersed everywhere (5.3). The reality of the 'communion of the saints', then, is based on two requirements. First, the church has only one 'head', Jesus. Second, all who are in communion with Him by faith are the church (5.4). Following this, it is illegitimate to claim a temporal, human as the head of the church. This honor—and this reality—is Jesus Christ's alone (5.5). Even though Jesus Christ is the head of the church, and even though His saints have real communion with Him and with each other, there is still true human authority within the church. What's necessary, though, is to derive that authority from its rightful source. Jesus 'so governs this church by His Holy Spirit that nevertheless He uses men as instruments to plant and to water.'[44] The church must be oriented around the word of God and, specifically, reestablish the biblical pattern of discipline in order to glorify God.

This discussion leads Beza to ask how one may discern if an assembly is a true or a false church. The key is that the true church is one that looks to, and looks like, Christ Jesus, the head of the church. For this reason, there are three distinguishing marks by which one may discern a true church. The first 'mark of the true church is the preaching of the lively Word of the Son of God.' Following this are the two marks of 'the sacraments duly ministered with ecclesiastical discipline established conformable to the holy and pure doctrine of God.' In these three marks we are

---

44. Beza, *Brief and Pithy Sum*, p. 300.

able to 'acknowledge the true church of God ... however small in number or little in appearance it is before men.' In the same way that we can discern a true church so we can also discern who the true members of this church are. The key marker is faith. This faith, though, is much more than just intellectual; it demonstrates itself in changed lives. Those with faith are marked by 'flying from sin, following righteousness.' They 'love and fear the true and eternal God only, and love their neighbors according to the Word of God, without turning or swerving either to the right hand or to the left.' They are not perfect, yet sin does not reign in them as it did before. So, when it is evident that the Spirit of grace is at work in a person, we can conclude that he is a member of the church, for the Spirit works in the elect alone. So Christians must join themselves with a true church when one is in their environs, separating from the Catholic church which is clouded by 'false doctrine' and led by a succession of unholy bishops.[45]

After these introductory comments on the nature of the true church, Beza moves on to discuss 'what the power and authority of the true church is.' Most basically, it consists in obedience to 'her only spouse, Jesus Christ'.[46] More needs to be said, though, and Beza examines the authority of the church in 5.11-22. This section demonstrates the historical setting of Beza's writing clearly, inasmuch as his anti-Roman polemic is heated here. In the first place, he acknowledges that there should be such things as 'universal councils' which are composed of representatives of the entire church, based on the precedent of the council in Acts 15 (5.11). The authority to convene such a council first falls to a Christian magistrate (whether emperor or monarch) who should be concerned with the welfare of his people and the church. If the magistrate is not a believer, pastors have the authority to call a council (5.12). The question of who the representatives to this council should be is central since in the Roman councils it would be hard to find a prelate willing to have his life and

---

45. Beza, *Brief and Pithy Sum*, pp. 301-2.
46. Beza, *Brief and Pithy Sum*, p. 304.

doctrine examined. This is why Beza expresses hopelessness that a council called in his day would be able to solve the disputed questions separating Catholics and Protestants, even though he thinks such a council should be convened to quiet the Catholics (5.13). At such a council order needs to prevail, but all should be allowed to speak since the Holy Spirit distributes gifts to all His people, indeed often to those one least expects (5.14). Since the ideal (for the emperor to preside over a council) will not happen, there are numerous princes who can do it. The bishop of Rome was not afforded special treatment in the ancient councils, nor did he call the council. So, his authority to call and preside over a council is nonexistent (5.15).

Beza continues, addressing the authority of councils and pre-empting Roman claims to papal preeminence and their attempts to supplant biblical clarity and power. Rightly-called councils have authority, but that authority must never supplant the power of God's word, as the church fathers argued (5.16). Councils do not have authority to make a new article of faith, for all that is necessary for salvation has been written in the Bible. Again, the fathers, especially Augustine, agree with that. Councils' authority only extends to maintaining pure doctrine against heretics and to laying down regulations for ecclesiastical discipline, orienting the polity of the church in different times and circumstances (5.17). Here, though, Christians must make a careful distinction. The doctrine of the church is one, and must never be changed. But the way the church regulates what it does—i.e., its discipline—may be changed according to different needs and times (5.18). However, when considering the church's discipline, all must be done in such a way as to support 'the doctrine of the gospel'. But many of the Roman ceremonies are additions to Scripture, unfortunately promoting superstition and idolatry. Instead, 'certainly the purest simplicity is the best, and the more Jesus Christ is plainly and simply declared, the more it is agreeable to His Word.'[47]

---

47. Beza, *Brief and Pithy Sum*, pp. 312-13.

Summarizing the Faith

Beza now discusses the different offices Christ has ordained to serve in His church. He does this in 5.23-38. In general, there are four types of office recognized by the Scripture: those whose duty is to preach the word, those who are 'to distribute ecclesiastical goods', those charged with overseeing ecclesiastical discipline and government, and those with the power of the sword to 'maintain the tranquility of the whole church.' Beza then addresses the first of these positions, noting the five offices of teacher in the church since Christ's coming. The first three—apostle, prophet, and evangelist—'served only at the beginning.' The other two—pastor and teacher—continue at the present time. The pastor's duty consists largely of four functions. He is to devote himself to doctrine, prayer, administering the sacraments, and blessing the marriages of believers. Since the only way one can be a Christian is by faith, and since faith is formed by the preaching of the word and the sacraments, pastors are said to have the keys of the kingdom.[48]

In expounding the role of pastors, Beza presses three points (5.25). First, there is a difference between teachers (also called doctors) and pastors. Teachers 'ought to expound the Scriptures simply and truly', especially to new converts. Pastors, though, go further than this. They are to preach and apply the Scripture to the congregation as well as to pray publicly (5.26). Second, although the ultimate binding and loosing in the Kingdom—giving 'remission of sins' and saving and condemning 'body and soul'—belongs to God, He has entrusted His ministers, who preach the word and administer the sacraments, with derivative authority in this regard. Third, not everyone who claims to be a pastor is one. A shepherd must be found faithful, and God's people need to follow a devoted pastor, one who has been commissioned by the Lord, who has been rightly elected in the church, who lives a godly life, and who feeds the sheep. Deciding whom to follow and obey is bound by faithfulness to Scripture, for there are many false pastors:

---
48. Beza, *Brief and Pithy Sum*, p. 315.

Theodore Beza

They are false pastors who are not able or fit to execute the office and responsibility; likewise those who do not execute their office and duty, for he is no pastor who does not feed his flock. Likewise those who exceed their commission (i.e., who do not faithfully expound the Word of God) either exchanging, adding to, or diminishing it, but declare their own fantasies or other men's traditions instead of the Word of God: all such persons, I say, are declared (namely, by the ancient canons) to be false pastors and ministers of Satan, and not of God.

All pastors have equal authority, but each convened group of pastors needs to operate in order, and so a 'president' of the pastors should be elected to lead their meetings (5.29). Deacons are also a church office, meant to administer and distribute ecclesiastical goods (5.30). The ancient church had four other offices, whose role was largely to serve the pastor and the church: door keepers (to keep out those persons not allowed to take the sacraments), followers (who served the pastors), readers of the Scripture in the assembly, and exorcists (5.31).[49]

Regarding authority within the church, Beza notes that according to Scripture 'spiritual jurisdiction ... was committed' to elders. Their 'jurisdiction does not lie in worldly and temporal things, but altogether in those things which concern the conscience. So it is fully distinct from the office of a civil magistrate.' Believers are to be subject to the magistrate in temporal matters, but the church has an authority of its own. Ecclesiastical jurisdiction has just one end: 'That the whole body of the church in general and every member of the same in particular is preserved and edified in doctrine and doing good, according to the will and Word of God.' To this end, the church must, first, establish doctrine, morality, and external discipline; second, the church must punish transgressors (5.33). This is why the church has elders; they are the ones who are to 'watch that the church which is committed to them is

---

49. Beza, *Brief and Pithy Sum*, pp. 316-18.

governed by good order according to the rule of the gospel; and that the ecclesiastical laws and ordinances, either universal or particular, are maintained and executed diligently according to their responsibility.' Their authority largely resides in their power to elect those within the church who are to serve in different capacities. Ecclesiastical elections are essential to protect the church. No one should be put into office in the church without its consent, even though the pastors and civil magistrates have the duty of making sure all is done in order (5.35). Those elected to office are to be men of highest character and doctrine (5.36). There are no set directions in Scripture of how elections are to be done, but the church should do them according to their time and place (5.37). To confirm elections, these things should take place: the magistrate should consent to it, the people should agree to it as done by the elders, and prayers should be offered (5.38).[50]

The final seven articles of chapter five cover various topics related to the church. Beza discourses, first, about marriage. Celibacy is a special gift, often given for a short period of time, for a few Christians. Others are to marry. To be married is honorable before God. Divorce is awful and not to be encouraged, although it may be permitted at times. Beza next considers fasting, noting that it has often been abused in the church. It has been pressed for wrong motives and in incorrect ways. Sunday is to be the day devoted to gathering together to hear the word of God. Beyond that, no days are to be viewed as special, in the same way that all foods—provided they are taken moderately—are permitted.

Beza then moves to a discussion of church discipline, which must be done according to 'the pure Word of God'. The causes for discipline are threefold: false doctrine, bad morals, or offences against the order of the church, all of which will be determined by the church's elders. In the process of discipline, the elders are to exercise wisdom, recognizing, for instance,

---

50. Beza, *Brief and Pithy Sum*, pp. 322-3.

the difference between a first-time and a serial offence (5.40). Beza's discussion of excommunication is lengthy. First, he defines it:

> We call excommunication a sentence by which the ecclesiastical elders, after knowledge of the cause, declare in the name and authority of God and His holy Word, that such or such, one or many, are justly excluded and separated from the company or communion of the saints, i.e., the church of God. They are consequently delivered to Satan, because outside the church there is no salvation. Yet this is not to continue forever, but so long as they remain unreformed and until they have satisfied for the slander of offense given.[51]

The authority to excommunicate comes from the word of God. There are varying degrees of excommunication, sometimes consisting only in suspension from the Lord's Supper or other more gentle punishments. The right to excommunicate is given to the elders, never to a single man. And these elders cannot excommunicate rashly. They 'cannot and may not use it at their wills, since we see that all men are subject to many infirmities. But this power is limited and appointed by the Word of God.'[52] Finally, the reasons God instituted this act were, first, to keep the church pure; second, to keep sin from spreading in the church; and, third, to provoke God's people to fear sin (5.41).

Beza concludes the fifth chapter by noting how the church is to interact with its temporal rulers. The Lord has appointed Christian magistrates largely to punish heretics and so to protect the church (5.42). However, not all magistrates are good or godly. When they mandate that the church disobey God, they are not to be obeyed, because 'it is not rebellion to disobey princes when they would cause us to do what God forbids or to

---

51. Beza, *Brief and Pithy Sum*, p. 330.
52. Beza, *Brief and Pithy Sum*, p. 330.

forbid what God commands.' We do this, not by harming those who harm us, but by suffering harm even like our Lord did.[53]

Our temptation might be to skim over this chapter as just a relic of sixteenth-century bigotry. There is indeed a great deal in this chapter that seems to be from a different world. However, we should try to understand Beza since he—like us—was trying to understand what Scripture says on these points. Beza's belief in scriptural authority led him to write this chapter so that God's people would be rightly organized and would rightly glorify Him.

Chapter 6: Of the Last Judgment

The sixth chapter is extremely short but essential to understand Beza's purpose. 'Of the Last Judgment' clarifies why Beza wrote the whole treatise. Based on the authority of the Bible, Beza believes that a time of judgment will come for all people. The Lord will judge everyone according to His word. When Jesus returns in judgment,

> those who believe (as will appear by the fruits of their faith) will be made partakers of the kingdom of God, not only in their soul (which even before and after the first death has been in the joy of their Lord), but also in their bodies, which will be unclothed from all imperfections and infirmities and again clothed with incorruption and glorious immortality to behold what eye never could see nor heart think; and in brief, to receive fully the fruit of their faith and hope, only by the goodness of God in Jesus Christ. On the contrary, the wicked, condemned and those vanquished by the testimony of their own conscience, will be made immortal eternally to suffer the pain prepared for the devil and his angels.[54]

It is this vision of the reality of eternity that has bolstered Beza to write the entire treatise. Each of his readers will go to one

---

53. Beza, *Brief and Pithy Sum*, p. 332.
54. Beza, *Brief and Pithy Sum*, p. 333.

of two eternal destinies. They need to prepare themselves for God's impending judgment.

Chapter 7: A Brief Comparison of the Doctrine of the Papists and That of the Holy Catholic Church

The seventh chapter, 'A Brief Comparison of the Doctrine of the Papists and That of the Holy Catholic Church', in many ways serves as an appendix to the treatise, comparing what Beza has written to the teachings of Rome. Here Beza again is quite polemical as he remonstrates against the errors of the Catholic church. Rather than rehearse every possible error of the Catholics, Beza compares their teaching to the main points he's composed in the treatise so far. He does this under fifteen articles. Beza's polemic here—although at times it might seem harsh to some twenty-first-century readers—has a purpose. Rome's errors will lead people to hell. Salvation is in the balance.[55]

In the first article, 'The papists worship a false God who is neither righteous nor merciful', Beza argues that the differences between Protestants and Catholics aren't merely a matter of disagreements over a few ceremonies. At its heart, the debate is over salvation: 'The principal difference concerns the substance of doctrine in which our salvation consists.' And the debate is substantial; the two sides are opposite one another concerning how one goes to heaven: 'I say then that black is not more contrary to the white than the religion of Roman Catholics is to this religion of the church of God.'[56] This is why Protestants have separated from the false Roman church.

The second article, 'If the doctrine of the papists is true, it follows that Jesus Christ is not true man', is a short paragraph. Beza argues that though the Catholics give lip service to the deity and humanity of Christ they betray their real view of Jesus when they say absurd things about Him. By giving Him

---

55. Perhaps because of the polemical nature of this chapter it was often left out when the book was published, from the sixteenth century on.
56. Beza, *Brief and Pithy Sum*, p. 334.

an invisible body, which they do in the eucharist, they distort His humanity. Similarly, arguing that Christ can be bodily in more than one place at the same time shows they've concocted a being that's not truly human.[57]

According to the third article, 'The Roman Catholic doctrine makes the sacrifice of Jesus Christ of no effect', the Catholics have so maligned the work of Christ that they rob it of its saving power. This is especially seen in the relatively recent Catholic invention of purgatory, in which Christians have to pay for their sins before arriving in heaven. Of what use, then, is Christ's work?, Beza asks. He continues with the next article, 'The papists abolish the true intercession of Jesus Christ.' Christ's praying for His people is a wonderful biblical truth which should call for their wholehearted crying out to Him. But the Catholics skew this, arguing that Christ is too lofty to be approached. Instead, they purport, Mary and the saints are the ones to whom we should pray. They will then intercede for us. This mashing up of the truth results in something that is both unbiblical and also unsatisfactory to hurting souls.[58]

The fifth article, 'The papists do not acknowledge Jesus Christ to be the perfect declarer of the will of God, nor the holy Scripture to be the sufficient doctrine of salvation', gets to the question of authority. The Catholics teach—in a way that derives from Satan—that their authority is Scripture plus the church's tradition. In truth, though, Jesus declares His will for His church in the Bible alone. 'And if the Scriptures are sufficient, where does this infinite number of human traditions and commandments come from which are imposed on poor consciences as necessary to salvation, not only above but contrary to the Scriptures?'[59] The sixth article, 'The papists spoil Jesus Christ of His office as head of the church', points out the

---

57. Beza, *Brief and Pithy Sum*, p. 335.
58. Beza, *Brief and Pithy Sum*, pp. 335-7.
59. Beza, *Brief and Pithy Sum*, p. 337.

Roman error of adding the pope and ecclesiastical hierarchy above that of Jesus' authority exercised through the Scripture.

These first six articles, then, deal largely with Jesus' person and work and the nature of authority in the church. Now Beza turns to issues specifically dealing with sinners' salvation. In the seventh section, 'By the doctrine of the papists, we can in no way understand how mortal the natural sickness of mankind is', he notes that the Catholics don't understand correctly the depth of their own sin. This inevitably leads to multifaceted problems with their understanding of personal faith and assurance, which he outlines in article eight, 'Another execrable error of the papists in the using of the only medicine of health, which is the benefit of Jesus Christ.' The reality is that there is only

> one means to be joined and united with Jesus Christ to have salvation in Him, i.e., faith, which is an assurance that all Christians ought to have of their election and salvation only by the grace and goodness of God in Jesus Christ. Faith and assurance are created and daily increased by the power of the Holy Ghost within the hearts of the elect by means of the preaching of the Word of God, the ministration of the sacraments. … So then this faith is as the hand which alone receives and apprehends Jesus Christ to the salvation of him that believes.[60]

The Roman church perverts this, teaching that 'to be assured of election and salvation in Jesus Christ and to pray with all trust and assurance, as St James says, is a presumption; not to trust in good works (as they call them) and to rest and wait on whatever they teach from their own brains is no presumption.'[61]

The ninth article spells out why the Catholics get these things wrong. They misunderstand both God's law and the gospel. By neglecting the judgment of God against human sin, they rob themselves of the good news of salvation through Christ alone. So, they misunderstand faith itself. The tenth article, 'In

---

60. Beza, *Brief and Pithy Sum*, p. 339.
61. Beza, *Brief and Pithy Sum*, p. 340.

popery, they do not know what good works are', recounts how they also misunderstand what the proper fruits of faith should be. Maligning Protestants for being antinomians (that is, those who have no role in the Christian life for obedience to God's commands), in reality they are the ones who misunderstand the nature of works, believing that our efforts put God in our debt.

The eleventh article ('In popery, they do not know what a sacrament is, nor what its use is') is a lengthy description of Catholic errors regarding the sacraments. Here Beza works through each of Rome's seven sacraments, showing their unbiblical practice. Concerning the baptism of infants, for instance, he notes that 'the grace of God is not tied or bound to the sacrament, as if the promise were not sufficient and strong enough of itself; rather the sacrament is only added to the promise for a confirmation, namely, when there is neither contempt nor negligence. And we do not doubt at all that the children of believers are sanctified from their mother's womb.'[62] Similarly, Beza notes that Rome errs regarding the eucharist because they have turned aside from the ancient practice of the church. For example, the Catholic notion of the ubiquity of Christ's body is unbiblical: 'But on the contrary, it is said that Jesus Christ has taken His body from us into heaven and will not remove Himself from there until He comes to judge the quick and the dead (although concerning His divine nature and power, He is over all).'[63] In sum, therefore, Rome's errors are great. They neither preach the word of God purely nor administer the sacraments rightly.

The twelfth article argues that 'in popery, there is no ecclesiastical government.' This lengthy section portrays the numerous ways in which the Roman church has created layer upon layer of positions and authorities within their hierarchy. All of them, though, are far from the biblical simplicity of church offices Beza has already outlined. Unfortunately, also, most of the Catholic prelates fall far short of biblical moral requirements.

---

62. Beza, *Brief and Pithy Sum*, p. 349.
63. Beza, *Brief and Pithy Sum*, p. 350.

The thirteenth article ('The abuse which is committed in the second part of ecclesiastical offices, which is the deacons') recounts how the Roman church fails to provide for the poor, not using the office of deacon as it was supposed to be employed. The manner in which priests abuse their power is recounted in the fourteenth section ('Of the abuse which is committed in the order of the priesthood and in the government of their spiritual jurisdiction'), where Beza also ventures into a discussion of the abuses of monks. The final section ('The papists are manifestly culpable of rebellion against the magistrate') handles the way in which the Catholic church has set itself up as a power on earth and, so, fails to submit to the magistrate as it should.

In conclusion, Beza encourages Protestants to diligently stay anchored to the truth, even if it's costly. The power of Rome is great. Nonetheless with God's help Protestants should continue to struggle for truth even if they suffer for it. Persecution will ultimately mean nothing, because God's truth will win out:

> Let them endeavor and do all that they may and do the worst to us they can, which is to cut us off and destroy us utterly—for that is the best that we can hope to have at their hands: But if it pleases the Lord, they will win no other thing. For despite them, our poor paper in the end will quench their fires, our pens will break their swords in their hands, our patience will vanquish their cruelty; and they will see with their eyes that truth will have the victory and their wicked kingdom should be overthrown. For it must be, will they nill they, that this Word pronounced by the Son of God will be fulfilled: 'Every plant which my heavenly Father has not planted will be plucked up.' Such is that faith for which we suffer, in which we now live, hope to die, and to live forever.[64]

Application

We can make three observations about Beza's summary of Christian doctrine. In the first place, we see the importance of Christian pastor-theologians concisely summarizing the Christian faith

---

64. Beza, *Brief and Pithy Sum*, p. 369.

Summarizing the Faith

for believers. Beza agreed with the later English and American Puritan tradition which rightly argued that theology is the art of living well. It should orient Christians in their thinking about the Lord, the world, and themselves. And it should drive them to act in God-honoring trust and love throughout their lives. It should be the purview of all followers of Christ, then, not just the few scholars who may read each other's theological tomes. Beza's summary works were distinctly popular in the sixteenth century; similar summaries would serve the church well in our day.

In the second place, we note that it is essential that evangelical theology must be evangelical. By 'evangelical' I mean gospel-oriented and gospel-saturated. Beza never lost sight of the gospel and its centrality to all of Christian living. As we have seen, he regularly brought everything back to the cross of Christ and to the realities of judgment to come in the future for all people. For our theology to honor Christ, it must also keep its bearings on the cross. And we must similarly constantly trumpet the reality that we will all stand before the judgment seat of Christ (2 Cor. 5:10). No one can escape this reality.

Finally, we see in Beza's *Confession* that all human doctrinal work is time-specific. Even when we try merely to summarize what the Bible says (i.e., 'be biblical'), we inevitably address problems and issues of our day. We can't help it, can we? We must apply biblical truth to issues that affect our lives today—abortion, homosexuality, and countless other topics. Similarly, due to its genesis in the mid-sixteenth century, Beza's *Confession* was filled with polemic against the errors of the Roman Catholic church. We should both recognize that this might mean we need to tone down some of Beza's rhetoric, and we should also critically ask ourselves if Beza needs to teach us something in our latitudinarian, postmodern age. Perhaps we've been co-opted more than we know by the constant cry in our society for tolerance.[65] Perhaps we need Beza more than we think.

---

65. See D. A. Carson, *The Intolerance of Tolerance* (Grand Rapids: Eerdmans, 2012).

Uses

The text of Beza's Confession of Faith may be found translated as 'A Brief and Pithy Sum of Christian Faith', in *Reformed Confessions of the 16th and 17th Centuries in English Translation: Volume 2, 1552-1566*, edited by James T. Dennison Jr (Grand Rapids: Reformation Heritage, 2010), pp. 236-369.

1. Read through Beza's *Confession* noting every time he addresses: (a) the gospel, (b) eternity, and (c) the Catholic church of his day. What do you learn from this?

2. Compare Beza's *Confession* to Calvin's *Institutes*. How does this help you to understand Beza's purpose in the *Confession*?

3. Read through the Pauline epistles in the New Testament, recording every time the apostle speaks about the manner in which he and others are charged with teaching a definite body of truth in the church. How does this aid you in understanding what Beza was trying to do in the *Confession*?

4. Read through your church's or denomination's confession of faith. And read the biblical prooftexts for each of the points.

5. Thank the Lord that He has communicated His truth to us in words and that we can reproduce and summarize that truth in our own words. What a remarkable thing that the Lord hasn't left us to our own imaginations!

5
LETTING GOD BE GOD—
Theodore Beza's
Tabula Praedestinationis

Introduction

Theodore Beza is no more famous—or perhaps infamous—than for teaching a doctrine of double predestination. One of Calvinism's most vocal, and thoughtful, recent detractors criticizes both Beza and this teaching of double predestination. Roger Olson writes that Beza is 'one of the founders of the extreme type of Calvinist theology known as supralapsarianism.' In this theology 'God foreknows what will happen because he foreordains everything that happens, and he foreordains because he decrees it all from eternity.' According to Olson, 'Beza and certain other Calvinists were obsessed with the doctrine of predestination more than Calvin himself ever had been.'[1] Olson is scathing in his criticism.

Olson avers that the Calvinist belief in unconditional election is tantamount to belief in double predestination and is wrong for several reasons. It goes against several key texts of Scripture (such as Ezekiel 18:32; John 3:16; 1 Timothy 2:4; 2 Peter 3:9; and 1 John 4:8), and it raises several key questions about the character of God:

> How can God be said to *be good, loving, and just in the face of these doctrines of high Calvinism?* How is God good, loving,

---
1. Roger Olson, *The Story of Christian Theology: Twenty Centuries of Tradition and Reform* (Downers Grove: InterVarsity, 1999), pp. 456-7.

and just toward the reprobate? How is God not arbitrary in his choosing some to save unconditionally while leaving others to damnation? And a related critical question is: How can the gospel call be given out as a well-meant offer to all if some have already been chosen by God for damnation and thus have no chance at all, whatsoever, of being accepted by God?[2]

Non-Calvinists' frustration with the Calvinistic understanding of the doctrine of predestination has a long pedigree. John Wesley expressed sentiments like Olson's when he argued that the doctrine of election implied the doctrine of reprobation (which defamed the love and justice of God); therefore, he did not believe in election. 'Unconditional election I cannot believe, not only because I cannot find it in Scripture, but also (to waive all other considerations) because it necessarily implies unconditional reprobation.' So, Wesley challenges Calvinists: 'Find out any election which does not imply reprobation and I will gladly agree to it.'[3] In other words, for God to choose some for salvation necessarily means that He did not choose others. And since this calls into question God's real love for humanity, the doctrine of unconditional election can't be true. God's non-election of some is false; therefore, His election of others is false. No more need be said to disprove the Calvinistic belief in double predestination.

At least on this point, Arminians like Olson and Wesley are correct: the Calvinistic doctrine of election implies also the doctrine of reprobation. We see this in Calvin's very definition of predestination. In short order he says predestination is that 'by which God adopts some to hope of life, and sentences others to eternal death.' More extensively, he notes,

---

2. Roger E. Olson, *Against Calvinism* (Grand Rapids: Zondervan, 2011), p. 11; his italics.

3. John Wesley, 'Predestination Calmly Considered,' in *John Wesley*, ed. Albert C. Outler (New York: Oxford University Press, 1980), p. 434.

> We call predestination God's eternal decree, by which he compacted with himself what he willed to become of each man. For all are not created in equal condition; rather, eternal life is foreordained for some, eternal damnation for others. Therefore, as any man has been created to one or the other of these ends, we speak of him as predestined to life or to death.[4]

Both of Calvin's definitions show that predestination does not only have a 'positive' referent (i.e., the elect), but it also has a 'negative' component. God eternally decrees to damn some.

Before we enter into a discussion of 'reprobation', we should understand its meaning. Knowing what it entails, as well as what its concomitants are not, is important. Muller helpfully defines it based on his study of Reformed theologians:

> *reprobatio*: 'reprobation'; the eternal decree (*decretum*) of God according to which he wills to leave certain individuals in their corrupt condition, to damn them because of their sin and leave them to eternal punishment apart from the divine presence. *Reprobatio* is, therefore, distinct from *damnatio*: whereas the cause of *damnatio* is the sin of the individual, the cause of *reprobatio* is the sovereign will of God.[5]

The questions before us are simple and important: Is double predestination biblical? And is it beneficial? To that end, we will look at one of Beza's better known works, his *Tabula Praedestinationis*.

Perhaps no work of Theodore Beza's is as well known in our day as the chart he produced at the beginning of his *The Sum of All Christianity*. With its stark symmetry showing God's eternal love for the elect worked out in history from their election to their eternal life, on the one hand, and God's eternal hatred of the reprobate from eternity past to eternal death, on the other hand, Beza's *Tabula* (as the work was often called)

---

4. Calvin, *Institutes*, 3.21.5.
5. Muller, *Dictionary*, p. 263.

Theodore Beza

presents a view of human destiny that is completely under the sovereign control of God. Having taken a quick glance at the chart, many have discounted Beza's theology as rigid, God-dishonoring, and unnecessarily humanity-shrinking.

This is a shame for several reasons. The simplest is that a more careful perusal of the chart would disabuse readers at the outset of some of these conceptions. For example, when Beza heads up the right column about the reprobate, he speaks of God's decree 'to doom to eternal punishment' those He's not elected. But he doesn't stop there. He points out the reprobates' culpability from the start, saying that God rejected them 'because of their own voluntary guilt'. He is not asserting a sort of robot theology. Another reason that this is a faulty approach is that it fails to pay attention to the asymmetry Beza paints in the chart. God's dealings with the elect proceed completely from grace since they are 'corrupt in themselves' and deserve nothing but judgment. The elect and the reprobate are in the same condition: both are corrupt and deserve only God's wrathful judgment. God's punishing of the reprobate is, therefore, pure justice. His saving of the elect is pure grace. The head of the chart already answers the objection people most often have to such a conception of reality: How can this be fair? Beza alerts his readers that God's 'ways are inscrutable'. To us, He's an enigma whose decisions are unfathomable to our reasoning. We do not have the right to sit in judgment over Him. He is God. Indeed, echoing Luther's heart that we must 'let God be God' is Beza's burden throughout this treatise.[6] God is a complex being who loves, judges, and does a whole host of other things. He has true affections for people. But over all of these things, God desires that He receive glory. Indeed, this is Beza's cry at the head of the chart. God decreed 'in himself' (that is, for His own reasons apart from anything setting one person apart from another) 'certain men

---

6. A classic book that gets to the heart of Luther's theology is Philip S. Watson, *Let God Be God: An Interpretation of the Theology of Martin Luther* (London: Epworth, 1947).

for his glory' (that is, He eternally and in time deals with each individual in such a way that He receives glory).

The greatest misreading of the treatise, though, is reading the chart in isolation from the rest of the treatise. The table is a visual summary of what Beza exposits at length in the heart of the treatise. It is in this exposition—complete with 578 'proofs from the word of God' footnoted and included as an appendix to each section—that Beza intended to convince his readers of the truthfulness of his position. The chart merely functions as a short reference tool. The critical doctrinal discussion is in the text. Too often though, this exposition is absent from discussions of the merits of Beza's *Tabula* as if it didn't exist and Beza only cared about charts. That is a shame because it's in the exposition where Beza persuasively brings forth biblical proof for his position. And there he also makes two other significant contributions: he answers objections to his position, and he shows his readers the profit of this biblical doctrine for their lives. What might have been a rigid, polemical, and scholastic tome if only in chart form thus becomes pastoral, personal, and profitable because of Beza's careful exposition.

The Historical Setting

The notion that God is completely sovereign in a person's salvation is found throughout the pages of Scripture. It is not my intention to rehearse that point here.[7] Throughout the history of the church, this biblical view has been attacked by different persons who for various reasons have done the same thing: magnifying the role of the human agent in the salvation process, they have downplayed the extent of God's role in a sinner's salvation.

---

7. The literature on this is legion. For a start, readers could consult J. I. Packer, *Evangelism and the Sovereignty of God* (Downers Grove: InterVarsity, 1961); Michael Horton, *For Calvinism* (Grand Rapids: Zondervan, 2011); and John Piper, *Five Points: Towards a Deeper Experience of God's Grace* (Fearn: Christian Focus, 2013).

Theodore Beza

The Protestant Reformation of the sixteenth century had at its disposal several streams of information concerning God's predestinating activity. After the Bible—both in time and importance—stood Augustine (d. 430) whose works included a strong attack on various forms of Pelagian and semi-Pelagian thought, thinking which wrongly prioritized the human will in the salvation process to the exclusion (or at least a secondary place) of God's will. The Reformers rode on the crest of the wave of this revived late medieval Augustinianism. In addition, they had recourse to the writings of Thomas Aquinas (d. 1274), the hugely influential teacher of Catholic doctrine and whose doctrine of predestination was closely akin to that of Augustine.[8]

The Reformers' works showed their familiarity with the Christian tradition on predestination. Reacting against Erasmus's semi-Pelagian thought, Martin Luther (an Augustinian monk!) asserted the biblical fidelity of the doctrine of predestination in his *On the Bondage of the Will*, which surely has to be one of the strongest defenses of this doctrine in the history of the church.[9] It was the Reformed, or Calvinistic, tradition that taught the doctrine of predestination in an unadulterated Augustinian manner. Reformed theologians, however, were not monolithic in their exposition of the finer points of predestination, as Donald Sinnema avers:

> There was a range of formulations that were forged in individual circumstances, often in polemical contexts in reaction to such opponents as Pighius, Bolsec, and Castellio. Thus, beside

---

8. For some of the history of the doctrine of predestination, see Gregg R. Allison, *Historical Theology: An Introduction to Christian Doctrine* (Grand Rapids: Zondervan, 2011), pp. 453-73.

9. Later Lutheranism, however, abandoned much of Luther's predestinarian thought—as much out of political expediency as out of theological conviction—and sought to present a kinder face to the world while distancing themselves from what they considered to be the too rigid systems of the Calvinists.

Letting God be God

the double predestination view of Calvin, influenced by Bucer, there was the more philosophical, causally oriented position of Zwingli, the cautious, moderate position of Bullinger, and the single predestination stance of Vermigli and Musculus. Vermigli, who developed his position independently of Calvin, advocated predestination of the elect only, but alongside reprobation.[10]

Yet Sinnema also asserts that there were 'some common themes in Reformed formulations' of the doctrine that unite Calvinistic churches in the main on this doctrine.[11] For our purposes, he helpfully spells out eight themes present in Beza's presentation of the doctrine that are part and parcel of the tradition. Not only do these eight themes alert us to some of Beza's idiosyncrasies, but they also differentiate some Reformed theologians' views from others. There was great agreement among the Calvinists yet enough differences of opinion to be noteworthy. Not surprisingly, we notice that Beza followed the thought of Calvin quite carefully. This is what Sinnema notes:

(1) 'In holding to double predestination (consisting of election and reprobation) Beza shared the stance of a major stream within the Reformed tradition, a view advocated by Bucer and Calvin before him. Double predestination had its roots in Augustine,' saw expression in the ninth century by the Saxon monk, Gottschalk, 'and was revived in the *schola Augustiniana moderna* of the late middle ages' by such figures as Thomas Bradwardine and Martin Luther.

(2) 'Beza shared in the Reformed consensus that emphasized that predestination was an act of the divine will—a decision or decree.' He was thus part of the voluntarist school going

---

10. Donald Sinnema, 'Beza's View of Predestination in Historical Perspective,' in *Théodore de Bèze (1519-1605)*, ed. Irena Backus (Geneva: Librairie Droz, 2007), p. 220.
11. Sinnema, 'Beza's View of Predestination,' p. 220.

back to the thirteenth century, which prioritized God's will over his intellect.

(3) 'Beza shared the assumption of the Reformed tradition that predestination was a decision that God made from eternity (*ab aeterno*).' Of course Reformed theologians knew that for God there is no before or after. But they felt it was important to heed Scripture's injunction that we were predestinated 'before the foundation of the world,' since from a Christian's perspective (and our perspective is 'subject to time'), 'predestination really happened "before" creation.'

(4) Beza was in the Augustinian tradition expressed by such medieval theologians as Aquinas, Bradwardine, and Gregory of Rimini (thus agreeing with both Reformed and Lutheran theologians) 'that the sole cause of election is the good pleasure of God's will.' Along with them he opposed 'the prominent semi-Pelagian strain in Catholic theology that identified foreseen faith as the cause of election.'

(5) He was typically Reformed in believing 'the cause of reprobation lies hidden in the unfathomable divine will.' This view was starkly different from both the Catholics and the Lutherans, who believed that 'foreseen sin or unbelief is the cause of reprobation.'

(6) Beza agreed with the Reformed consensus 'that, while the cause of reprobation lies in God's will, the actual condemnation of the reprobate is caused by their own sin, and so their punishment is justly deserved.' This distinction Reformed thinkers made 'between reprobation and condemnation' allowed them to defend God against the charge that He 'arbitrarily condemns people to death.'

(7) 'Beza shared the common Reformed idea that the fall into sin was somehow willed by God, but in such a way that he is not culpable as the author of sin.' God permitted, but was not the author of, sin.

(8) Beza also agreed with both Calvin and Bucer 'that the ultimate end or purpose of both election and reprobation is to manifest God's glory in showing his mercy to some and his justice to others.'[12]

These points allow us to see some of the different streams that flowed in the pre-Reformation and Reformation eras regarding the Bible's teaching on predestination. Beza was not, then, unique in discussing this complicated doctrine. He was, rather, in a long line of thinkers who had tried to make sense of it. And as we have seen from his arrangement of material in his *Confession*, Beza was not obsessed with predestination as if it were the *sine qua non* of all theology. Predestination was important, but it was not all that Christians needed to know about. What, then, were the historical circumstances that called forth the publication of a treatise devoted to this doctrine?

The Immediate Setting

Theodore Beza didn't compose the *Tabula* in a vacuum. Jérôme Bolsec's unflagging opposition to Calvin's teaching on predestination was the *raison d'être* for Beza's treatise. We must take a quick look at Bolsec and try to understand why his attack on Calvin's doctrine of double predestination caused the Genevan leader such consternation.

Bolsec's life story is quite exciting. He was a French Catholic, a Carmelite monk, who converted to the Protestant faith sometime around 1545. A medical doctor, he was a theologian by avocation. Fearing persecution, he settled eventually near Geneva. He lauded Calvin's theology, agreeing with almost all of it, except for his doctrine of double predestination. His concern was 'that Calvin's doctrine made God partial to some humans and the author of sin. Bolsec espoused a type of universalism: humans were of the elect because of their faith, and they were condemned because they refused the election common to all.

---

12. Sinnema, 'Beza's View of Predestination,' pp. 220-2.

He wished to view election within the realm of history and human responsibility instead of in terms of a pretemporal double decree.'[13] He made the fateful decision to oppose Calvin's theology publicly at an October 1551 Friday Congregation, a weekly early morning meeting to hear sermons and discuss theological topics. Arrested and imprisoned, Bolsec was tried for heresy. Having sought the opinion of other Reformed churches, the Genevan magistrates found him guilty and exiled him for life in December of that year. He spent an uneasy exile in the Swiss territory of Berne from 1551 until 1563. After his unsettled stay in Berne, Bolsec was exiled from there in 1563. He returned to France, reverted to Catholicism, and before he died wrote two scathing biographies—one of Calvin (1577), the other of Beza (1582)—composed mostly of material he dreamt up that accused both the Genevan leaders of heresy, greed, hypocrisy, and sexual deviancy. He died in France in 1584.[14]

In order to understand the Genevans' response to Bolsec, especially Beza's *Tabula*, we need to notice three factors. First of all, the Genevan position on predestination was not the only option in Reformed circles. Berne, a very powerful Protestant Swiss canton, disagreed with Calvin's view of double predestination. As Bruce Gordon notes, this mattered greatly given the political realities of the day: 'Geneva had few friends. Precariously perched on the edge of Catholic French and Savoyard lands, it remained dependent on the protection of the Bernese. During the years 1548 to 1550 Genevan attempts to join the Swiss Confederation had come to nothing and the alliance between Berne and the city expired in 1550, though it was eventually extended for another five years.'[15] Not only the

---

13. J. Wayne Baker, 'Bolsec, Jérome (c. 1524-1584),' in *The Oxford Encyclopedia of the Reformation*, ed. Hans J. Hillerbrand (New York: Oxford University Press, 1996), vol. 1, p. 188.
14. Baker, 'Bolsec,' pp. 188-9.
15. Bruce Gordon, *Calvin* (New Haven: Yale University Press, 2009), p. 204.

Bernese, but the Zurichers led by Heinrich Bullinger as well, disagreed with the implications of Calvin's doctrine. Their fear was that the Genevan implicitly made God the author of sin since He had eternally decreed that some would go to hell apart from their works.[16] The Bernese, inhabiting both German-speaking and French-speaking regions, were concerned about Calvin's influence outside of Geneva, especially in Lausanne. Calvin's friends Theodore Beza and Pierre Viret both taught at the Academy in Lausanne, and the Bernese city council and pastors thought them to be puppets of Calvin.[17] It was these Bernese who received Bolsec into their region after he'd been exiled from Geneva. Such a tense situation called for Calvin to defend his position.

In the second place, when Bolsec was in Geneva and attacked Calvin's doctrine, Calvin's position in Geneva was not secure. It was only in 1555 that Calvin's theological and political allies won control of Geneva's political authority. From then on, Calvin was able to exercise more than just moral authority in the city. But in the early 1550s, facing opponents on many sides, Calvin's position was not secure. Had he allowed Bolsec's attack on Calvin's interpretation of Scripture to go unanswered, Calvin's authority as a teacher of the Bible would have dissipated. Calvin—for political as well as theological reasons—needed a strong biblical defense of his views.[18]

In the third place, Calvin was not immune to theological controversy and the type of response necessary to his critics. His teaching had caused quite a stir already, and he'd needed to respond to challenges to his doctrine of predestination before. Specifically the Dutch Catholic, Albert Pighius, had

---

16. See Gordon, *Calvin*, pp. 205-9.
17. Gordon, *Calvin*, pp. 209-11.
18. See Richard A. Muller, 'The Use and Abuse of a Document: Beza's *Tabula Praedestinationis*, The Bolsec Controversy, and the Origins of Reformed Orthodoxy,' in *Protestant Scholasticism: Essays in Reassessment*, eds Carl R. Trueman and R. S. Clark (Carlisle: Paternoster, 1999), pp. 36-7.

contradicted Calvin's doctrine. In 1543 Calvin responded to the first six sections of Pighius's attacks on Calvin's and Luther's doctrines of predestination and human freedom, publishing his *Bondage and Liberation of the Will*.[19] Pighius's work was significant enough that Calvin felt the need to continue his response to the last section of Pighius's attack. So Calvin published his response to the final four sections of Pighius in 1552. His *On the Eternal Predestination of God* is a comprehensive response to Pighius as well as a Benedictine theologian called Georgius Siculus.[20] Calvin had already been responding to doctrinal attacks before the Bolsec affair, and he was writing an apology to Pighius while it was going on. His involvement with Pighius, in fact, was probably why he asked Beza to deal with Bolsec's attacks.

The actual genesis of Beza's *Tabula* is not totally clear. He published it in 1555, three years before relocating to Geneva. We can reconstruct from letters to and from Beza that he began work on the treatise at the time of the original controversy between Bolsec and Calvin in Geneva. In fact, it's possible that he completed a first draft before Bolsec was banished in December of 1551.[21] Beza continued to seek input on his work—from Vermigli and Bullinger, as well as Calvin—and revised it over the next few years. We have seen that Calvin published quite a few works on the issue of predestination during this time, so the obvious question is why there was the need for another apology for the Genevan position. Beza, it seems, felt that Calvin's defense of predestination up to this point had been hampered by attempting to answer his opponents' charges, following their arrangement of material. Calvin had assumed too much of a

---

19. John Calvin, *The Bondage and Liberation of the Will: A Defense of the Orthodox Doctrine of Human Choice Against Pighius*, ed. Anthony Lane, trans. G. I. Davies (Grand Rapids: Baker, 2002).

20. See Wulfert de Greef, *The Writings of John Calvin: An Introductory Guide*, trans. Lyle D. Bierma (Grand Rapids: Baker, 1993), pp. 58-9.

21. Muller, 'Use and Abuse of a Document,' p. 37.

defensive posture. In other words, Beza did not believe a positive statement of the doctrine of predestination from the Genevan point of view had come forth. That's what he was attempting to do when he published the *Tabula*.[22] Calvin thought his younger friend was successful in his attempt. Towards the end of his life, Calvin preached through Genesis and allowed his sermons dealing with Jacob and Esau to be published as a stand-alone volume. In the conclusion of that body of sermons, Calvin noted the views of some of those who disagreed with his interpretation of God's interaction with Jacob and Esau and the manner in which Paul employs them in Romans 9. Calvin thought Paul's words, 'Jacob I loved, but Esau I hated', represented God's attitude of grace towards the elect, on the one hand, and His attitude of just condemnation towards the reprobate, on the other hand. Rather than rehearsing his own doctrinal position in detail, though, Calvin urged his readers to 'consider those places which are gathered in a little book that our brother, master Beza hath made thereof, and you shall be fully satisfied therein.'[23] Thus, even after the final edition of his *Institutes* was published (1559), Calvin referred in 1562 to Beza's treatise as a helpful summary of the matter with which he agreed.

The *Tabula* was a popular work during Beza's lifetime. It was included in his *Tractationum theologicarum*, his collected theological treatises, published in three volumes in 1582. The *Tabula* was translated into English and published in 1556, 1575, 1576, and 1581. It was issued in French translation in 1560 and in Dutch in 1571.[24]

---

22. Muller, 'Use and Abuse of a Document,' pp. 38-9.

23. John Calvin, *Sermons on Election and Reprobation*, trans. John Field (London: 1579; repr., Audobon, NJ: Old Paths, 1996), pp. 310-11. See also Sinnema, 'Beza's View of Predestination,' p. 220.

24. Wright, *Our Sovereign Refuge*, p. 235. For accounts of the publication of this work in the sixteenth century, see Gardy and Dufour, *Bibliographie des Oeuvres Théologiques*, pp. 47-53.

Theodore Beza

Before we look at Beza's work in outline, one other word is in order. Why was it titled the *Tabula*? Beza titled the complete work *Summa totius christianismi*, but it was often simply called *Tabula praedestinationis*. As Richard Muller notes, the problem with the former title is that it easily misleads readers into thinking that Beza intended this to be a *Summa theologiae* akin to Thomas Aquinas's.[25] As John Bray indicated, the title should rather be understood as 'the sum total of the Christian life'.[26] In other words, it explains the existence of Christians from eternity past to eternity future. The text in no way indicates that Beza intended this to summarize all of Christian doctrine, or even be the most important aspect of theology. Rather, here Beza controverted an error and set forth the correct doctrine of predestination. That is all. Unfortunately, too often Beza's chart at the start of the *Tabula* has been reprinted with no reference to his 'aphorisms' (his biblical and theological discussions of the points of the chart) or his biblical references for each section.[27] At best this is to neglect what Beza attempted to highlight. At worst it is to intentionally misread his purpose in this treatise. Muller correctly, on the other hand, summarizes Beza's intent in this treatise:

> Beza's fundamental intention is to demonstrate how such a doctrine [as the order of the causes of salvation and damnation]

---

25. Muller, 'Use and Abuse of a Document,' p. 33.
26. Bray, *Theodore Beza's Doctrine of Predestination*, p. 72; referenced by Muller, 'Use and Abuse of a Document,' p. 34.
27. See, for example, Heinrich Heppe, *Reformed Dogmatics: Set Out and Illustrated from the Sources*, trans. G. T. Thomson, rev. and ed. Ernst Bizer (London: George Allen & Unwin, 1950), pp. 47-8. Paul Zahl's work is a grievous example of this wrong-headed approach. He argued that Beza 'said the whole of Christian theology could be condensed on a single sheet of paper. He did this, and it remains an epigrammatic touchstone for all who come after him.' As proof of this, Zahl reproduced Beza's 'table' with no explanation. Paul F. M. Zahl, *A Short Systematic Theology* (Grand Rapids: Eerdmans, 2000), pp. 96-7.

belongs to Christian instruction and is a support of piety. In short, the intention of the *Tabula* is to show that the doctrine of the decree and its execution, as presented through the collation of biblical texts, is a source of consolation and strength—in this particular context, against the claims of Bolsec that the doctrine was not based on a simple reading of Scripture and was a monstrous distortion of the gospel.[28]

The Content

We are now prepared to examine the contents of the *Tabula*.[29] Approaching it for the first time, though, one must strive to rid oneself of the notion that one is going to jump head first into a pool of arid scholastic, irrelevant theological disputation. That would be a great misconception.[30] Rather, readers should be on the lookout for several distinctive features in the *Tabula*. In the first place, there is certainly technical theology. As we'll see, Beza didn't shy away from treating difficult doctrines such as election and reprobation. He didn't handle these doctrines, however, in a philosophical manner. Another feature of the treatise is Beza's biblicism. His desire was to understand the Bible, not to insert a logical formulation on top of it that muted its truth. His numerous biblical references show this. And

---

28. Muller, 'Use and Abuse of a Document,' p. 35.

29. I appreciate the work that Philip C. Holtrop has done on Beza's doctrine of predestination in its historical context. Interested readers should consult Philip C. Holtrop, *The Bolsec Controversy on Predestination, from 1551 to 1555*, 2 vols. (Lewiston, NY: Edwin Mellen, 1993). I do not agree with all of Dr Holtrop's conclusions about Beza's doctrine, but I thank him for allowing me to use his fine translation of Beza's *Tabula* found in his unpublished *The Potter and the Clay: The Main Predestination Writings of Theodore Beza* (Grand Rapids: Calvin College, 1982). At the time of this writing, Dr Holtrop is near completion of what should become the publication of a multi-volume English translation of several of Beza's works.

30. As we observed in our study of Beza's life, he had no scholastic training in theology when he composed the *Tabula*. The non-scholastic nature of this treatise, therefore, should not surprise us.

we'll be able to see it in much of the reasoning that he uses to make his points. Two other features of the *Tabula* remind us that Beza had pastoral concerns as he wrote this treatise. He wanted, first of all, to show the usefulness of the doctrines he was discussing. Whether it was calling Christians to humility as they considered predestination, reminding unbelievers that the truth of reprobation should make them flee the wrath to come, or encouraging believers to share the truth of the gospel with all people since they were not privy to God's eternal determination of those who had not yet submitted to Christ, Beza applied the truth of predestination to his readers. He was a consummate pastor. Additionally, he exemplified shepherding qualities in anticipating concerns and answering them throughout the *Tabula*, especially in the final chapters. An overview of the entire work clarifies some of Beza's main emphases.

Beza divides the *Tabula* into eight chapters. The relative amounts of time that Beza spends on different aspects of the discussion is significant. After an unexpected introduction which comprises the first chapter, chapters two through six are his doctrinal exposition. Chapters seven and eight show its use and application. The approximate percentages of each unit are significant. The introduction (chapter one) is about 7 per cent. The exposition is about 59 per cent, and the application comprises about 33 per cent. This simple observation shows that Beza's intention was not just to be an adept theologian but also a thoughtful pastor while dealing with this thorny doctrinal issue.

Chapter One: Predestination is the Historic Position of the Church
Chapter one, titled 'That the Question of God's Eternal Predestination is Neither a Matter of Curiosity Nor of Little Necessity in the Church of God', is Beza's introduction. Significantly, one of the first words in the whole treatise is 'Augustine'. As Calvin did in the *Institutes* in his discussion of predestination,

Letting God be God

Beza appeals to the great fourth- and fifth-century theologian of the Catholic church (Augustine lived from 354 to 430) in order probably to demonstrate that his notions were not new-fangled. No, he was in line with historic Catholic dogma. Others were the new (read 'heretical') kids on the block. In his four well-chosen selections from Augustine's anti-Pelagian treatise, *On the Gift of Perseverance*, Beza is intent to both introduce what he will argue and what he will not say.

First, belief in predestination does not rob the church of the ability to preach. No, one should both believe in predestination and also preach, following the example of Paul. Augustine argues: 'They say that the doctrine of predestination is a hindrance to preaching and is unprofitable. As though it were a hindrance to the apostle, who preached it. Did not that teacher of the Gentiles uphold predestination repeatedly and incessantly preach the word of God?'[31]

Second, there is no denying that such a doctrine is difficult for us to conceptualize and grasp with our finite understanding. Christians need to preach the gospel to everyone indiscriminately, but only the elect hear the words of the gospel to their salvation: 'Those having ears that hear us, hear us in obedience.' Others hear but don't understand. Why? Ultimately, we do not know, but God does. So, Augustine avers, 'But why some have ears to hear and others do not have, or why some are given by the Father to come to the Son, and others are not—who has come to know the mind of the Lord? Must something obvious be denied because what is hidden cannot be understood?'[32] We are responsible to obey what is clear in Scripture, leaving the rest with our good and sovereign God.

---

31. Theodore Beza, *The Sum of All Christianity, or the Description and Distribution of the Causes of Salvation of the Elect and the Destruction of the Reprobate, Collected from the Sacred Writings*, in *The Potter and Clay: The Main Predestination Writings of Theodore Beza*, trans. Philip C. Holtrop (Grand Rapids: Calvin College, 1982), p. 26.
32. Beza, *Sum of All Christianity*, p. 26.

Third, our allegiance must first and foremost be with God and the veracity of his word, not with what men will think of us if we teach this doctrine. They may not like what we say about predestination. Even more, they may misuse predestination as an excuse for inaction on their parts. That is a shame we should seek by all means to avoid in our explanations and exhortations. But we absolutely cannot evade the Bible's clear teaching on predestination.

Fourth, we are obligated to preach predestination to believers. It will have the salutary effect on them of proving their responsibility to God. And, conversely, it will lead them to glory not in themselves but in God. Augustine perceptively encouraged this:

> If the apostles and those doctors of the Church who followed them both discussed piously God's eternal election and held the faithful to the discipline of pious living, why is it that these fellows of ours, being bound by the invincible power of truth, think it right to say that whatever is stated on predestination must not be preached to the people, no matter how true it be? On the contrary, it must certainly be preached, that 'he who has ears to hear may hear.' But who 'has' them, unless he 'received' them from him who makes the promise to 'give' them? Certainly, let him who does not receive, reject; but let him who desires 'take and drink,' and let him drink and live. Just as piety must be preached, that God may be worshipped in a proper ritual, so predestination must be, that 'he who has ears to hear' may glory, from God's grace, not in himself but in God.[33]

In the doctrine of predestination, God receives the glory, and this is Beza's burden in the *Tabula*.

Concluding his foray into Augustine's thought, Beza notes the two conditions which the great doctor of the church lays down for us. First, all discussions of predestination should follow 'the prescription of God's word'. Second, how the

---

33. Beza, *Sum of All Christianity*, pp. 26-7.

discussion proceeds is important. The exposition must be done 'in a fitting manner and for edification'. Beza will do the first of these in his discussion of 'the doctrine itself', in chapters two through six. The fitting manner and edification will occur at the end of the treatise (chapters seven and eight) where he will show 'its use and application'.[34] Beza has thoughtfully laid out the structure of the work. We now turn to an examination of it.

Chapter Two: God's Mysterious, Eternal Plan is Known by Its Effects

Beza titles this chapter, 'On the Eternal Plan of God, Which is Hidden in Him, But Ultimately is Understood from Its Effects.' Here he makes seven distinct points by way of seven aphorisms. Having shown in the previous chapter that his view is the historic view of the church, here he attempts to outline in brief fashion his view of election.

In the first aphorism Beza says three things. First, we aren't able to understand God's ways and choices: 'The ways of the omnipotent God are completely inscrutable.' Second, God has decreed everything that comes to pass in His creation: 'Nothing comes to pass anywhere, by anyone, in general or particular, without his eternal and immutable decree.' Finally, God has mysteriously (at least to us) decreed even evil, but He remains good in this, for evil instruments carry out the evil they want to do. God has decreed 'those things that are evil and that therefore must be detested; not, of course, inasmuch as they are decreed by God, who is always good and righteous, but inasmuch as they are evil, from Satan and other evil instruments.' This is the most foundational point Beza makes: we have absolutely no right to sit in judgment over God. He decrees everything—the good and the bad—yet He is always holy.[35]

The second aphorism makes the point that God has decreed two entirely different ends for different people. Nothing outside

---

34. Beza, *Sum of All Christianity*, p. 27.
35. Beza, *Sum of All Christianity*, p. 27.

of Him determines His actions; He decrees 'from eternity ... in his own times' exactly what He wants. The Lord's guiding principle in relation to all humankind is 'his own glory'. First, He decided to save some 'according to his secret will,' to make them 'participants of his glory through mercy.' These are the elect. But towards others He wanted to display 'his wrath and power'. So He raised them up 'for that purpose' so that He might be glorified in their punishment. The key to this aphorism is that God's eternal choice is the driving force in the eternal destinies of all persons, the elect and the reprobate alike.[36]

The third aphorism highlights that nothing outside of God's choice determined His election of His people to salvation. 'It does not emanate, as some would think, from the presence of either their faith or works, but from this one point alone: in the good pleasure of God itself, from which, then, election, and faith, and all works flow forth.' Salvation flows from God's choice alone.[37]

In the fourth aphorism Beza deals with the issue of assurance. At times Christians may doubt their 'faith and calling' or not be able to see evidence of 'the fruits of faith' in their lives. At that point, the only source of assurance they have is God's eternal choice of them in Christ. In Him, 'our Head, we are really elected and adopted; and it mounts from there all the way up to that eternal purpose that God has set forth in no one else than himself alone.' Believing in the Lord's eternal choice of a people in Christ is not a hindrance to assurance of salvation. Indeed, it's the only ultimately stable hope they have.[38]

The fifth aphorism turns to the reprobate, those whom God decreed for destruction. Beza stresses that at the back of reprobation—like election—is the inscrutable, eternal plan of God. This is the 'high mystery that precedes in order all causes

---

36. Beza, *Sum of All Christianity*, p. 31.
37. Beza, *Sum of All Christianity*, p. 32.
38. Beza, *Sum of All Christianity*, p. 34.

of their damnation. Indeed, no other cause for this secret is known to men than his just will, which we must accept with reverence. For it certainly proceeds from him who is just in himself—and in no way can it be comprehended by man or by anything else.' This is the most foundational cause of their reprobation, but Beza admits an important asymmetry not present in God's election of His people. Election is purely of God's grace; the elect don't deserve it. But the reprobate deserve what they receive: 'The total blame remains within themselves.'[39]

The sixth aphorism makes this asymmetry clearer. The 'purpose of reprobation', i.e., why God chose to damn one and not another, is hidden to us. But 'reprobation itself' has clear causes: 'The corruption, infidelity, and iniquity of the vessels made for dishonor.' They are responsible for these causes, for they are 'voluntary'.[40] The seventh aphorism establishes the point that we can also distinguish between 'the purpose of election' (which God decreed in Himself) and 'election itself, which is constituted in Christ.'[41]

Chapter Three: God's Common Actions towards both the Elect and the Reprobate
In the third chapter, 'On the Execution of the Eternal Plan in What is Common to the Elect and Reprobate', Beza makes several essential points by means of six aphorisms. The burden of this chapter is to demonstrate the justice of God in the damnation of the reprobate and the gracious character of His election of a people for Himself. The way that God accomplished this was through creating humanity good, as we will see.

The first aphorism makes the commonality between the reprobate and elect clear. In wisdom the Lord determined a

---

39. Beza, *Sum of All Christianity*, pp. 35-6.
40. Beza, *Sum of All Christianity*, p. 37.
41. Beza, *Sum of All Christianity*, p. 38.

'common way for both those to be elect and those to be reprobate.' This would be 'a distinguishing proof of his mercy in the salvation of the elect' while at the same time displaying 'his just judgment in the condemnation of the reprobate.' To this end, the Lord included both the elect and the reprobate 'under obstinacy and sin'. This was essential so that God 'could have mercy on all who believe—that is, all the elect (for faith is the peculiar gift of God to the elect)—and on the other hand he could find a reason for justly condemning those to whom it was not granted to believe or to know the mysteries of God.' Both groups were sinful and deserving only of the Lord's eternal wrath.[42]

This might sound like God is the author of sin, but Beza denies that charge most vociferously. So in the second aphorism his burden is to show that God created all humanity in 'his own image: in purity and holiness'. God is the author of good, not evil. Yet humanity sinned, as the Lord determined in His wisdom that they would do. Therefore, 'the entire guilt of the damnation of the reprobate remains in themselves, but the entire praise of the salvation of the elect must be referred completely to his own mercy.' God is glorified in damnation and salvation. He is shown to be perfectly just in both of these determinations.[43]

The third and fourth aphorisms account for humanity's fall into sin. In the first place, 'man spontaneously and freely, in rebellion against God, surrendered his integral nature to sin and to both kinds of death, being compelled by absolutely no one, and thus impelled by no necessity of inordinate desire as far as his will was concerned (for it was not yet sold under sin).' But 'this fall did not take place by chance—for God's providence extends to even the very smallest details.' Mankind chose to sin, but that spontaneous fall into the deep abyss was undergirded by God's exact providence.[44]

---

42. Beza, *Sum of All Christianity*, pp. 38-9.
43. Beza, *Sum of All Christianity*, pp. 39-40.
44. Beza, *Sum of All Christianity*, p. 40.

Letting God be God

The fifth aphorism attacks the issue of God's permission. Beza struggles to show, as Calvin had done, that God's providence over sin is not just 'some bare or neutral permission, which was separated from his will and decree.'[45] This would potentially leave the outcomes of events to chance and discredit God's omnipotence, as Augustine remarked. Beza concludes that

> this fall proceeded from Adam's voluntary act in such a way that nonetheless it did not occur apart from the will of God, whose pleasure, in some wondrous and incomprehensible manner, was that even what he does not approve (because it is sin) does not happen apart from his will. And he does that, as we said above, to show for the riches of his glory toward vessels of mercy and to declare his wrath and power in those vessels that he made for the purpose of showing forth his glory by their just damnation. For neither the salvation of the elect nor the destruction of the reprobate is the ultimate end of God's plans, but rather, the illustration of his glory, in some to be saved by mercy, and in others to be damned by just judgment.[46]

The Lord's ultimate aim is that He should receive glory. He will receive this glory in salvation and damnation. To accomplish this end, He even 'in some wondrous and incomprehensible manner' ordains what He hates, namely, sin.

The sixth, and lengthy, aphorism repeats the content of the previous five, especially answering the charges of those who would accuse God of injustice since our parents 'could not have resisted this will of God' that led to humanity's plummeting into sin. Beza stresses on the one hand that everything happens according to the will of God, but that, on the other hand, 'the whole fault of destruction inheres in man.' So, if people want to charge God with injustice, they should be prepared to face His justice which will immutably come against them due to

---

45. Calvin, *Institutes*, 3.23.8.
46. Beza, *Sum of All Christianity*, p. 41.

their sin. The response of those whom God has saved should be to preach His mercy to all, recognizing that all humanity alike deserves His wrath: 'But let us, instead, respect what supercedes the capacity of our nature and turn all the senses of our mind to the preaching of the mercy of him who saved us by his own goodness alone. We are no less wicked than they, and are worthy of every kind of punishment.'[47] No group of people should stress the Lord's goodness and mercy in their gospel proclamations more than those who are convinced that his mercy alone saved them. We will never understand God's reasons for acting as He has done. But there is much we can comprehend and much we can do in response to that truth.

Chapter Four: The Order of Causes in God's Election
Thirteen aphorisms make up the fourth chapter, 'By What Order of Causes the Lord has Made Known the Way for Declaring His Election and, to a Certain Extent, Bringing it to Fulfilment.' Beza labors in this lengthy section to delineate the Bible's teaching on God's eternal choosing of His people for salvation. He struggles to clarify here what can easily be confusing and misunderstood by sincere Christians.

The first aphorism sets the stage for all that follows, showing again the necessity for God's choice since mankind is totally absorbed in sin:

> Apart from man's being too weak to sustain the passion of God's wrath, he delights himself so much in his own utterly miserable blindness that he does not even see it. For he is totally enslaved to the rule of sin, to the point that God's law delivers him to death. That is how impossible it is that he can either bring himself back to liberty or satisfy God's law in even its minutest aspect.

Man can, therefore, do nothing to save himself. God's mercy will save, but it can only express itself in justice. Indeed, since

---

47. Beza, *Sum of All Christianity*, p. 42.

Letting God be God

God 'is not obliged nor able to forgo his justice,' 'therefore it was necessary for some Mediator to be appointed.' And we can trace the steps that the Lord took to appoint this one who would justly save the elect.[48]

The second aphorism claims that God, therefore, 'as the most merciful Father of the elect, tempered his justice by an infinite mercy and designated his only Son, of the same substance as himself, eternal God, to become a true man at the appointed time.' The eternal divine Son added a human nature to His being. He did this for three purposes. First, according to the third aphorism, He did it so that 'when the two natures were conjoined in the one Jesus Christ, the entire corruption of man might be utterly removed in one man.' Second, according to aphorism four, he did it so that

> this one might fulfill all righteousness and appear both powerful enough to sustain God's judgment and a priest worthy enough to pacify the heavenly Father. Thus he died as a just man for the unjust, wiping out the obstinacy of Adam by his own obedience, and expiating all the iniquities of us all, which were laid on his shoulders.

Last, as aphorism five avers, he did this so that 'by his one sacrifice he might sanctify all who were to be elect, and might destroy and bury sin by the communication of his own death and burial, and might vivify the elect in a new life by his resurrection, to such an extent that they find in him even more than they lost in Adam.'[49] The Father thus eternally determined that His Son would be equipped with all things necessary, and that He would have the proper status, to procure the salvation of the elect.

All this, though, would not avail to the elect's salvation were it not certain that they would be found in Christ. So at the

---

48. Beza, *Sum of All Christianity*, p. 43.
49. Beza, *Sum of All Christianity*, pp. 44-6.

same time He decreed to appoint His Son as the Mediator. God decreed 'to give his Son to those whom, as we said, he destined to eternal salvation, and to give them, in turn, to his Son,' according to the sixth aphorism. Beza next traces the stages that accomplish this union of the elect with Christ in the following several aphorisms.

First of all, according to aphorism seven, God makes the elect aware of their dire situation outside of Christ: 'He suddenly thrusts before their eyes the very great danger in which they are walking.' To rouse their consciences he adds the preaching of the law 'along with examples of his judgments, that they may shudder in recalling their own sins.' But the Father's intention in doing this is not to torment them but to give them reason to turn to Christ, to 'flee, having turned to contemplating the magnitude of the danger that surrounds them, and being converted to that one Mediator, Jesus Christ.' This is the first step in the experience of salvation for the elect.[50]

Next, after the law, comes the gospel. According to the eighth aphorism: 'Therefore, after that strict preaching of the law he sets before them the grace and generosity of the Gospel, adding the condition, however, that they believe in Christ, who alone can release them from condemnation and can grant them the right to obtain the heavenly inheritance.'[51] Yet, all this would avail nothing if the Lord merely tried to convert the elect through the outward preaching of the gospel, according to the ninth aphorism. The problem is that man in his sin hates what the gospel proclaims and has no 'free will' that's not radically affected by his sin. 'For whatever remains of the will in us is posited in this: We sin voluntarily; flee from God; practice hatred; and are even unable to hear him, or believe him, or acknowledge the gift of God, or even to think any good thing at all; and we are finally completely subject to wrath and curse.' Given this, Beza notes that God must first of all change

---

50. Beza, *Sum of All Christianity*, p. 48.
51. Beza, *Sum of All Christianity*, p. 51.

the hearts of the elect to want to receive the gospel. He does this by conjoining 'with the preaching of the external word the internal power of the Spirit.' The Spirit 'changes hearts of stone into flesh; he leads them along and instructs them; he illumines the eyes and opens the mind, the heart, the ears, and the understanding.' This is the essential first work of the Holy Spirit in the lives of the elect.[52]

In the tenth aphorism Beza notes that the purpose of the Spirit's work in the elect is to create faith in them so that 'they may be able to meet the condition connected with the preaching of the Gospel.' Faith may be considered in two different ways. It can refer, on the one hand, to a belief in the veracity of facts about Jesus. This is not saving faith, though, for it is 'a faith that is granted, on occasion, even to the reprobate themselves.' Saving faith, on the other hand, belongs only to the elect. Its distinctiveness is a personal grasping of Christ for salvation. It 'belongs to the elect in particular and is posited in our applying to ourselves, as our very own, the Christ offered universally and for all men, and our being rendered individually more certain of our election, which formerly was hidden in God's secret but was later revealed to us.' This saving faith has two sources: the individual's conscience pricked by the Spirit through preaching and the Spirit's changing the elect's orientation away from self to the things of the Lord: 'It is revealed partly by the internal witness of conscience through God's Spirit, conjoined with external preaching, and partly by the power and efficacy of that same Spirit who leads his individual elect, emancipated from the slavery of sin, to freedom, that they may begin to will and do the things that are of God.' The Holy Spirit grants this saving faith to the elect alone.[53]

The eleventh aphorism notes that in addition to 'that precious and peculiar gift of faith by which [the elect] lay hold on their salvation in Christ,' the Lord also gives them other

---

52. Beza, *Sum of All Christianity*, p. 52.
53. Beza, *Sum of All Christianity*, pp. 54-5.

gifts necessary for their perseverance in the faith. These include, especially, the sacraments of baptism and the Lord's Supper. 'For surely, the main end of these sacraments is that there be definite and efficacious seals, or even attestations, of the communion of the faithful with Christ, that he may become, for them, "wisdom, justice, sanctification, and redemption".'[54] Sacraments are aids, then, to keep the elect faithful to Christ. Indeed, perseverance is essential for the elect, as aphorism twelve reiterates. Beza here demonstrates pastoral sensitivity that is worth noting in full:

> He who has obtained the gift of true faith and has trusted in that same goodness of God must also be concerned about his perseverance. Yet he should not doubt, but should rather call on God in every kind of temptation and affliction, with the sure hope of attaining what he asks, at least as far as it is expedient, since he knows himself a child of God, who cannot fail him. Besides, he never strays from the right way without returning finally to that path, by the aid of that same grace. For though faith in the elect is occasionally buried for a time and may even seem entirely lost, to make them recognize their weakness, it still never recedes so far that the love of God and one's neighbor is entirely ripped from their minds.

Good works are essential for the perseverance of the elect. Yet these are not self-efforts of Christians, but are rather gifts the Lord will prepare for them to walk in.[55]

The last aphorism of this chapter acknowledges that steps recounted in the previous aphorisms are the normal manner in which the Lord acts in His elect 'while they are still in adolescence.' However, in the covenant of grace He also calls some 'into his kingdom while they are newly-born or in the first years of their lives.' For these the way of salvation is shorter. He 'pronounces them "holy"' so that 'there can be no shadow of

---

54. Beza, *Sum of All Christianity*, pp. 56-7.
55. Beza, *Sum of All Christianity*, p. 58.

doubt that he has handed over to the Son (who will never cast them aside) the saints' children, who belong to the election.' We don't know who these elect are. 'He only knows.'[56]

Chapter Five: How the Lord Reprobates

In the previous two chapters Beza discussed election. The next two chapters parallel this discussion by dealing with the doctrine of reprobation and how the Lord carries out His eternal decree among those whom He has chosen for destruction. Beza begins this sensitive discussion in chapter five titled, 'By What Order the Lord Begins to Carry Out the Plan of Reprobation and to Make It Known in Reality', consisting of seven aphorisms.

The first aphorism frames all the subsequent discussion on reprobation. The reprobate are those whom God 'created in order to glorify himself in their own just condemnation.' Their condemnation is just due to the headship of Adam over all of those destined for destruction. Drawing on Romans 5, Beza notes that 'as Christ, the second Adam from heaven, is the foundation and entire substance of the salvation of the elect, so too the first Adam from earth, since he fell, is therefore the first author of the hatred and destruction that awaits the reprobate.' All humanity is under one of two heads—either Jesus or Adam—and the reprobate are found under the latter.[57] The second aphorism, though, makes it clear that it's not due to Adam's sin alone that the reprobate are condemned. Rather, Beza here sketches out the steps God has ordained that they take which proves that 'the whole fault of the destruction of the reprobate would remain in themselves.' God is thus just in condemning them: 'Therefore, since man fell into that miserable condition by his own free will, the Lord rightly condemns the reprobate, because they are corrupt.' This is essential. They are corrupt in Adam and therefore they warrant condemnation. In fact, Beza avers that on some—apparently infants and young

---

56. Beza, *Sum of All Christianity*, p. 60.
57. Beza, *Sum of All Christianity*, p. 61.

children—God chooses to exercise 'his just wrath on some of them as soon as they are born.'[58] The asymmetry that Beza draws is essential for us to repeat. Some infants are included in the covenant of grace merely due to God's gracious election; but reprobate infants are condemned for their sin in Adam.

The steps leading to reprobation work out in an orderly sequence in adults, among whom there are four different types of reprobate. The third aphorism speaks in the first place of those whom God doesn't even allow to hear the gospel of Jesus. The Lord 'allows them to proceed in their own ways and to hasten on to a sure end.' They are responsible for their own lack of faith, though, for 'they have nothing but their own guilt to use as a pretension.' They were born in corruption and from it flows their ignorance and folly. So they are culpable. Beza shows the miserable end of these:

> whatever they can behold in the divine realm by the light (or rather, the darkness) of nature, is such that it cannot, in any way, be enough for salvation. It is necessary, for salvation, that we know God not only as God but also as Father in Christ—which secret 'flesh and blood does not reveal' but the Son himself, finally, to those whom 'he has received from the Father.'[59]

The fourth aphorism speaks of the second type of reprobate. These hear the gospel and because of that 'the situation is even worse' for them than for the first type of condemned. Beza does not blame them alone, nor does he remove God's sovereign will from the equation of their condemnation. No, they are condemned because though hearing, they both can't and won't respond. And they are also condemned because God doesn't allow them to believe.

> Although he dignifies them by external preaching, they are not willing, once they are called, nor are they even able to

---

58. Beza, *Sum of All Christianity*, p. 62.
59. Beza, *Sum of All Christianity*, p. 63.

respond. For they delight themselves in their blindness so much that they even say that they see. It is not granted them to embrace the Spirit of truth and to believe. Therefore, their stubbornness, though necessary, is nonetheless spontaneous.

Showing their ultimate guilt, Beza notes that 'they refuse, although they are invited, to come to the "banquet", and the word of life itself is "foolishness" for them, and a "stumbling block", and finally a "deadly odor unto death".'[60]

Aphorism five speaks of the third type of reprobate person, the one to whom God grants a general faith. This faith will not avail to save them. But the final two aphorisms speak of the most culpable group, the fourth type of reprobates. They are 'the most miserable of all,' the ones God allows to 'rise up still higher, that they might fall the harder.' These are the ones who appear to be Christians, yet they turn away from Christ, showing that they were never true believers. God grants them a 'certain grace,' allowing them to 'taste the heavenly gift,' to receive the seed, to appear 'to be implanted in the church of God and to display to others the way of salvation.' All this is not salvific, though, for God has not chosen them to salvation: 'The Spirit of adoption, which we said they possess who are "never cast out", and who are "written down" in secret as God's people, is never communicated to them. For if they were among the elect they would certainly remain with the elect to the very end.' But it's not merely due to God's choice that they aren't among the elect. Beza insists that their condemnation is due both to them and to the Lord's decision. It's both a result of God's mysterious will and also because of their insistence to be their own gods and not submit to the gospel. In other words, their turning away happens both 'necessarily and yet voluntarily'. Beza avers,

> They are abandoned by God, I say, who, according to his will, which 'no one can resist,' even though they are moved by their

---

60. Beza, *Sum of All Christianity*, p. 64.

own corruption and depravity, 'hardens' them, and 'dulls their hearts,' and 'closes their ears,' and finally 'blinds their eyes.' To accomplish that he uses in part their own wicked desires, to which he 'hands them over to be ruled,' and in part that 'spirit of falsehood' that keeps them 'ensnared' on account of their own corruption.[61]

This corruption of theirs is what leads God justly to condemn them.

Chapter Six: God's Ultimate Glory in Election and Reprobation

Chapter six, 'On the Final and Full Execution of God's Plan, Not Only in the Elect But Also in the Reprobate', serves as the doctrinal and biblical conclusion to the treatise. Here Beza especially is intent upon showing his readers the ultimate end of both the elect and the reprobate. More than all else, though, his desire is to highlight how God receives glory through both reprobation and salvation, since both of these actions focus our attention on different aspects of God's perfect character.

The first aphorism recounts the manner in which God saves the elect: 'Only those are just among men who are united and ingrafted in Christ by faith, and are rooted in him, and made one body with him, and thus are justified and sanctified in and through him.'[62] The next aphorism, though, speaks of the manner in which God treats the reprobate: 'On the other hand, God rightly hates those who remain in the pollution of Adam and in death. He therefore condemns them without exception,' even those who never sin consciously as Adam did.[63]

These first two aphorisms show the big picture. The next two cover the stages God uses to accomplish these things. God brings both the elect and the reprobate through three stages

---

61. Beza, *Sum of All Christianity*, p. 66.
62. Beza, *Sum of All Christianity*, p. 69.
63. Beza, *Sum of All Christianity*, p. 70.

to usher them to their respective ends. Aphorism three deals with God's elect. The first stage comprises 'that very moment in which they received the gift of faith.' At that point 'they "passed over" in some sense from "death to life".' The second stage, their bodily deaths, frees their souls 'from the chains of the body' and allows them to enter 'into the "joy of its Lord".' Finally, in stage three, they receive the consummation of the salvation they've been yearning for their entire Christian lives:

> Finally, on that day appointed for the 'judgment of the living and dead,' when this corruptible shall have 'put on immortality' and God shall be 'all in all'—at that time, and only then, will they gaze openly on his majesty and enjoy to the full that 'inexpressible joy' predestined them from eternity, because of that reward that is owed to the justice and holiness of Christ. He was 'delivered up for their sins' and was 'raised from the dead for their justification.'[64]

The fourth aphorism shows the mirror of these stages in the reprobate. They are, first, 'conceived, born, and nurtured in sin, death, and the "wrath of God which remains in them".' Second, they 'rush down, when they depart this life, into another abyss of destruction' so that '[t]heir souls are thrown down headlong into eternal dread.' They are in grave fear until the third stage, 'that day when, with body and soul again conjoined, they enter into that "eternal fire which is prepared for the devil and his angels".'[65]

The final aphorism of this chapter shows that all of this—God's myriad dealings with the elect and the reprobate from eternity past to eternity future—will resound to the glory of God as all of His actions show His character to be perfect. Indeed, when the elect are in heaven and the reprobate are in hell, 'that final outcome of God's judgments will show forth his

---

64. Beza, *Sum of All Christianity*, p. 71.
65. Beza, *Sum of All Christianity*, p. 72.

glory to all men.' God will be glorified among the elect since He will be seen to be 'supremely just and supremely merciful.' His justice will be magnified in the manner in which He treated their sin: 'He will be just in that he will have punished, with the greatest severity, all the sins of his elect in the person of his Son, and will not have allowed them into his fellowship before he justified and sanctified them, fully and wholly, in that same Son.' But His mercy will be magnified as well; indeed He will be seen to be 'infinitely merciful': 'Having proposed in himself to elect them by grace, he will have adopted them freely in his Son, as he proposed, by calling, justifying, and glorifying them, by means of that intercession of faith which he himself grants them, being moved by that same goodness.'

God's actions towards the reprobate, on the other hand, will show Him to be completely, and severely, just: 'In regard to the reprobate, their own corruption and infidelity, with the fruits that rise from them, and the testimony of their conscience, will have accused them in such a way that no matter how they resist, God's highest justice will nonetheless appear in their just condemnation, with no excuses for any of them.'[66] Beza has thus reached the end for which he began the trek at the start of the treatise. God's glory is ultimate, and both His reprobating and His electing display and magnify His glory.

Chapter Seven: How to Publicly Teach this Doctrine

Not willing to leave the doctrine of predestination only in the ethereal realm, Beza turns in the last two chapters to his application of the doctrine. Chapter seven, 'In What Way This Doctrine Can Be Set Forth Publicly, in a Fitting Manner', is unusual in that Beza doesn't include aphorisms to show how the doctrine should be preached and taught publicly. Instead, he divides those who oppose his doctrine into two categories: the willfully ignorant (who understand the doctrine but rebel against it) and the unsophisticated. It's the latter category he

---

66. Beza, *Sum of All Christianity*, p. 73.

addresses in this chapter, since he recognizes that predestination is hard to understand and its difficulty is compounded by the wrong way in which some people teach predestination. Recognizing that 'it is for God alone to correct the error of those in the first category', Beza notes that he has found several approaches helpful when addressing the category of people who misunderstand the biblical doctrine of predestination. He makes six points.

First, the top priority of a faithful preacher is to avoid speculation. Teachers 'must guard diligently lest they bring forth vain and curious speculations instead of God's simple truth.'[67] The simple truth of Scripture should be the content of their teaching. But too often they fall into several errors in an effort to work out how God's mysterious plan of predestination can fit with human responsibility. They often 'distinguish' and 'separate foreknowledge from God's purpose'; or they imagine that God's permission of things is 'a bare and indifferent permission'; finally, they 'make God's purpose twofold.' In the process of doing these things, they are often 'compelled … to deny those [things] that are necessarily implied' in predestination; 'and, at times, they contrive a multitude of distinctions that are useless and obscure.' This path leads to grave trouble: 'The further they are thrust into those distinctions, the more they are entangled, until they can never emerge from those labyrinths.' This is a shame. Given the difficulty of this subject, Beza urges that 'no subject is more fittingly taught, in a pure and sincere way, in God's church.'[68] This is what is required of teachers.

The place to begin—the second point Beza makes—is only to speak in the language of the Bible. So,

> no manners of speaking should be used that are foreign to Scripture, as far as that is possible (for in the interest of

---

67. Beza, *Sum of All Christianity*, p. 74.
68. Beza, *Sum of All Christianity*, pp. 74-5.

teaching we must sometimes hazard something in a holy and reverent way). The teachings that are found in the Word of God should be explained by proper interpretation, so that one who is less sophisticated will not have reason to stumble.[69]

Beza's third point is a reiteration of what introduced this chapter. Teachers must 'put great stress on the condition of the hearers.' Two types of people rebel against predestination. They are either 'malicious' and 'willfully ignorant', or they are 'unsophisticated' people 'who labor under simple human ignorance.' God will judge the former category. Unlearned people 'must be led gradually into the knowledge of the truth' though. A caring teacher, however, will remember that even while caring for the weak in his audience he must also remember his responsibility to speak to those who are stubbornly opposed to God's truth, even as Paul did in Romans 9:10-15.

In the fourth place, Beza finds Paul's pedagogical approach in Romans to be the best. Teachers 'should strive from the lowest to the highest stages, as Paul, in the epistle to the Romans (which is the method of all theology) proceeds from the law to forgiveness, and from there gradually to the highest stage.' Paul doesn't address predestination until the end of chapter eight, at which point he has already taught about God's righteousness, His holy law, human rebellion and condemnation, and a whole range of other doctrinal material. Only then does the apostle deal with predestination. Teachers in the church should follow his model so that predestination will make more sense to those confused: 'For the brightness of divine majesty, if thrust before them all at once, usually hurts their eyes so much that they are blinded from later distinguishing other things, unless they are first accustomed to looking on that light for a long time.'[70] Wise teachers will build up to the doctrine of predestination, not thrust it on people prior to any foundation being laid.

---

69. Beza, *Sum of All Christianity*, p. 75.
70. Beza, *Sum of All Christianity*, p. 75.

Fifth, Beza urges that teachers and preachers be balanced in their teaching of predestination. Indeed, 'they must take care not to hasten from one extreme to the other, and thus to overlook the means.' It seems that Beza had heard young preachers who liked to dwell on reprobation, especially focusing their teaching on the fact of God's eternal choice of the damned. In doing so they have neglected Beza's previous teaching that persons are responsible for their damnation because of their sin. This middle position must be struck: 'One can rush from God's purpose to salvation, or, even more so, from salvation to his purpose, or else from his purpose to damnation; and, on the other hand, he can ignore the causes of God's just judgment that are nearer at hand.'[71] People must be taught that the reprobate are condemned because of their sin.

Sixthly, Beza urges that preachers should never apply this doctrine to a particular person, 'unless some prophet of God is possibly warned by some special revelation.' Even here, instead of discounting this as never happening, Beza cautions that 'we should not believe that rashly, since it does not happen very often.' What's clear, though, is that pastors should approach people in one of two different ways. Either they should encourage believers by the reality of their eternal election, or they should admonish unbelievers by the fact of God's future judgment. In both cases, the minister needs to relinquish final judgment to God.[72]

Chapter Eight: Using the Truth of Predestination Personally

The eighth and final chapter, 'How Individuals, With Some Profit, Can Apply this General Doctrine to Each Other', is comprised of five lengthy and wide-ranging aphorisms. Beza's primary point here is to convince Christians that, applied to them, the truth of predestination should lead to confidence

---

71. Beza, *Sum of All Christianity*, pp. 75-6.
72. Beza, *Sum of All Christianity*, p. 76.

instead of producing doubt. He labors to prove that and to show believers how they can derive comfort from this doctrine.

The first aphorism makes the argument that only those who agree with Beza about predestination can in reality have assurance of salvation. Beza acknowledges that 'it is clear that God's gospel is completely overthrown by those who teach that man's salvation depends entirely or in some part on works.' In opposition to this, 'those who teach a free justification by faith rest on a sure foundation.' Yet if we think about this a little, we see that they only do this by agreeing with the Bible's teaching on God's absolute sovereignty: 'They only do so if they set faith under that eternal decree of God in which finally even Christ himself stands, as well as the apostle Paul, who followed in Christ's footsteps.' Only believing in God's eternal decree gives us certainty. Why? Here is how Beza reasons:

> For since perseverance of faith is necessary for salvation, why do I have faith unless I am certain of the gift of perseverance? But we must not fear that this doctrine renders us careless and dissolute. For that peace of conscience, of which we now speak, differs totally from foolish indifference; and he who is God's child, since he is moved by God's Spirit, can never find an occasion for idleness in contemplating God's benefits. Therefore, even if this doctrine brought this fruit only—that being protected by it we learn to strengthen our faith in all future events—it is obvious that the main basis of our salvation is destroyed by those who attack this heading of religion. For they measure God according to the standard of their own genius.[73]

Predestination, rightly understood and correctly taught, should strengthen a Christian's sense of assurance and lead him to persevere in faith in Jesus. Indeed, a Christian has no other true reason to persevere in the midst of the vicissitudes of life than in being convinced of the invincibility of God's sovereignty in his life.

---

73. Beza, *Sum of All Christianity*, p. 78.

Letting God be God

In the second aphorism Beza teaches his readers how to apply this doctrine to themselves.[74] The problem we face is that

> the works of God, even the smallest, are of such a sort that a man cannot judge them except in a twofold way: either after they have already happened or from the ordered arrangement of secondary causes. As one comes to know from long experience, these latter point forward to a certain end. That is commonly the case in natural events, but men are remarkably blind as far as those events are concerned.[75]

If we're dependent on the Lord for information in every area, of course we're dependent on Him when it comes to our election, since this doctrine 'is by far the most difficult to grasp.' We must beware lest our thinking run wildly on its own. Rather, we must turn to God's word. Apart from the Bible, our 'total judgment rests on observing these causes that surpass every power of nature.' Therefore, we 'must find recourse in something else: God's utterances, which are written down fully in his word. Since these utterances are more certain, in their infinite parts, than all the conjectures of men, they also lead us

---

74. Beza wrote a letter to Gaspard de Coligny to console him on the death of his wife Charlotte de Laval in 1568. It shows us that to Beza predestination should be a comforting doctrine. 'But the sovereign remedy is that which you have taken, namely, the power, the wisdom, the good will of the Lord: power to assure you that he lacks no means; wisdom to enable you to understand well that he knows better than anyone, even you, what is best for you and yours; good will which is proper to God's elect, namely, that he who has chosen us by his eternal and unchangeable council (to which our vocation is an infallible witness resounding in our ears by the preaching of his word accompanied by his sacraments and in our hearts through the Holy Spirit), and since he can do all, he wishes nothing and consequently does nothing except for the salvation of his own.' *Correspondance de Théodore de Bèze*, vol. 9, eds H. Meylan, A. Dufour, C. Chimelli, B. Nicollier (Geneva: Librarie Droz, 1978), pp. 97-8; translated in Raitt, 'Theodore Beza, 1519-1605,' p. 99.

75. Beza, *Sum of All Christianity*, p. 80.

to a more certain and indubitable judgment.'[76] The way to gain true assurance, therefore, is to turn to the Bible.

What Christians find when they turn to the Bible is that their Father has done everything necessary for their salvation, from beginning to end. Echoing Romans 8:29-30, Beza notes:

> The Scripture witnesses that whoever God has predestined by his eternal purpose to adopt as sons for himself through Jesus Christ are called at the appointed time, that they may hear and embrace the voice of the one who calls. The Scripture witnesses that, being justified and sanctified by this faith in Christ, they are necessarily also glorified.[77]

Of course, thoughtful people will desire to be assured, then, that they have been predestined to life. How can they have this certainty? This question is doubly important since 'all the attacks of Satan' lead them to doubt. The answer is to follow the orderly arrangement of the Bible's material from the lowest to the highest:

> Take care, and be diligent that you do not begin at the highest stage, for otherwise you will not endure the immense light of God. Therefore, begin at the lowest stages; and when you hear God's voice resounding in your ears and heart and calling you to Christ, the only Mediator, consider step by step, and inquire carefully if you are justified and sanctified by faith in Christ. For these are the effects, and from them we understand that faith is the cause.[78]

In other words, don't seek to read God's mind about your election. Instead, look to your life now. Are you being sanctified? Do you have faith in Christ? If so, you can have certainty from these effects that you have been called by God's voice to Christ.

---

76. Beza, *Sum of All Christianity*, p. 80.

77. Beza, *Sum of All Christianity*, p. 80.

78. Beza, *Sum of All Christianity*, p. 81.

Even more than this, though, a Christian has a third means of gaining assurance (the first two being: to see if one is being sanctified and to consider if one has faith in Jesus). The third ground of assurance is the Holy Spirit's testifying to the believer that he's safe in Jesus' arms: 'You will know this [assurance] partly from the Spirit of adoption who inwardly cries, "Abba, Father," and partly from the power and efficacy of that same Spirit within you—if, that is, you experience and also demonstrate in reality that sin, though it "dwells" in you, does not "reign" in you.'[79] The Spirit, then, is the third means of providing certainty of salvation for doubting, struggling Christians. Look to see if there's evidence—either a sense that you're a believer, or indications that you are fighting sin—of the Spirit's presence in your life. The Spirit's work within us is the strongest evidence of our salvation:

> Is it not the Holy Spirit who causes us spontaneously not to give free reign to our wicked and depraved desires, as those are wont to do whose eyes the prince of this world has blinded? Who else 'exhorts us to prayers,' no matter how cold and sluggish we are? Who arouses in us those 'inexpressible sighs?' Who implants in us after we have sinned (sometimes intentionally and knowingly) that hatred for the sins that we commit—not because we fear punishment but because we offend our most merciful Father? Who, I say, bears witness to us that our sighs are heard? Who urges us even to dare entreat God, our God, and still our Father, even after we have offended him? Is it not the Spirit, and he alone, whom 'freely we received,' as 'freely he is given' for a sure pledge of our adoption? But if we can infer faith from these effects, we can only conclude that we are efficaciously called and drawn, and that from this calling in turn (which we have shown is peculiar to God's children) we comprehend entirely what we are seeking. We therefore were given to the Son, since we were predestined by God's eternal counsel, which he

---

79. Beza, *Sum of All Christianity*, p. 81.

proposed in himself, to be adopted in the Son. From this it follows, in short, that since we were predestined by that most unshakable will of God, which depends on itself alone, and since 'no one can snatch us from the hand of the Son,' and since perseverance in faith is necessary for salvation, we have a sure expectation of our perseverance, and consequently our salvation. And therefore it is wicked to have any more doubts concerning that matter.[80]

The Spirit's ministry of assuring Christians is supreme.

Moreover, the Spirit's assuring ministry makes Christians active in pursuing righteousness. Indeed, assurance of salvation makes Christians more, not less, active in seeking holiness. Certainty of election leads Christians to pursue God, not sin: 'The apostle clearly witnesses that when we have come to know these "depths" we learn not to conduct ourselves negligently but to persevere bravely, and to worship, love, fear, and call on him; so that daily, more and more, as Peter says, as far as we are concerned, we "make our calling and election sure".' The harsh realities of this fallen world and of the Christian's sojourning to a true, final home are such that only the truth of God's predestining work can give the struggling Christian the assurance he yearns for:

> How can anyone remain firm and constant to the end, against so many dangerous internal and external temptations, and so many 'strokes of chance,' as the world likes to say, if he has not first established in his mind what is utterly true: that God does all things according to his good will, no matter what, or whatever instruments he uses, in the interest of his own, and that the man who is set in such a plight may number himself among 'those in his book'?[81]

Conviction of God's sovereign election will fortify believers to persevere to the end.

---

80. Beza, *Sum of All Christianity*, pp. 81-2.
81. Beza, *Sum of All Christianity*, p. 82.

In the third aphorism, Beza argues that Christians shouldn't avoid the doctrine of reprobation. They just need to handle it circumspectly and humbly. We do not have the right to edit what God has spoken: 'Those who want to bury that side as though it were a matter of curiosity or hardly necessary do great injustice to God's Spirit.' Like Calvin (remember his definition of predestination at the start of this chapter), Beza avers that it's impossible to think of God's election without also noting His reprobating: 'For no one can even think of the purpose of electing unless he reflects on its opposite, at the same time, and in the same measure, to say nothing of what is obvious: that these two are very frequently interconnected to God's word.'

The key to handling reprobation in a biblical manner is to approach it cautiously, with the correct emphases. One 'must treat it with such moderation that the depth of God's justice puts a bridle on man's curiosity.'[82] Specifically, we need to speak of its truth while never pointing to a person and saying, 'You are reprobate.' In this sense, reprobation is profoundly different from election:

> In short, we must treat it so that it is not applied privately to any single man or any particular group. For it also differs from election as follows: The latter, as we have shown, is revealed to us by God's Spirit, not in others, whose mind we cannot see through, but in ourselves, while reprobation is almost always hidden to everyone unless it is revealed by God, as it were, in an extraordinary way. For does anyone know if the Lord has decided to have mercy, at the last moment of life, on one who has wasted his whole life in shameful activities and sins? Yet, that hope must not confirm anyone in his perversity, for I am speaking of those things that we ought to observe in others; and the examples of this forbearance are rare; and no wise man can promise himself, in a vain assurance, what does not lie in his own power. Suffice it for us to understand in general

---

82. Beza, *Sum of All Christianity*, p. 86.

that some vessels are prepared for destruction. But since the Lord has not revealed them to us, we ought to invite every single person to salvation, as eagerly as we can, by the example of our living and by prayer. We ought to invite even those of whom we dearly despair when we look at their sins.[83]

Rather than driving us to lethargy and despair, then, the doctrines of election and reprobation should propel us to seek everyone's salvation, with the deep confidence that the Lord will act sovereignly as He chooses.

In the fourth aphorism Beza encourages his readers that holding to the doctrine of predestination will lead to much fruit in a Christian's life. He notes four benefits that should follow from embracing this truth. 'First, we shall learn from the knowledge of it to bow our hearts willingly before God's majesty, so that the more we fear and revere him the more we shall work in confirming within us the witness of our election in Christ.' It will lead us to greater assurance. More than that, second, holding to this truth will lead us to exult in God's incredible goodness to us: 'When we ponder carefully that chasm established by God's mercy (among men who are otherwise equally subject to curse) we cannot refrain from knowing and embracing that extraordinary goodness of God, much more eagerly than if we made his grace common to all men or sought the reason for its inequality only in men themselves.' In the third place, holding to this doctrine will result in further growth in the Christian life. Beza writes that 'when we acknowledge that the gift of faith is particular, shall we not receive more eagerly what is offered us and be more concerned about its growth than if we imagined (as some do) that it inheres in all men's power to repent as often as they want? For God (they say) "wills to save all men," and "does not will the death of a sinner".' The fourth point Beza makes is that embracing this doctrine will be an encouragement as

---

83. Beza, *Sum of All Christianity*, pp. 86-7.

Letting God be God

we look around and see that the vast majority of mankind despises God:

> when we see that the doctrine of the gospel is not only ignored by almost the whole world but is even treated very crudely, what will strengthen us more than if we affirm that nothing happens by chance; that God knows his own; and that finally those who commit such errors (unless they are given to repent) are predestined, not accidentally but by the sure, eternal counsel of God, in order that in them (as in a mirror) God's just wrath and power might shine forth?[84]

As Christians struggle for faith in this hard world, knowing that God has sovereignly called them and will hold them close to Him is their ultimate hope.

In the final aphorism of the book Beza reminds his readers that even with the clearest of explanations many people will continue to oppose this doctrine. Even so, their consciences will condemn them. Seeing nay-sayers oppose God for this truth, Christians should, conversely, exult in it as we look forward to the judgment day: 'Our hearts, however, being confirmed by God's goodness, will be free in that day of Christ.' So, Beza ends where he had begun, in offering praise to the triune God for His work of salvation: 'To him, with the Father and the Holy Spirit, be glory, praise, and honor, for ever. Amen.'[85]

Application

If you read this summary of Theodore Beza's *Tabula*, you almost certainly know more about it now than many scholars who have written about Beza, especially those who claim that Beza's chart proves his deviation from John Calvin. Several themes punctuate this short treatise by Beza: God's utter sovereignty in our salvation, our inability to do anything to save ourselves,

---

84. Beza, *Sum of All Christianity*, pp. 87-8.
85. Beza, *Sum of All Christianity*, p. 88.

God's justice in the damnation of sinners, human responsibility to respond to God's invitation in the gospel, the manner in which Christians can find assurance from the Lord even while contemplating predestination, and the need for teachers to be cautious while speaking about this, and to make sure that they are communicating the truth of Scripture, not just their ideas.

Before we move on, we should stop and consider what we can learn from Beza, specifically how we can apply some of the truths he taught. In the first place, just like Beza, we need to come to grips with the fact that God is God. We're not. And we have to allow Him the right (in our hearts and minds) to be God and to be in complete charge of our destiny and the destinies of those whom we love. Reflecting on Paul's thought in Romans 9 may be a useful exercise for us at this point. Rather than attempting to re-cast God in our own image, we need to allow Him—through the Bible—to change the way we think about Him.

We also need to wrestle with the question of assurance of salvation as it relates to the doctrine of predestination. Maybe you're a person who struggles with assurance and who finds the idea of God's sovereignty unsettling in this regard. Beza, as you have seen, though, believed the opposite. He thought the only grounds for our assurance was God's complete sovereignty. Left to ourselves, we are impotent to keep ourselves in the way of salvation. But the Lord is well able to keep His children from falling away. Perhaps reflecting on Paul's great assuring words in Romans 8:28-39 would be useful for you.

In the last place, as Beza admonished us, let's be careful as we talk about the doctrine of predestination, especially double predestination. We can hold them to be true without stressing them in an unbiblical fashion to our listeners. Beza would remind us: know who you're talking to, know where they're coming from, realize you don't have to say everything all the time. Speak of sin. Speak of Christ. Beg people to come to Christ for forgiveness. It's that call to salvation that should be our great theme. If people respond in repentance and faith, it's because our sovereign God has predestined them to be His own. Let us be like Paul who believed in predestination and also preached the gospel relentlessly. Reflect on Paul's almost super-human labors in this regard in the book of Acts.

Uses

The text of Beza's *Tabula* may be found translated by Philip C. Holtrop as *The Sum of All Christianity, or the Description and Distribution of the Causes of Salvation of the Elect and the Destruction of the Reprobate, Collected from the Sacred Writings*, in *The Potter and Clay: The Main Predestination Writings of Theodore Beza*, edited by Philip C. Holtrop (Grand Rapids: Calvin College, 1982), pp. 21-94.

1. As you approach the question of predestination, what background and personal experience do you come with? Are you predisposed to like, or dislike, Beza's doctrinal formulation?

2. Do you agree with the manner in which Beza speaks of the similarities and differences of election and reprobation? Why or why not?

3. Read Romans 8:28-39 and Ephesians 1:3-14. Notice that Paul can employ the truth of predestination in two different ways. How does this help you understand the usefulness of this doctrine?

4. Does the doctrine of predestination lead you to greater comfort in your relationship with God? Why?

5. Does the doctrine of predestination encourage you to share the gospel more widely? Should it? Why?

6

Trusting God in Life's Difficulties—
Theodore Beza's *Treatize of the Plague*

In the previous chapter we noticed one of the treatises Theodore Beza is most known for authoring. Now we turn to one of his lesser-known works. We will see here, though, a great deal of commonality as Beza wrestles with an implication of the doctrine of God's sovereignty that he so ably defended in the *Tabula*. If God is completely sovereign, does that mean that human beings have no real decisions to make in this life? Is everything determined by fate? This charge, of course, has been one of the complaints made against Reformed theology's vision of God. As he discusses Christians' responses to the onset of the plague, Beza doesn't shy away from addressing these life and death questions. He doesn't turn away from teaching the same comprehensive view of God's sovereignty that he'd put forward in the *Tabula*. And in a similar manner to his defense of double predestination, his work on the plague is filled with pastoral wisdom that is fueled by his eschatological vision of the eternal end that awaits all persons.

The Setting
Every age of human history since the fall of Adam into sin has been traumatized by the effects of sin. Consequently, in many epochs of history people have felt like they were in a period of

crisis, a time of unusual tumult, a traumatic period from which there seemed to be little hope of escape. Late medieval and early modern Europe's conflict with the plague qualifies as one of those times of crisis, if only because of the sheer number of persons killed by it. Theodore Beza was not immune to the disease's dire effects.

The plague brought terror both because of the speed at which it killed previously healthy people and also because of the stealthy mode by which it spread. No one knew why it struck a community or how it was transmitted. Due to the rapidity with which it spread, it was often termed the 'pestilence', recounting God's judgment on Egypt. Because of the black blemishes that formed under the skin of those infected, it was also given the moniker, 'the Black Death'. It caused numerous anxieties for centuries and untold heartache. At the very foundation of Christian Europe, it made people ask themselves, 'Why did God allow this pestilence to come to us and devastate us?'

Contemporaries described its horrendous effects. Jean de Venette (d. ca. 1370), a French Carmelite friar, left a chronicle of his days, including his account of the plague and the destruction it brought on France beginning in 1348:

> All this year and the next, the mortality of men and women, of the young even more than the old, in Paris and in the kingdom of France, and also, it is said, in other parts of the world, was so great that it was almost impossible to bury the dead. People lay little more than two or three days and died suddenly, as it were in full health. He who was well one day was dead the next and being carried to his grave. Swellings appeared suddenly in the armpit or in the groin—in many cases both—and they were infallible signs of death ... . Wherefore in many towns timid priests withdrew, leaving the exercise of their ministry to such of the religious as were more daring. In many places not two out of twenty remained alive.[1]

---

1. Jean de Venette, *Chronicle*, in *The European Reformations Sourcebook*, ed. Carter Lindberg (Oxford: Blackwell, 2000), p. 4.

Well did Petrarch say of the plague, 'Everywhere is woe, terror everywhere.'[2]

The plague, first introduced to Europe from the east in the mid-fourteenth century, still devastated communities throughout the sixteenth century. Andrew Pettegree says this of the plague's continued devastation in the time in which Beza lived:

> Sixteenth-century Europe made no progress whatsoever in grappling with the scourge of epidemics. Indeed the growth of cities, unaccompanied by any breakthrough in public sanitation or public hygiene, may indeed have intensified its impact. Many cities suffered incidence of epidemics at least every ten years. In the middle of the sixteenth-century England was twice laid low by the sweating sickness, a mysterious if deadly affliction which modern medical science has struggled precisely to identify. Most terrifying of all was the Black Death, the bubonic plague, introduced to Europe in 1348, and a regular visitor thereafter. Epidemics could kill up to one third of a city's population in one year, a rate of mortality that left few households untouched. While its cause was still unknown, the plague sent terror through communities that recognized the tell-tale signs of a new outbreak. Panic led to the wildest accusations: some believed that plague was deliberately spread by malign individuals, and communities turned on these plague spreaders with a ferocity that in the next century would be reserved for witches.[3]

The plague's mortality rates were astounding. Two examples show this. Eight years of pestilence struck Augsburg in the early sixteenth century, killing about 40,000 people, even though the city's population only rose to 45,000 later in the century. London experienced the plague twice in the second half of the

---

2. Petrarch, *Rerum familiarium libri* 8.7.1, in *European Reformations Sourcebook*, ed. Lindberg, p. 3.
3. Andrew Pettegree, *Europe in the Sixteenth Century* (Oxford: Blackwell, 2002), pp. 2-13.

century. In 1563, 27 per cent of the population succumbed to the pestilence, and in 1593 about 18 per cent were struck down by it. In all, a total of about 40,000 Londoners met their death by the plague in these two years.[4]

The plague came in at least three different forms. Bubonic attacked the lymph nodes, pneumonic the lungs, and septicaemic the blood. Carter Lindberg tells us of the horror of the disease:

> The gruesome nature of the disease increased its horror: large painful boils (the term 'bubonic' comes from *buba*, Latin for groin, where lymph nodes were often the first to swell since many flea bites were on the legs) accompanied by black spots or blotches due to bleeding under the skin were the prelude to the final stage of violent coughs of blood. A contemporary description is less clinical: 'All the matter which exuded from their bodies let off an unbearable stench; sweat, excrement, spittle, breath, so fetid as to be overpowering; urine turbid, thick, black or red ...'
>
> It is difficult for us today to realize the profound personal and social impact the plague had upon its survivors. It was an inexplicable and swift disaster. People did not know its whence and wherefore. The plague could strike down a healthy person within days or, in the septicaemic version where the bacillus entered the bloodstream, within hours. The widespread fear of both an imminent and a horrible death broke down customs and norms. Parents deserted their children, and children deserted their parents. The horror extended to the nursery, as suggested by the rhyme, 'Ring Around the Rosey.' The 'rosey' was the reddish 'ring' that preceded the skin blotch; the 'pocket full of posies' refers to the use of flowers to mask the stench and supposedly ward off infection; 'ashes, ashes' is shorthand for 'ashes to ashes, dust to dust;' and 'we all fall down' is the inevitable result.[5]

---

4. Richard Mackenney, *Sixteenth Century Europe: Expansion and Conflict* (New York: St Martin's, 1994), p. 84.

5. Carter Lindberg, *The European Reformations* (Oxford: Blackwell, 1996), pp. 27-8

Ministers felt the effects of the plague dramatically, as Rudolph Heinze comments: 'Priests and doctors who came to minister to the sick often died, and many people became so fearful that they avoided the sick, whose suffering was thereby increased. In many instances it was the most caring clergy who died, because it was they who ministered to the sick and dying.'[6] The result of this was that 'the shortness of life was never far from people's minds.'[7]

The plague killed Catholic and Protestant alike. In 1519, in Zurich, the early Protestant reformer Ulrich Zwingli almost died of a deadly plague that struck the city. He survived, but his brother wasn't so lucky. In all, about 2,000 of Zurich's 7,000 citizens were slain by the pestilence. While he was suffering, Zwingli penned his 'Plague Song', a desperate plea to God for help:

> Help me, O Lord
>   My strength and rock;
> Lo, at the door
>   I hear death's knock.
> Uplift thine arm,
>   Once pierced for me,
> That conquered death,
>   And set me free.[8]

Luther's Wittenberg also was struck in 1527, forcing most of the citizens to flee for their lives. Luther, however, remained to care for the sick. Later that year he wrote an open letter, 'Whether One May Flee from a Deadly Plague', seeking to offer guidance to Christians should the pestilence strike their city.[9]

---

6. Rudolph W. Heinze, *Reform and Conflict: From the Medieval World to the Wars of Religion*, A.D. 1350-1648 (Grand Rapids: Baker, 2005), p. 24.
7. Lindberg, *European Reformations*, p. 27.
8. George, *Theology of the Reformers*, pp.113-14.
9. Timothy F. Lull, ed., *Martin Luther's Basic Theological Writings*, 2nd ed. (Minneapolis: Fortress, 2005), p. 479.

Geneva wasn't spared either. During John Calvin's ministry in the city, the pestilence struck twice, first from 1542 to 1544 and again in 1560. The 1542 outbreak was likely the result of 'the passage of ten thousand French troops through Genevan lands in 1542' because 'twelve months later the city was firmly in its grip.' The city magistrates responded, first sending spies into surrounding regions to find those who were intentionally spreading the disease. They also called for volunteers from among the city's pastors who would minister to the plague victims, 'a dangerous job rewarded with almost certain death.' Calvin volunteered, but his application was rejected. 'Unsurprisingly, none of the ministers was eager for the position and for this they were rebuked by the council, which declared that all were to serve in the plague hospital except John Calvin, who was vital to the church.'[10]

The reason the magistrates disallowed Calvin from ministering to the plague victims was likely due to Pierre Blanchet, one of Geneva's pastors. When the plague struck the city, he volunteered to move out of the city's walls and minister to plague victims who were housed in the plague hospital. Calvin wrote of this to Viret, noting the difficulty that would come on the Company of Pastors if something happened to Blanchet:

> The pestilence also begins to rage here with greater violence, and few who are affected by it escape its ravages. One of our colleagues was to be set apart for attendance upon the sick. Because Pierre [Blanchet] offered himself, all readily acquiesced. If anything happens to him, I fear that I must take the risk upon myself, for as you observe, because we are debtors to one another, we must not be wanting to those who, more than any others, stand in need of our ministry. ... So long as we are in this ministry, I do not see that any pretext will avail us, if, through fear of infection, we are found wanting in the discharge of our duty when there is most need of our assistance.

---

10. Gordon, *Calvin*, pp. 24-5.

Trusting God in Life's Difficulties

When the plague came to Geneva again the next year, Blanchet again volunteered to serve the victims. He contracted the disease and was dead by the end of May 1543. It was at this time that the magistrates decided that there would be an election of which pastors would go out of the city to serve the victims. Only Calvin was exempted from the pool of candidates. The pastors opposed this mandate and insisted that only volunteers should go outside of the city where they might be infected. The impasse was breached when Mathieu de Geneston, a young pastor, volunteered to serve the hospital's patients. He also died of the plague. But the epidemic was over for the time.[11]

Something like paranoia seems to have gripped the city due to the mysterious nature of the plague's onset and spread. As Andrew Pettegree recounts:

> Three times in the sixteenth century Geneva initiated proceedings against unfortunate individuals who it was alleged had deliberately spread plague in the city. Evidence collected under torture revealed a bizarre conspiracy to spread the disease by smearing door lintels with grease concocted by rendering fat from the foot of a corpse removed from the town gibbet. Incredible though this might seem to us, the magistrates were in deadly earnest. In the third episode, in 1570, 115 persons were prosecuted and 44 executed.[12]

The psychological effects of the pestilence must have been severe. 'Between 1568 and 1571,' in Geneva, 'as many as three thousand townspeople died of the plague.'[13] During these years, it was not uncommon for families to abandon simple love

---

11. Manetsch, *Calvin's Company of Pastors*, pp. 285-6.
12. Pettegree, *Europe in the Sixteenth Century*, pp. 3-14. The precedent for the 1570s' executions was Calvin's allowance for the interrogations and executions of suspected 'greasers' in 1540s since he believed their activity involved some sort of witchcraft. See Diarmaid MacCulloch, *The Reformation: A History* (New York: Viking, 2003), p. 550.
13. Manetsch, *Calvin's Company of Pastors*, p. 287.

for one another for fear of contracting the disease from their afflicted loved ones. Scott Manetsch recounts the experience of the Bourgeois family in the village of Malval near Geneva in the fall of 1571:

> A daughter of the family contracted the plague while in the final days of pregnancy. Fearing infection, the young woman's mother, brother, and sister abandoned her. Even when the pains of labor overcame the sick woman, neither family members nor neighbors responded to her desperate cries for help. In the end, she delivered her baby alone, all the while screaming for water and assistance. Both mother and infant died within hours. The woman's family, listening to the entire ordeal outside the family's house, had already dug a grave for the woman.[14]

The Genevan church's response was swift. The family was suspended from participation in the church. The pastors begged the magistrates to demand 'that sick villagers should be cared for, either by people from the city or from their own villages' lest anyone 'suffer a similar thing ever again.'[15] The Genevans were all too familiar with both the heroism, and the shame, of the townspeople's response to the plague.

Theodore Beza also had first-hand awareness of the plague. After he fled France, while teaching in Lausanne, he was struck by the pestilence in 1551. A letter Calvin wrote in June of that year—possibly to a relative of Beza still in France—tells us of some of his feeling for his younger friend:

> I was informed ... that he had been seized with the plague. I was therefore not only troubled about the danger he was in, but from my very great affection for him I felt almost overpowered, as if I was already lamenting his death; although, indeed, this grief did not rise so much from private regard, as from my public anxiety for the prosperity of the Church.

---

14. Manetsch, *Calvin's Company of Pastors*, p. 216.
15. Manetsch, *Calvin's Company of Pastors*, p. 216.

Indeed, I were destitute of human feeling, did I not return the affection of one who loves me with more than a brother's love, and reveres me like a very father.[16]

The year of Calvin's death, 1564, when Beza was taking over the reins in the church, the plague broke out. It showed up again in 1567-8 and in 1570-1. The latter episode struck down Theodore's brother, Nicolas, who had just fled hostile France to the relative safety of Geneva. Beza was devastated, as we notice in a letter he wrote to the reformer, Heinrich Bullinger, in Zurich: 'My mourning is deep. ... I would like you and your honored brothers, your colleagues, to sustain me by your prayers in the extreme exhaustion that I feel.'[17] This particular onset of the plague almost shut down the Academy in 1572, when only four students enrolled for ministerial training. The council eliminated all professors except Beza. He had run-ins with the city council regarding the pestilence, since he and the city's other pastors argued against the council's decision to keep Beza from ministering at 'the plague hospital during the outbreaks of 1564 and 1567.' When the council forbade him from plague service again in 1570, 'Beza successfully persuaded the government not to exclude him from the lottery.'[18] Finally, in 1588 during a later episode of the pestilence, Claudine, Beza's wife of almost forty years, died from the horrible disease.[19]

Theodore Beza, then, was all too familiar with the plague's devastation and the emotional, psychological, and, above all, spiritual questions it raised in those who suffered from its

---

16. Calvin, *Selected Works*, 5:314.
17. H. Clavier, *Théodore de Bèze: Un apercu de sa vie aventureuse, de ses travaux, de sa personnalité* (Cahors: A. Coueslant, 1960), p. 52.
18. Monter, *Calvin's Geneva*, p. 211. Manetsch helpfully explains Beza's and the other Genevan pastors' attempts to make their whole company's care for plague victims fair in Manetsch, *Calvin's Company of Pastors*, p. 284-9.
19. Baird, *Theodore Beza*, p. 332.

effects. His own experience of the plague, as well as his desire to shepherd those suffering its dreadful consequences, led him to write *A Learned Treatize of the Plague* in 1579, as a sixty-year-old, seasoned pastor, well-acquainted with the realities of life and death.[20] Moreover, he was obviously concerned to help Genevans, and other Christians, know how to think and act correctly when the plague struck. Specifically, he yearned for them to understand how they should consider God and His goodness, as well as their duties, at such times. Another impetus for his treatise was the faulty logic of a reformed pastor in Aarberg, a village in the canton of Berne. Christophe Lüthard had denied that God used any secondary causation to bring about His purposes in sending the plague. He taught, rather, that 'plagues are deadly, not because they are contagious, but because they are an expression of God's punishment against sinners.' So, he urged, rather than flee the plague, Christians should never take precautions or run from the pestilence.[21] These practical realities along with the theological questions of the Lord's relationship to the sickness were, then, at the heart of Beza's treatise on the plague.

The Content

Beza wrote the *A Learned Treatize of the Plague* in order to answer two questions that were being asked in his day. First of all, was the plague an infectious disease? Was it disseminated from person to person by natural means, or was it, rather, an instance of God's direct activity in human affairs? How one answered this question had ramifications for faithful living during tumultuous times when the plague struck. For instance, should one minister to those afflicted with the plague, regardless

---

20. For accounts of the publication of this work in the sixteenth century, see Gardy and Dufour, *Bibliographie des Oeuvres*, pp. 78-80. I will use Theodore Beza, *A Shorte Learned and Pithie Treatize of the Plague*, trans. John Stockwood (London: Thomas Dawson, 1580).
21. Manetsch, *Calvin's Company of Pastors*, p. 288.

of the fear of contracting the illness from them since it was sent by God upon whom He willed apart from human contact? The second question was related to the first: when the plague struck, was it appropriate for believers to flee from it in order to protect themselves and their families? Or was fleeing, instead, an example of lack of faith on their part? In answering both of these questions, Beza alerts us to several realities. His conception of the relationship of a disease to God's providence was nuanced because he had a robust understanding of God's providence, specifically of God's use of secondary causes to accomplish His will. We also see that Beza's thought process was driven by his biblicism. Far from trying merely to arrive at what he thought was logical, Beza was intent on finding answers from the Bible. Lastly, we note the manner in which Beza sought to apply biblical truth in a difficult situation. This is a clear instance demonstrating that he was far from an ivory tower theologian intent on dotting all his *i*'s and crossing his *t*'s. The reason he cared about the truthfulness of biblical doctrine was that this doctrine affected how people lived and died. God's providence was the most practical of doctrines, and Beza reasoned well and shepherded his readers into seeing its practicality.[22]

Introduction

The 'preface' Beza prefixes to the work introduces several themes he will come back to later, and in it Beza also evinces his motivation for writing the treatise.[23] He expresses tremendous surprise that he's even having to write the work, because it should be obvious to all that the plague is infectious. Some, though, 'within these few years' have begun to question whether or not the plague is spread by natural means. Ironically, though, the result

---

22. For more interaction with Beza's handling of God's providence, see Wright, *Our Sovereign Refuge*, pp. 34-66.
23. He calls the preceding portion of the treatise a 'preface'. See Theodore Beza, *A Shorte Learned and Pithie Treatize of the Plague*, trans. John Stockwood (London: Thomas Dawson, 1580), p. 3.

has more often than not been that those questioning the plague's infectious nature have been quick to flee when the plague strikes their region. Beza is realistic that many 'greatly fear this disease and the death which commonly follows' it.[24] As we have seen, Beza had first-hand experience with the heinous nature of the disease. People had good reason to fear catching it. In responding to these fears in the preface, though, he introduced three themes that should guide Christians in responding to the plague.

In the first place, Beza stressed that duty was essential. When asking whether or not one should flee the plague, the first question to answer was, What is my duty in this situation? In fact, 'not only Christians but all humanity' need to answer this question, because everyone has particular responsibilities they must attend to.[25] The plague and its consequences were traumatic, so in the midst of such a whirlwind it was essential at the outset to fight against 'forgetfulness of all duty' which so often accompanied those figuring out their appropriate response to the plague. In fact, Beza argued that people could go wrong at this very point, thinking that the most essential thing in this crisis was the preservation of their lives. Protecting one's life, though, may not be the most important matter. We all have duty that 'we owe to God, to our country, and which we owe to men' either because of family or civil ties.[26] Beza says that this, in fact, is what he wishes he could write the treatise on, rather than dealing with the odd question of whether the plague was contagious. He will return to this theme later.

Related to the propriety of duty, in the second place Beza stressed the role of conscience in influencing what decision one should arrive at regarding fleeing the plague. It is all too easy for believers to fly from the disease only to mourn later the harm they did to their fellow men by their absence. No one,

---

24. Beza, *Treatize of the Plague*, p. 1.
25. Beza, *Treatize of the Plague*, p. 1.
26. Beza, *Treatize of the Plague*, p. 1.

he averred, 'with a good conscience' can claim that the plague 'without exception should be fled from.'[27] Not all decisions in life are either black or white. We have to act with biblical wisdom. Thus Beza wants to help instruct his readers so that after the plague has come and gone they might not question themselves about their prior decisions. He wants to produce a wise person who follows 'the golden mean so that he doesn't flee when he should tarry nor, when he should go aside, ... by his rash tarrying offend against the same love which seemed to counsel him to stay.'[28] Already, then, Beza has alerted his readers that at times the answer to the question will be 'stay', and in other instances it will be 'flee'. Conscience needs to be followed.

Conscience must be heeded because people are living in the sight of God. This is the third theme Beza introduces in the preface, a theme he will come back to and stress at the conclusion of the treatise. The 'chief cause of this sickness,' he notes, is the wrath of God.[29] The Lord is the one who sends the disease and He does so in order to get men's attention. Beza cannot get away from the reality that men live with eternity in the balance. Even things as tangible and earthy as caring for those dying from the plague and fleeing it out of fear that one may die a painful death need to be approached with the reality of God and eternity in view. God is behind the plague and we must deal with Him.

First Question: Is the Plague Infectious?

As Beza moves into the heart of the treatise, his first burden is to answer the initial question asked in this controversy: 'Is the plague infectious or not?' The first thing to decide is what recourse we have in order to answer the question. His opponents argue that all we need is the Bible since God's word is full of talk of disease coming directly from the hand of God without

---

27. Beza, *Treatize of the Plague*, p. 3.
28. Beza, *Treatize of the Plague*, p. 3.
29. Beza, *Treatize of the Plague*, p. 2.

any secondary means being noted. Before he examines their biblical hermeneutic, Beza critiques the logic of their position. He notes it is a faulty contention that one's authority has to be either the Bible or modern medicine. In effect his detractors have created a false dichotomy. Rather, something can be both 'natural' and flow from the decree of God at the very same time. One need not look further than death. It always has natural causes, yet it only occurs by the eternal decree of God.[30]

This leads Beza to assert that subservient to the decree of God are secondary causes He ordains to use to accomplish His will. 'The infection itself is to be reckoned among secondary causes,' he trumpets.[31] He then explodes with a litany of events that must be reckoned as both eternally decreed by God and also coming about by natural, secondary causes. Doesn't sin proceed both from Adam and God's decree? What about other causes of death? His opponents are inconsistent; he lampoons their lack of integrity in this regard, for if their logic follows 'Let us neither eat nor drink nor seek any remedy against any diseases. Let soldiers go unarmed to battle, because death ordained by God cannot be avoided. Neither should we eat or use remedies against diseases or put on armor against enemies as if we meant to withstand God'[32]; they are guilty of gross inconsistency.

One way for a Christian to gauge what to do when the plague strikes is to look to duty, recognizing the way in which God uses secondary causation to accomplish His will. Seeing this, a believer should do his duty, for 'he shall be greatly blamed who rather casts himself and his family into the danger of infection, when as the apostle bears witness, he is worse than an infidel who has not so great care over his family.'[33] Duty is commensurate with understanding secondary causation.

---

30. Beza, *Treatize of the Plague*, p. 3.

31. Beza, *Treatize of the Plague*, p. 4.

32. Beza, *Treatize of the Plague*, p. 4.

33. Beza, *Treatize of the Plague*, p. 4.

Trusting God in Life's Difficulties

Scripture is replete with examples of secondary causation. Beza's detractors, though, exercise poor biblical interpretation. They argue that since the plague is denominated 'the hand of God' in 2 Samuel 24, the 'word of God' in 1 Chronicles 21, and 'arrows' in Psalms 38 and 91, 'it doesn't come from infection, since neither hand nor sword nor arrows wound by infection.'[34] Beza responds on two levels. First, he points out their poor hermeneutic since, for instance, in Psalm 17 David refers to his enemies as 'the hand of God', even though it's clear from this psalm that he had in view only the natural means by which his opponents attacked him. Besides, it's manifest 'that in the Scripture all evils and punishments whatsoever that God sends to mankind—using either ordinary laws or nature alone, or else using the service of angels—are called "arrows".'[35] Besides, wasn't leprosy also from the 'hand of God'? It was not on that account less contagious, with the result that leprous people were to live outside the city for fear of the disease's spread. Beza's final example displays the tenor of his day. He turns to the 'pox', a common way of referring to syphilis. It has different varieties—French, Spanish, and Dutch—but each is 'a punishment sent by God for whoredom.'[36] Of course it's contagious, for 'this most filthy sickness is gotten, not only with lying together, but also by breathing and handling, and is sucked out by infants from their nurses' breasts. And the nurses get this disease by giving suck to the infant, who is either conceived by an unclean father or born of an unclean mother.'[37] These natural, secondary causes, however, are compatible with God's decree, for at the same time 'there is no man who dares deny that it is indeed the "hand", "sword", or "arrow" of God, which strikes

---

34. Beza, *Treatize of the Plague*, p. 5.
35. Beza, *Treatize of the Plague*, p. 5.
36. Beza, *Treatize of the Plague*, p. 6.
37. Beza, *Treatize of the Plague*, p. 6.

whoremongers.'[38] Up to this point, then, Beza has established that the plague may be both from the eternal decree of God and also have its spread accounted for by natural, secondary causation. In other words, one need not deny the active role of God in the spread of the plague in order to be able to affirm at the same time that it is spread by natural causes. It is both infectious and also spread by God's decree.

But Beza is not done with this first point. He wants to drive home the manner in which God uses secondary agents to accomplish His will. Some deny that God ever employs others to accomplish His will, and in so doing they are able to assert that no plague or infection ever comes from natural causes. Beza's response flows from the Bible.

His detractors' main reason for denying secondary causation is that God sends angels, not natural causes, to spread plague. Of course, they're right that the Lord employs angels, but that doesn't mean that He does not at the same time use other natural causes:

> But what hinders God from so commanding the natural causes themselves to be stirred up by the angels? For surely it cannot be doubted that they—both the good and the bad—stir up the mind of man after a certain sort, what kind of moving whatsoever it be, when as Satan is said to have entered into the heart of Judas (unless we shall perhaps say that the good angels have somewhat less power than the bad).

The Bible is on Beza's side in this debate. That's where he now turns.[39]

Beza marshals four chief examples to prove that God uses agents to accomplish His will. First of all, both Judas and Ahab are examples in which we see compatibilism at work, meaning the person's will is active (and they are thus responsible), but

---

38. Beza, *Treatize of the Plague*, p. 6.
39. Beza, *Treatize of the Plague*, p. 7.

at the same time God acts decisively through angels (so the Lord is responsible too). 'Who can deny that the will of man is to be reckoned amongst the very chiefest causes of men's actions?' Beza asks. 'But if the will of man is not debarred from the ministry of angels, why shall we think that other natural causes have to by the same be taken away?' Secondly, the plagues God sent during the time of Moses are certainly an example of God's use of angels, but they also arose from 'natural' causes. Beza urges us to consider this: 'But did not therefore the lice and flies come of rottenness, the hail of vapors growing together suddenly by restraint on the contrary, and the boils and botches also of corruptions of the humors?' Those imprisoned in the book of Revelation provide a third example of this 'both-and' reality. 'The devil sends the godly to prison (Rev. 2:10), but [they are sent] by tyrants and persecutors of the church (Rev. 6:8).' Fourth, Beza turns to God's use of the devil and the wind in Revelation, as indications of His causation in the spread of the plague. The rider represents death, and he is certainly an angel too. This rider is ready to kill with the sword, famine, beasts, and by infectious pestilence. Since all four of these means are natural, it demonstrates that angels can use natural means to accomplish their ends. And in Revelation 7:1 we are told that angels are commanded to keep the winds back. Thus, the winds, which are the chief agent in spreading the plague, are in God's control:

> From which it is doubtless manifest that many infections of the air ... proceed. So that natural causes, when they are moved by little and little of their own force planted in them by nature, or otherwise beyond order—God commanding them so—they are in a moment carried to their effect. They are natural, and so far forth are their effects also worthily judged to be natural, which no man of reason can deny.[40]

---

40. Beza, *Treatize of the Plague*, p. 7.

One of the major faults of Beza's opponents is that they have missed the main point of the Bible, which is to teach us and bring us 'great profit so that we may learn both to fear and to love God.' The Lord uses all kinds of means to accomplish this end, including very fearful things. Such fear-inducing realities make us look to God and consider eternity. In pursuit of this purpose, the Lord uses secondary agents, like the wind (the 'contagious air') to do His will. Others buck at this, arguing that the plague is sent only by 'the singular and special providence of God'. Acknowledging God's utter providence, Beza still denies their conclusion. 'The certainty of God's providence' fails to prove 'that the plague is not infectious.'[41]

Beza tenaciously keeps drawing our attention to Scripture, showing the 'both-and' nature of life. God is sovereign, and He often employs agents to accomplish His will. Regarding the plague, he notes that 'as therefore God has appointed some which shall not die of the plague, so also has he appointed remedies, by which, so far as in them lies, men may avoid the plague.' Five biblical examples model this: first, Joseph's actions while serving Pharaoh in Egypt ('God without doubt when he sent a famine to Egypt and the regions around there had determined who should die in that scarcity; yet for all this Joseph ceased not with best diligence and most wise counsel to provide for the Egyptians'); second, Agabus's prophecy ('The [same] things which the churches in the times of the emperor Claudius also did, when they understood by Agabus the prophet that a famine should shortly come'); third, Israel's reaction to Assyrian attack ('The Lord also knew who should die in that most cruel war of the Assyrians in the days of Ezekiel; and yet both Ezekiel and the prophet Isaiah himself secured themselves within the walls of the city'); fourth, Paul's actions in shipwreck ('What should I say more, when as Paul knew certainly that neither he himself nor any of those which were with him should perish in the shipwreck, yet he said to the mariners who were preparing

---

41. Beza, *Treatize of the Plague*, pp. 8-9.

to fly out the ship, "You cannot be saved unless these stay"?'); finally, Jesus' saving of his own life ('Christ also, though he knew well that his hour wasn't yet come, yet he did more than once withdraw himself when the Jews sought to kill him'). Each of these five examples shows that God both sends disaster and appoints how men are to avoid it.[42]

Some of those disagreeing with Beza, however, appealed to Augustine, who wrote that 'the will of God is the necessity of things.' They insisted that God's will is singular and includes no secondary, or as Beza terms them, 'middle' causes. Their problem, he pronounces, is threefold. In the first place, they don't understand Augustine rightly, because the North African bishop also wrote that 'it does not follow, that though all things which God has decreed shall come to pass, have to come to pass, that therefore they come to pass of necessary causes.' In the second place, their reasoning is closely aligned with that of the Stoics whose fatalism was well known and clearly unscriptural. Finally, two examples from Jesus' life show the error of this approach. On the one hand, Jesus' bones could have been broken; on the other hand, they couldn't: 'For don't we believe that Christ had man's bones; therefore such as of their own nature might at any time have been broken, and yet indeed they could not be broken, for it was otherwise decreed by God?' Additionally, Jesus could have been killed when He was a child; but at the same time He couldn't have been killed:

> All Christians confess that Christ from the very time that he took upon him our human nature was endued with a mortal body. Therefore of his own nature he might have been slain by Herod with the other little children. But by God's decree he could not. Therefore, that he wasn't then slain fell out by chance, if you consider the nature of his body, when it might have chanced otherwise. But by God's decree he could no more be slain by Herod than the will of God could be

---

42. Beza, *Treatize of the Plague*, pp. 9-10.

changed. Christ, when he was carried to be crucified, was then undoubtedly of such health that he didn't need at that time to have died; he died therefore by chance, if you consider the cause of his natural death. And yet he died of necessity if you look to the unchangeable appointment of his Father, because his hour was come. And withal he died willing, because he laid down his life for us. Thus far therefore is neither 'chance' nor 'will' repugnant to the most certain decree of God.[43]

Beza concludes this first point of the treatise against his 'unskilled' detractors by interacting with their final argument. They aver that the plague is not contagious due to the reality that not all in an area are infected with the pestilence. Their reasoning is wrong. It doesn't comport with experience. Nor does it mesh with Scripture, which teaches in places like Psalm 91:6 and Mark 16:18 that the 'almighty God governs natural causes and their effect as it pleases him.' Beza drives home this point, trumpeting: 'Therefore this argument also is not of force to prove there is no infection in the plague, because many who keep company with those who are sick of the plague are not taken; and on the contrary those who are absent are infected. As if the poison of a viper were not deadly because Paul was bitten by one but felt no harm at all (Acts 28:5).'[44]

Beza has proved in this first point, then, that the plague is indeed contagious. Experience proves this. But experience and the Bible also nuance this, teaching us that the pestilence's contagious nature is governed by God's providence. Saying that the plague is contagious does not relegate its onset to bare chance. The Lord is sovereign over who is infected by the deadly blight.

Second Question: Is it Appropriate to Flee the Plague?
Midway through the treatise Beza turns to the second major point of the work: Is it appropriate for Christians to flee an area

---

43. Beza, *Treatize of the Plague*, pp. 10-11.
44. Beza, *Treatize of the Plague*, p. 11.

when the plague strikes, or are they obligated out of Christian love to remain and care for those afflicted? Here we see Beza the pastor shining through the printed page. His reasoning shows both biblical fidelity and human honesty. It's a hard question with nuanced answers. But at the end of the day, whatever one decides regarding running from the infection, one should use the plague as a reminder that eternity is just around the corner for all of us.

Beza notes the two major answers to the question people tend to have. First, some argue that all fleeing from the plague is sin. These 'without exception find fault with going aside on account of the plague' and 'count it a very heinous offense.' Conversely, some reason that everyone should flee when the plague strikes, holding 'that every man, so soon as the plague comes, ought to provide for himself, having no or very little regard of the fellowship and duties which Christian love commands.' Beza is going to handle each argument in turn, but he says at the outset that if he only had to choose between these two options he'd opt for the first. Better to stay than to flee. But there's a lot more to it than just that.[45]

The first view is that Christians should never flee from the plague. This argument was made philosophically, using Plato to reason that 'he cannot seem to be a temperate person who flees death because it proceeds from too much delight in life.' More than that, though, it is based on at least nine biblical arguments. Beza concludes that they are wrong at each point.

First, some say that those who flee the plague don't realize that God's providence includes His unchangeable decree that includes the limits to a man's life. This is true, Beza concurs, but they fail to consider that even though God's decree is unchangeable, He also decrees to us lawful means to save our lives:

> Albeit God's decree is unchangeable and that his eternal providence has set the unremovable bounds of our lives, yet this does not take away the ordinary and lawful means to save

---

45. Beza, *Treatize of the Plague*, pp. 11-12.

our lives—no, not even if a man has received an answer from God of prolonging his life, as we have shown by the manifest examples of St Paul (Acts 27:24 and 31) much less that we may not use these means, when it is yet hidden from us what God from everlasting has decreed concerning the prolonging and ending of our life.

Second, some argue that those fleeing the plague don't trust God's promise to be their God and the God of their children, for they act like they—not God—will preserve their lives. This is wrongheaded reasoning for one doesn't mistrust God when he uses God's ways to avoid evil: 'Why should he be said to distrust God's promises who follows the ways appointed by God to avoid evil' and in so doing 'depends wholly on God?' In the third place, some argue that those fleeing the plague have no love or pity for others. Beza responds by noting that a person may serve others by the act of fleeing: 'It is also plain that he not only doesn't offend against Christian charity, neither yet tempt God, who in such a way by going aside avoids the plague so that in the mean time he lets pass no act of piety towards God or of charity towards his neighbor.'[46]

Beza dispenses with the fourth argument—that fleeing tempts God like the Israelites tempted Him to wrath (Exod. 17:3 and Ps. 78:18)—quickly, noting that if one shows love to his neighbor he will not provoke God to wrath. The fifth argument is more intricate. His opponents aver that if one flees the plague it proves one doesn't sincerely love God, 'for being enamored and in love with earthly goods, they neglect and are careless of the heavenly.' They argue that Christians should want to depart and be with the Lord immediately instead of flying for their lives. This is wrong, Beza warns. Three biblical instances prove this. In the first place is Paul who on the one hand wants to be loosed from the world to be with Christ (Phil. 1:23) but who 'also wishes for his brethren's sake to be separated as a thing accursed'

---

46. Beza, *Treatize of the Plague*, pp. 12-13.

(Rom. 9:3). Paul again demonstrates this tension: 'Neither does he deliver up his life into the hands of those that lay in wait for him, appealing to Caesar (Acts 25:11) and gives thanks for his health restored to him (2 Cor. 1:11).' The final example comes from David who fled from Saul, Absalom, and death itself. Beza concludes: 'Therefore, whoever flees death is not rashly to be judged or censured not to love God, since contrarily whoever desires death isn't to be thought to love God, but only he who lawfully and with a good conscience, obeying God's will, prepares himself either to suffer or avoid death.'[47]

The sixth argument is that escaping the plague shows that the one fleeing fears death from God's hands, but God's will is always good. Beza won't submit to this logic. Rather, 'fear of death ... if it is grounded on good reason and is moderate, is not only not to be condemned but also to be allowed as a preserver of the life grafted in us by God.' Beza ushers examples from church history, especially that of Athanasius who fled death more than once. But he needn't go further than Scripture, which gives ample examples of those who fled death. 'No man that is godly, and of right understanding, ever condemned Jacob's going aside; no man ever condemned David's flying the fury of Saul and Absalom's conspiracy, nor Elijah avoiding Jezebel's rage by his flight.' Appealing to Christ's unwillingness to flee His final hour won't do because this is the central component of our salvation, a mystery not to be mirrored by us.[48]

The seventh appeal is weighty because it seems to give due reverence to God's sovereignty. Some argue that one shouldn't flee the plague because everything the Lord sends is good. Their argument sounds good at first. 'There can be nothing sent from God, they say, but that which is good. No, there is nothing good but that which comes from God. But the plague is sent from God; therefore, it is good—if not of its own nature, yet in respect of the good end, namely, to punish our sins, to try our

---

47. Beza, *Treatize of the Plague*, p. 13.
48. Beza, *Treatize of the Plague*, pp. 13-14.

faith, to drive us to repentance, and to bring forth hypocrites to light.' The one fleeing, therefore, doubts the Lord's goodness. More than that, fleeing attempts to deviate from God's good intention for His people.

These disputations ultimately hold no weight for Beza, though, because his opponents never define what 'good' and 'evil' are. All their argumentation is thus vain. We can see this, he asserts, by simply looking at sin. 'Are sins, I pray you, therefore good, and does he who resist them resist God?' Of course, Christians are to fight sin, even though it's part of God's ordination. Beyond that, 'Abraham himself, Isaac and Jacob fled hunger, which nevertheless was sent by God; yet they cannot be said to have fled a thing that was good or to have sinned.' We should resist and flee certain things—things ordained by God—because they're evil or harmful.[49]

The eighth argument is simple: fleeing breaks the golden rule of doing to others as you would have them do to you. Beza responds that one can flee the plague having already served those afflicted and so having already obeyed Christ's command to love. Besides, we are responsible not only to care for those afflicted but also for those who haven't been infected with the plague.[50]

The ninth argument of those saying one should never flee the plague is that there are no instances of this in biblical history. Beza shows the wrongheadedness of this tack in three quick strokes. First, the Bible doesn't record everything ever done in history. Second, if there's no specific biblical command, we are to follow general biblical guidelines. Third, the Bible doesn't record every instance of the plague or people's response to it.

But his opponents still have some biblical examples which, they think, prove fleeing the plague to be sin. They appeal, first, to David who 'did not fly that very sore plague of which mention is made (2 Sam. 24), nor did he remove his household to any other place.' Beza's reply, however, is devastating:

---

49. Beza, *Treatize of the Plague*, pp. 14-15.
50. Beza, *Treatize of the Plague*, p. 15.

I grant this, but many peculiar circumstances forbid us to make a general conclusion of that. For [David] himself was the cause of that plague and deservedly so far forth troubled, that he is ready even with his own destruction to redeem the public calamity; further, when as this plague didn't continue more than three days at the most, what place was there left him to take advice or to flee to?

They also appeal to Jeremiah. This prophet 'and Baruch also, with other godly men, didn't flee out of the city being besieged by the Chaldeans, even though a great part of the people died as well of the plague as of famine.' This is faulty reasoning because 'neither do we say that we may worthily shun the plague by going aside, if we depart from that which we owe to God, our country, and each of our neighbors. But I cannot but wonder, that those who allege this example of Jeremiah have forgotten that he was taken at the gate of the city when he attempted to get out (Jer. 37:12).' The ninth argument of those arguing one should never flee the plague—like the first eight—is wrong.[51]

Up to this point, Beza has answered the two questions he set out to address. He has proved that the plague is infectious and also ordained by God. And he has argued that going aside from the plague is not in every case to be condemned. Summarizing this second argument, he notes, 'as God by his everlasting and unchangeable decree has appointed the course of our life, so has he also ordained middle causes, which we should use to preserve our lives.'[52]

Application of the Treatize to Particular People
Now Beza addresses the application of all that he's discussed up to this point: exactly when is it appropriate for one to flee the plague? Everything up to this point is foundational, and preliminary, to this application. Here we see Beza the pastor

---

51. Beza, *Treatize of the Plague*, pp. 15-16.
52. Beza, *Treatize of the Plague*, pp. 16-17.

reasoning carefully and gently with those coming to him for advice. And his advice is nuanced, leaving persons to consider their calling before the Lord.

By way of introduction, Beza asserts that this is an 'indifferent' matter, one on which Scripture doesn't speak definitively. So a person may 'use fleeing both well and ill.' Even though there is no one correct answer, Beza avers that it's almost always better to stay than to flee: 'They offend much less, who when they might otherwise with a good conscience withdraw themselves, had rather yet tarry; and to venture and endanger their lives, rather than … seem to have forsaken their neighbor or family.'[53]

In applying the treatise to his readers more specifically, Beza makes four distinct points. First, he urges his readers to use the plague as a warning of the judgment each will face. Beza's eschatological worldview—including judgment and either eternal heaven or hell for every person—shines through here. Whether an individual decides to stay or flee the plague, he should reflect on its proleptic character of future judgment and benefit from it. 'Every man [should] summon himself to the judgment seat of God, to the plague as the coming of news of God's wrath, condemning himself that he may be acquitted by' God. That person should remind himself 'that this rod cannot be avoided by change of place, but of manners; and that he must die, that this is decreed for the good of men who die, forasmuch as they are blessed who die in the Lord.'[54]

Secondly, Beza writes that when deciding whether to stay or flee the plague, people must follow their consciences. There is no easy answer that applies equally to all. Rather, individuals will vary in their decisions. They will do so by following their consciences. That conscience, however, is not an autonomous power. It must be informed by God's word to orient people in a biblical direction. So, the rule Beza propounds is that 'no man either goes aside or tarries with a doubtful conscience. But

---

53. Beza, *Treatize of the Plague*, p. 17.
54. Beza, *Treatize of the Plague*, p. 17.

when as he shall have learned out of the word of God what his duty is, that commending himself unto God' he should do it. Duty flows from a Christian conscience informed by the Bible and a believer acting in faith.[55]

The third directive is quite diffuse because Beza's point here is that the Bible doesn't set down one rule for everyone. Scripture gives us general principles by which to judge whether we should stay or flee. It is, he says, 'no hard matter to give certain general precepts agreeable to the word of God, by which as a certain rule singular cases may afterwards, as they say, be tried.' He begins by asking a couple of questions. If one wants to stay when the plague comes, he should consider God's prohibition against murder, even self-inflicted murder. Are you sinning by murdering yourself if you stay? 'Know that it is the commandment of God, "You shall not kill". Therefore neither their own nor the lives of any belonging or depending on them are rashly to be put in danger of deadly infection.'[56]

But Beza asks the one who wants to leave if he is failing to love those God's called him to care for. He urges this point because 'no man ought to have so great regard either of himself or his family that he forgets what one owes to his country and fellow citizens. ... for love doesn't seek the things which are her own.' But Beza isn't tacitly trying make those fleeing feel guilty. Leaving may be legitimate as long as they meet one of four different criteria: first, if their age or infirmities make it impossible for them to help others by staying, they may leave; second, if their staying would be a detriment to the entire commonwealth, robbing the city or country of a necessary person, they may leave; third, parents may leave because they are to look out for the well-being of their families; finally, magistrates—who are called to care for all their citizens, not just those stricken by the plague—may need to leave in order to secure the well-being of the weak ones in their midst, as

---

55. Beza, *Treatize of the Plague*, p. 17.
56. Beza, *Treatize of the Plague*, p. 17.

long as they have provided care for plague victims. Here is Beza's reasoning:

> I confess that I cannot see by what reason at all any man is forbidden to depart, which either because of age or of sickness—past hope of recovery—cannot help others, and if they tarry, they may therefore seem only to be staying that they may die to the great loss of the commonwealth. For as their cruelty can never be blamed enough who thrust them out of their cities, especially if they are of the poorer sort, so both the pious natures of parents in time providing for the preservation and life of theirs, without prejudice or hurt to any man, seem to me to be greatly commended. And also the providence of the magistrates is much to be praised where their care shall be extended—without damage to the common welfare—to see that those weak ones, as seed-plots of citizens, are well looked unto.[57]

The fourth directive is that one must consider his calling in order to determine if he should flee or stay. Private individuals have a different set of obligations than public persons. Each person has different bonds to others, and the strength of those bonds will influence the obligation one has to stay or leave. All persons have general bonds that bind them to fellow humans, first, and to fellow citizens of their city or country, second. 'Both these bonds I affirm to be natural and universal.'[58]

Most people are private persons and need to consider the bonds—and, therefore, the obligations—they have to others. Often this will mean that they should stay when the plague strikes: 'Therefore, let man help man, citizen help citizen, that needs his help, according to his power, and let him not think of fleeing, by which it may justly appear likely to him to come to pass that by this means somebody shall' not be cared for. He shouldn't allow fear of death to keep him from his 'duty to humanity'. At other times, though, it will mean that he can,

---

57. Beza, *Treatize of the Plague*, pp. 17-18.
58. Beza, *Treatize of the Plague*, p. 18.

and should, depart, if by fleeing he 'may be careful both for himself and his.' In such cases, he is bound to leave.[59]

Private persons have several potential bonds of responsibility to others. Husbands and wives, parents and children, masters and servants—all of them are held together by unique levels of obligation:

> As touching private persons, their bonds of friendship and amity are diverse and manifold; among these, this is the chief one, unto which all natural conjunction of blood (as God witnesses) must give place, I mean the bond and tie of wedlock, so that in my judgment the husband cannot with a good conscience go from the wife or the wife from the husband, especially if one of them be visited by the plague. And how much parents owe to their children, and children to their parents, kinsmen to kinsmen, the very laws of nature declares, which Christian love is so far off from letting loose that on the contrary it draws them more and harder together. Yes, and for servants to forsake their masters, or masters to look slenderly to their servants being sick (which comes too often to pass) who have made use of their service when they were well, is cruelty.

The rule Beza sets down is that one should look first to the closest bonds he has, and move out from there, in considering when he's obligated either to stay or to leave. Because, as Beza points out, it is not the case that 'the bond of all these friendships [is] alike or equal, and therefore that which is not so near must give place to the nearer, forasmuch as many cannot be discharged at once.'[60]

Relatively few people are public persons—those serving in 'public offices—either civil or ministry'. These people have special obligations to the commonwealth due to their positions of general responsibility and authority. Under God, they are to care for a larger group of people than private persons are. They

---

59. Beza, *Treatize of the Plague*, p. 18.
60. Beza, *Treatize of the Plague*, pp. 18-19.

have more bonds. Their first obligation upon the onset of the plague is to deal with the carriers of the pestilence, making sure that the disease doesn't spread. As Beza says, 'it is the duty of a Christian magistrate to provide that those things which either breed or nourish the plague, so far as they may, be taken away and that regard may be had of those who are visited with this sickness.' Out of obligation for the good of those under their care, public persons—including pastors—should usually not leave when the plague strikes. They're to care for those afflicted: 'How they that serve in any public civil office may leave their charge in the time of the plague, I do not see. And for faithful pastors to forsake but one poor sheep at that time when he most needs heavenly comfort, it were too shameful, no too wicked a part.' Summarizing the role of magistrates, Beza says they have two great responsibilities: 'that the infection may be prevented, and also that those sick with the plague want nothing.'[61]

There is a final obligation to consider, the obligation of those afflicted towards those not stricken. On the one hand, of course, it is right for them to seek care from others. However, the sick shouldn't abuse their position of sickness unnecessarily so that it will cause those who are well to become sick. They must see 'that they do not abuse the love of their family and friends, while they desire to have themselves provided for.' Beza offers himself as an example of one who didn't seek for undue care when he was taken down with the plague: 'But how others are affected and disposed in craving their friends' presence I don't know, when as myself being visited with the plague, and that diverse of my friends offered to me all kinds of courtesy, I suffered none to come to me, lest I might have been thought to have provided for myself with the loss of my friends.' Even those who stay to care for the afflicted are obliged to be wise and not let themselves be placed in harm's way unnecessarily. Those 'who continue in doing their duties' must see 'that they cast not themselves rashly into the danger of infection.'

---

61. Beza, *Treatize of the Plague*, pp. 18-19.

Instead, they should use true and Christian judgment. Since, as he established in the first point, the plague is infectious, one should avoid situations where he is likely to contract it. One can care for others, and provide for their needs, while also avoiding contact with them.[62]

Where does all this leave his readers? Beza reminds them in closing of their final and most pressing obligation. They stand before God. The Lord will hold them accountable for all that they do in life. They must use the plague as a means God uses to draw their attention to the fragility of life and the certainty of life to come. Are they prepared for the final judgment that this disease foreshadows? 'Our sins are the chief and true cause of the plague,' Beza proclaims. So pastors must not dispute questions of causation; rather, by 'their life and doctrine [they should] stir up the people to repentance and love and charity one towards another.'[63]

Application

Theodore Beza exemplified Christian maturity in being able to stare the reality of the horrendous plague square in the face and not blink. He saw loved ones die from it, and he almost died from it himself, yet he didn't respond by questioning the goodness of God. Nor did he shy away from seeing God's sovereign hand controlling something even as devastating as this pestilence. The reality, of course, was that Beza lived in a fallen world and endured many things that were beyond his ability to comprehend. By faith, though, he struggled to hold on to the truth that 'God works all things together for the good of those who love God, who have been called according to his purpose' (Rom. 8:28). May we learn from Beza how to hold tenaciously on to God when things don't transpire as we expected them to go. Let us never lose our grip on the twin truths of God's

---

62. Beza, *Treatize of the Plague*, p. 19.
63. Beza, *Treatize of the Plague*, p. 19.

sovereign power and also His supreme goodness. He only desires our best, no matter what He brings into our lives.

Uses

The text I have used is Theodore Beza, *A Shorte Learned and Pithie Treatize of the Plague*, translated by John Stockwood (London: Thomas Dawson, 1580). It has not been republished since the sixteenth century, but it is available through the website, *Early English Books Online* (eebo.chadwyck.com).

Here are some practical ways for you to use the material discussed in this chapter.

1. Read back over the description of the devastating effects of the plague at the beginning of the chapter. Put yourself in these dear people's places, and try to imagine how you would have felt watching loved ones die such awful deaths. Reflect on God's use of secondary agents to accomplish His will.

2. Do you consider Beza's exposition of God's sovereign providence over evils like the plague to be biblically correct? Why? Look at Scripture to see what the Bible says.[64]

3. Even if you don't have to consider what to do when the plague strikes, you will face difficult decisions in dire situations. Reflect on Beza's advice that we consider our stations in life, specifically if we're private or public individuals. How does your role as a parent, a spouse, a church member, a pastor, an employer, or an employee influence how you should act when difficult situations arise?

---

64. For biblical and pastoral reflections on God's relation to evil, see Calvin, *Institutes*, 1.16-18; *The Westminster Confession of Faith*, chapter 5; John Flavel, *The Mystery of Providence* (1678; rpt., Carlisle, PA: Banner of Truth, 1963); and D. A. Carson, *How Long, O Lord? Reflections on Suffering and Evil* (Grand Rapids: Baker, 2006).

7

Struggling to Gain Assurance of Salvation—
Theodore Beza's
Treatize of Comforting such as are Troubled about their Predestination

Introduction

If you believed that predestination was the most controversial doctrine coming out of the Reformation, you would be close to the mark. But only close. Other doctrines would vie for the 'most controversial' title, doctrines such as the nature of the Lord's Supper, justification (by faith alone?), and the question of assurance of salvation. The debated point about assurance can be expressed pointedly: can Christians attain certainty that they are believers who will certainly go to heaven, and, if so, exactly how they can gain this assurance? This query was usually directed to those who believed in a doctrine of predestination like we observed in the previous chapter on this topic. After all, it was often asserted, if God was the sole cause of one's election (since man in his sin was unable to do anything to earn his salvation), how could one ever be certain in this life that God had chosen to save him? Maybe one's belief that he was saved was wrong and God had not chosen him for salvation. False assurance could lead a person to hell.

Why is this such a debated point? A couple of reasons rise to the surface in answering this question. There's the fact, first of all, that in the Catholic church assurance was impossible to attain, except for a very few saints whose exemplary lives made their salvation certain in the present.[1] One of Rome's most stringent attacks on the Protestants was in the area of assurance.[2] If it was true, as the Protestants said, that one could know today that he would definitely go to heaven, the inevitable result would be licentiousness and apathetic Christian living. After all, why struggle with mortification of sin and the pursuit of holiness if the gift of heaven was certain? Beza and the other Reformers battled to respond to these charges with both pastoral wisdom and biblical reasoning.[3] In fact, we have seen Beza address the issue of assurance of salvation at several points already. It was a major component of his teaching in the *Confession*, and it also played a prominent role in his *Tabula*.

---

1. Many medieval Catholics, 'since they regarded faith as a "work" of fallible man, thought that the believer's confidence and assurance should always be tempered by a certain humility, by a degree of uncertainty as to whether one really was forgiven. This spiritual state has been memorably described as an "oscillation between fear and hope". The classic text of such writers was the Vulgate's mistranslation of Ecclesiastes 9: 1: "a man does not know whether he is worthy of love or hatred"' (Euan Cameron, *The European Reformation* [Oxford: Oxford University Press, 1991], p. 18).

2. The Council of Trent, for example, responding to the growing Protestant movement in the middle of the sixteenth century, proclaimed, 'If any one saith, that he will for certain, of an absolute and infallible certainty, have that great gift of perseverance unto the end, unless he have learned this by special revelation; let him be anathema' (Council of Trent, session six, canon 16). For an insightful treatment of the medieval background of the doctrine of justification as well as its development in the Protestant reformers and the reactions of the Catholic church at the Council of Trent (1545-63), see Alister E. McGrath, *Iustitia Dei: A History of the Christian Doctrine of Justification*, 2nd ed. (Cambridge: Cambridge University Press, 1986), pp. 37-284.

3. Timothy George helpfully places the Protestant Reformation in its context, showing how it came on the edge of the later medieval Catholics' intense concern about whether or not they would go to heaven. See Timothy George, *Theology of the Reformers*, rev. ed. (Nashville: B & H, 2013), pp. 21-48.

Struggling to Gain Assurance of Salvation

As we come near the end of our study of Beza, it's fitting to look a little bit more at a short work he wrote that addressed assurance particularly.

But there's another reason the doctrine of assurance is such a pressing matter. As we noticed in chapter four, an entire school of historic interpretation has arisen which asserts that there is a massive chasm between the thought of John Calvin and that of the later English Puritans. And assurance of salvation is the fulcrum of the debate. It's asserted that with Calvin you have the simple belief that Jesus died indiscriminately for all people so that if one trusted in Christ, one could have immediate and true certainty of salvation. Things began to derail with Beza, though, and were finally wrecked with the Puritans who taught people not to look to Christ for assurance. After all, you couldn't do this since, they taught, Jesus died only for the elect. You couldn't look to Jesus since that's the question at issue: did He die for my sins? So, the Puritans urged doubting souls to look to their works to see if they were living like Christians should live. If so, they could have assurance that they were believers. If not, well, that's a problem, isn't it? Beza, then, is often accused of introducing an element of works righteousness into Reformed thought which really was a return to Roman bondage.[4]

At this point, we need to return once again to R. T. Kendall's views, since he has made this issue the major point of difference between Calvin and Beza. Fundamental to Kendall's view is his assertion that Calvin believed that Jesus' death on the cross was for all people indiscriminately; therefore, he urged doubting persons to look to Jesus for assurance. Since Christ had died for them all, they could find solace in His arms. But, Kendall urged, Beza didn't have recourse to such a pastoral response since he didn't believe Jesus' death was for all persons. Hampered by his logical system

---

4. For a very good treatment that puts both Calvin and Beza into their theological and methodological contexts, see Richard A. Muller, *Calvin and the Reformed Tradition: On the Work of Christ and the Order of Salvation* (Grand Rapids: Baker, 2012), pp. 244-76.

of limited atonement, Beza only had recourse to the 'practical syllogism' to help Christians find certainty of their standing with the holy God.[5] Unfortunately pastorally, the practical syllogism is a shaky foundation at best since it turns a troubled person's gaze on himself instead of on Jesus. Doctrinally it demonstrates a remarkable shift away from Calvin's belief to 'Calvinism'. Here is how Kendall points out the shift that took place:

> Fundamental to the doctrine of faith in Theodore Beza (1519-1605), Calvin's successor in Geneva, is his belief that Christ died for the elect only. Beza's doctrine of a limited atonement makes Christ's death that to which the decree of election has particular reference and that which makes the elect's salvation efficacious. It must therefore be argued that, as a result of this soteriological position, Beza's doctrine (1) inhibits the believer from looking directly to Christ's death for assurance; (2) precipitates an implicit distinction between faith and assurance; (3) tends to put repentance before faith in the *ordo salutis*; and (4) plants the seed of voluntarism in the doctrine of faith. In a word: Beza's doctrine requires the use of the practical syllogism in order for one to be persuaded he is one of those for whom Christ died.[6]

According to Kendall, Calvin discouraged persons from seeking assurance based on their sanctification because he believed that Christ died for everyone indiscriminately.[7] Doubting persons could simply look to Christ to find comfort for their souls. Beza advocated the opposite, though, since his doctrine of limited

---

5. A syllogism is a logical form of argument, usually containing a major premise, a minor premise, and a conclusion drawn from the relationship of the minor to the major premise. We will examine Beza's use of the practical syllogism in the pages to follow.
6. Kendall, *Calvin and English Calvinism to 1649*, p. 29.
7. In order to understand Kendall's perspective, as well as to understand some of Calvin's doctrine of faith and Beza's assurance teaching in his *Questions and Responses*, I am using material from Wright, *Our Sovereign Refuge*, pp. 73, 217-23.

atonement 'makes trusting Christ's death presumptuous.'[8] The only ground for assurance was to look at oneself, that is, to look for proof of one's salvation by means of the 'practical syllogism'. Thus Kendall argued, 'it is as though Beza says: all who have the effects [of salvation] have faith; but I have the effects, therefore (the infallible conclusion) I have faith.'[9] So Kendall concluded:

> Beza's doctrine of faith substantially diverges from that of Calvin; the difference is not quantitative but qualitative. The origin of this departure is linked to Beza's doctrine of limited atonement; when Christ is not held forth to all men as the immediate ground of assurance, the result is not only introspection on our part but a need to assure ourselves upon the very grounds Calvin warns against.[10]

Calvin urged persons to find assurance in Christ. Beza urged them to find it in themselves.

Many have responded to Kendall at this point, noting that his proposal hasn't taken into account the breadth of material, either in Calvin or in Beza, not to mention the rest of the Calvinistic tradition.[11] We can limit our interaction with Kendall to a few points. In the first place, we need to understand what is meant by the 'practical syllogism' and see if Calvin employed it. Here is how Joel Beeke defines it:

> A 'practical syllogism' (*syllogismus practicus*) is a conclusion drawn from an action. The basic form of the syllogism when it pertains to salvation is as follows:

---

8. Kendall, *Calvin and English Calvinism*, p. 32.
9. Kendall, *Calvin and English Calvinism*, p. 33.
10. Kendall, *Calvin and English Calvinism*, p. 38.
11. See, for example, Paul Helm, *Calvin and the Calvinists* (Carlisle, PA: Banner of Truth, 1982); Richard A. Muller, 'Calvin and the 'Calvinists': Assessing Continuities and Discontinuities Between the Reformation and Orthodoxy,' *Calvin Theological Journal* 30 (1995), pp. 345-75; 31 (1996), pp. 125-60.

Theodore Beza

Major premise:	Those only who do 'x' are saved.
Minor premise (practical):	But I do 'x'.
Conclusion:	Therefore I am saved.[12]

Second, let's see what Calvin taught about faith and assurance. In doing this, we'll see that Beza did not drift very far from his mentor's position on assurance. Calvin defined faith as 'a firm and certain knowledge of God's benevolence toward us, founded upon the truth of the freely given promise in Christ, both revealed to our minds and sealed upon our hearts through the Holy Spirit.'[13] Later, Calvin asserted that the essence of faith was certainty: 'As faith is not content with a doubtful and changeable opinion, so is it not content with an obscure and confused conception.'[14] Similarly, he made the blanket statement that 'he alone is truly a believer who, convinced by a firm conviction that God is a kindly and well-disposed Father toward him, promises himself all things on the basis of his generosity; who, relying upon the promises of divine benevolence toward him, lays hold on an undoubted expectation of salvation.'[15] If this were all the information Calvin left us, we should have to conclude that assurance was of the essence of faith since he stressed the Spirit's role in revealing and sealing

---

12. Joel R. Beeke, *Assurance of Faith: Calvin, English Puritanism, and the Dutch Second Reformation* (New York: Peter Lang, 1991), p. 97 n. 153. Johannes Wollebius (1589-1629) expressed it this way: 'In exploring our election we must advance by the analytic method from the means of execution to the decree, beginning with our sanctification, with a syllogism like this: Whoever feels in himself the gift of sanctification, by which we die to sin and live unto righteousness, is justified, called or presented with true faith and elect. But I feel this by the grace of God. Therefore I am justified, called and elect.' (in Heppe, *Reformed Dogmatics: Set Out and Illustrated from the Sources*, trans. G. T. Thomson, rev. and ed. Ernst Bizer (London: George Allen & Unwin, 1950), p. 76.) Also see Muller, *Dictionary*, p. 293.
13. Calvin, *Institutes*, 3.2.7.
14. Calvin, *Institutes*, 3.2.15.
15. Calvin, *Institutes*, 3.2.16.

the truth to the Christian. Where there was faith, there was *by definition* assurance. This was all that Kendall saw in Calvin.

This, however, was not all that Calvin taught. Soon after these spectacular statements of faith's certainty he qualified his exuberance. 'Surely, while we teach that faith ought to be certain and assured,' he resumed, 'we cannot imagine any certainty that is not tinged with doubt, or any assurance that is not assailed by some anxiety. On the other hand, we say that believers are in perpetual conflict with their own unbelief.'[16] So, Calvin qualified his insistence upon assurance. The Word and the Spirit worked in believers in order to seal the promises of God in their hearts, he said.[17] Yet, he reiterated, 'Faith is tossed about by various doubts, so that the minds of the godly are rarely at peace—at least they do not always enjoy a peaceful state.'[18] And even though he had previously lucidly stated that the final resting place of faith—and hence the *locus* of assurance—was Christ, not oneself,[19] Calvin did not shy from continuing his discussion in the next chapter by emphasizing the necessity of repentance in the lives of Christians.[20] So, for Calvin, the place of assurance, though ultimately it consisted of Word-induced faith in Christ, could be cloudy for Christians in this life. Assurance was of the essence of faith. Yet assurance

---

16. Calvin, *Institutes*, 3.2.17.

17. 'The Spirit accordingly serves as a seal, to seal up in our hearts those very promises the certainty of which it has previously impressed upon our minds; and takes the place of a guarantee to confirm and establish them' (Calvin, *Institutes*, 3.2.36).

18. Calvin, *Institutes*, 3.2.37.

19. Calvin said, for instance, that 'if you contemplate yourself, that is sure damnation. But since Christ has been so imputed to you with all his benefits that all his things are made yours, that you are made a member of him, indeed one with him, his righteousness overwhelms your sins; his salvation wipes out your condemnation; with his worthiness he intercedes that your unworthiness may not come before God's sight' (Calvin, *Institutes*, 3.2.24).

20. Calvin, *Institutes*, 3.3.

was almost never free from doubt in this life. Faith was central, but works were important as well.[21] This appears to me to be a very competent evaluation of the matter. Beza's use of the practical syllogism was not, then, so far beyond Calvin's as is often assumed.

In the third place, there are internal clues in Beza's works that he saw the 'practical syllogism' as just one means of finding assurance.[22] We see this even in one of Beza's more 'scholastic' treatises, his *Little Book of Christian Questions and Responses*. If we examine Beza's definition of faith, his pastoral emphasis on assurance becomes manifest. 'What is faith?' Beza asked. It was more than intellectual agreement, he said. It was, instead, 'a firm assent of one's mind accompanying that recognition of the facts, whereby it happens that each man applies particularly to himself the promise of eternal life in Christ Jesus, just as if he already were actually a possessor of it.'[23] Later, in the midst of his discussion of sanctification, he included another pastoral application. Beza answered a question about God's delay in making His children holy by asserting that instead of asking the question Christians should

---

21. Beeke has helpfully noted this in Calvin: 'By insisting that the Spirit's *primary mode* of bringing assurance is to direct the believer to embrace the promises of God in Christ, Calvin rejects any confidence being placed in the believer as he is in himself. Nevertheless, Calvin does not deny that a *subordinate means* to bolster assurance is realized by the Spirit on the basis of His own work with the believer which bears fruit in good works and various marks of grace.' What then of the 'practical syllogism' in Calvin's thought? 'Calvin did not use the *syllogismus practicus* in a *formal sense*,' Beeke concluded, 'for the formal usage of syllogisms to glean assurance belongs to a later date. But Calvin did utilize the principles of the syllogism in a *practical* sense (Beeke, *Assurance of Faith*, p. 72).

22. See Wright, *Our Sovereign Refuge*, pp. 194-217.

23. Theodore Beza, *A Little Book of Christian Questions and Responses, In which the Principal Headings of the Christian Religion are Briefly Set Forth*, trans. Kirk M. Summers (Allison Park, PA: Pickwick, 1986), p. 29.

marvel at His goodness, in that He instills any little drop of regenerating grace in man. Yet why He defers the full sanctification of us into another age, there are many reasons, and chiefly two. One, because we are of little faith, and therefore, as much as is in us, we impede the inworking of the Holy Spirit. The second, so that, as we are saved by grace alone, and not by works, he who glories, should glory only in God.[24]

However, Beza continued, those sanctified must be active in doing good works:

> For true sanctification is not able to be idle; and of what kind a fruitbearing tree is, so also is the fruit of that tree. Therefore, since our intellect is partly illumined with the knowledge of the true God, we also know in part; since we partly assent to the promise of God, and apply it to ourselves, therefore we believe in part; since our will is partly unchanged, therefore we will and do rightly only in part.[25]

Later he clarified what he meant in answer to the question, 'you say that good works are necessary to salvation?' He responded that 'if faith is necessary to salvation, and works necessarily flow out of true faith (as that which cannot be idle), certainly also it follows, that good works are necessary to salvation, yet not as the cause of salvation (for we are justified, and thus live, by faith alone in Christ), but as something necessarily attached to true faith.'[26]

But it was in his discussion of predestination that Beza showed his pastoral acumen most decisively in speaking about assurance. The interlocutor put forth the query, 'in the perilous temptation of particular election, where should I flee for succor?' Beza's delineation of assurance encompassed three means that Christians had for attaining assurance of salvation:

---

24. Beza, *Questions and Responses*, p. 53.
25. Beza, *Questions and Responses*, p. 53.
26. Beza, *Questions and Responses*, p. 61.

the fruits of sanctification, the testimony of the Holy Spirit, and Christ. Troubled persons should run

> To the effects whereby the spiritual life is rightly discerned. ... Therefore, that I am elect, is first perceived from sanctification begun in me, that is, by my hating of sin and my loving of righteousness. To this I will add the testimony of the Spirit, comforting my conscience as David said: 'Why are thou cast down, O my soul? And why art thou disquieted within me? Hope thou in God; for I shall yet praise him, who is the health of my countenance, and my God.' ... From this sanctification and comfort of the Spirit we gather faith. And therefore we rise to Christ, to whom whosoever is given, is necessarily elect from all eternity in Him, and will never be ejected from the doors.[27]

Even with this tri-fold approach to assurance, Beza knew that because of demonic attacks assurance would not be perfect until heaven; indeed, the testimonies of assurance would often be 'faint'. 'Yet still our minds must not be despondent,' Beza counseled, 'but must be strengthened by those indefinite promises, and again throw darts at our adversary. For although the struggle of our flesh against our spirit (especially as often as the Spirit seems to fall apart and be quenched) does bring great doubts to our consciences concerning the truth of our faith, still it is certain that this spirit which truly (although faintly) opposes the assaults of the flesh, is the spirit of adoption, whose gift is not to be repented of.'[28] Finally, in a rhetorical and pastoral flourish Beza noted that perseverance, although it was certainly made difficult by the devil's schemes, was certain for believers. They could be assured of their final salvation:

> I confess that the Spirit is now and then interrupted in severe temptations, and that the testimonies of Him who

---

27. Beza, *Questions and Responses*, pp. 96-7.
28. Beza, *Questions and Responses*, p. 97.

Struggling to Gain Assurance of Salvation

dwell in us are so made unconscious, that for a time He seems to be utterly departed from us. Nevertheless, I say that He is never taken away, since the decree of God to save His own must be firm, and therefore, at the right time, finally the clouds of the flesh are chased away, and the happiness of the salvation of the Lord always returns, and shines as the sun into the troubled consciences of the elect. ... those who have the Spirit of adoption have a sure pledge of eternal life. Therefore, in this most perilous struggle, the very thing by which Satan assaults us, can and must hold forth certain victory for us. For unless the Spirit of adoption (who also is the Spirit of sanctification, justification, life, and faith) is present in us, there would be no struggle, and the reign of sin would be peaceful in us.[29]

In one of his arguably most 'scholastic' treatises, Beza showed himself to be very pastoral while speaking of assurance, sanctification, and perseverance. This was no legalistic, introspective abuse of troubled souls. We will see the same to be true in Beza's response to Jakob Andreae.

The Context of the Debate

As with so much else in the sixteenth century, it is hard to separate the religious from the political in the Colloquy of Montbéliard of 1586. Whether or not magistrates said they believed doctrines from their hearts, often their expressed beliefs seem rather to have been motivated by political realities than by their understanding of Scripture. And the political pressures in 1586 were acute. We can sketch the background to the debate before noting the character of the debate itself.

Montbéliard was a town in the German duchy of Württemberg, which was part of the Holy Roman Empire. As such it was staunchly Lutheran. Not all within its environs, however, were Lutheran. In fact, Montbéliard had many residents of a Reformed persuasion and there had been a great influx of

---

29. Beza, *Questions and Responses*, p. 98.

French Calvinistic refugees there following a 1585 decree by Henry III of France exiling any who refused to practice Catholicism. Now the French residents of the city were showing their recalcitrance. They were unwilling to receive communion according to Lutheran doctrine, wanting, instead, to have it administered according to their French Reformed confession and liturgy. They followed Calvin's teaching that Christ was 'spiritually present' in the Lord's Supper; only the faithful, they said, received Christ's body and blood in the eucharist by the 'mouth of faith'. The Reformed population of Montbéliard resisted efforts to make them celebrate communion according to Lutheran teaching, especially its belief that Christ was bodily present in the elements and that everyone who partook of the elements actually ate and drank the body of Christ. Frederick, count of Montbéliard, was a staunch Lutheran and he would not allow the city to turn in a Reformed direction, especially since his uncle, Duke Ludwig of Württemberg, was also a committed Lutheran. Frederick decided to call a debate, or colloquy, to decide the matter.

He invited Theodore Beza to come up from Geneva to represent the Reformed position. Jakob Andreae, professor at the University of Tübingen and favorite theologian of Ludwig, was selected to defend the Lutheran position. Beza arrived, thinking the issue of debate was going to be the particulars of the eucharist. However, once the colloquy began four other matters were added to the agenda: Christology, baptism, the use of art and music in the church's liturgy, and predestination. Beza was flummoxed by the additions, but Frederick and Andreae showed themselves to be astute politically and theologically. Predestination was their strongest card, for Montbéliard's population had sided with the single predestination scheme of Berne against the double predestinarianism of Calvin and Beza. The sticky points of double predestination, they had thought, were the manner in which it called the character of God into question and how it worked against arriving at settled assurance of salvation.

Struggling to Gain Assurance of Salvation

From Beza's perspective the colloquy did not go well. Some partial rapprochement was reached on art and music in churches, but there was no compromise on the other topics of debate. Frederick required the population to accept the Lutheran understanding of communion before receiving the Supper. Not only had Beza been unsuccessful in winning the authorities of Montbéliard to his position; Andreae continued to plague him by publishing accounts of the Colloquy that called Beza's character and theological acumen into question. Beza responded by publishing his own account of the Colloquy, part of which was published as an appendix to William Perkins's *Golden Chain*, a treatise devoted to defending double predestination.[30] Richard Muller correctly highlights the on-going debate after the colloquy:

> So extensive was the disagreement that controversy continued after the Colloquy in the attempt to produce a transcript of it. Each side claimed to have emerged as the victor in the debate. The Lutherans went so far as to publish their own version of the Colloquy, demonstrating the orthodoxy of their position again the Reformed. Beza responded with a Reformed response to the Lutheran 'acts', indicating the superiority of the Reformed position.[31]

The Content

Beza was multifaceted in explicating means by which Christians could find assurance of salvation. This makes sense of the reality, as we have seen throughout this study, that Beza was first and foremost a Christian and a pastor. As a Christian he was well aware of his own struggles for assurance. And he was certainly

---

30. For details on the Colloquy of Montbéliard, see Jill Raitt, *The Colloquy of Montbéliard: Religion and Politics in the Sixteenth Century* (New York: Oxford University Press, 1993); Jill Raitt, 'Colloquy of Montbéliard,' in *The Oxford Encyclopedia of the Reformation* (New York: Oxford University Press, 1996), 3:84-85; Wright, *Our Sovereign Refuge*, pp. 87-8.
31. Muller, 'Theodore Beza (1519-1605),' pp. 217-18.

well aware of the manner in which different believers needed different types of help to arrive at certainty of assurance. For these reasons, as I have shown elsewhere, Beza in a sense provided Christians with different means to gain assurance of their salvation.[32]

We can get a bird's eye view of the debate quite easily. Andreae aggressively pressed the negative implications of Beza's doctrine of predestination since he saw this as the weakest link in the Reformed armor. Specifically he believed that Calvinists could not offer real assurance to anyone who doubted his standing with God. What could you tell him? Nothing, except to hope that God had eternally chosen him to be among the number of the elect. Not much comfort there! Andreae's answer to the conundrum of assurance was quite simple. Assurance was found in one's baptism. If a person doubted his standing before the holy God, all he needed to do was look back to his baptism. For baptism was baptism into the Christian faith and indicated a person's reception into the church. Baptism was not merely forward-looking (hoping that the infant baptized would come in time to embrace the faith); rather, it was in itself an initiation into the faith, holding within itself the promise of God's grace.

According to Andreae, baptism is essential for one's assurance of salvation. Other evidences of grace may be absent in a person. But one can always look back to the anchor of his baptism to find certainty that Christ has saved him. 'Unless regeneration is always united to baptism, and remains in such as are baptized,' he asks Beza, 'how should the troubled consciences of those be eased and comforted, who because they do not feel

---

32. I am using Theodore Beza, *An Excellent Treatize of Comforting Such, as are Troubled about Their Predestination. Taken Out of the Second Answer of M. Beza, to D. Andreas, in the Acte of Their Colloquie at Mompelgart.* In *A Golden Chaine, or, The Description of Theologie ... by that man of God, Mr William Perkins*, trans. Robert Hill, (London: John Legatt, 1621), pp. 563-75. For the editions of the *Acts* of the colloquy, see Gardy and Dufour, *Bibliographie des Oeuvres*, pp. 197-200.

in themselves any good motions of God's Holy Spirit, find no other refuge except the word and sacraments, especially the sacrament of baptism?[33] This is extremely powerful to the doubting soul because God 'in baptism has not only offered us the adoption of sons but has indeed bestowed the same on us.'[34] Baptism saves us because, according to Jesus, 'He that believes and is baptized shall be saved'; and Paul teaches us that 'You who are baptized have put on Christ.'

Andreae's arguments (Beza says they appear to be 'strong weapons') are both unbiblical and hurtful, Beza claims. For the doubting soul who sees nothing of Christ in him, Jesus's words are unhelpful. He will reason in this way: 'Truly I am baptized; yet, even having been baptized I do not believe in Christ; so, my baptism is of no avail; therefore, I must be condemned.'[35] Augustine is a better guide than Andreae, for Augustine pointed out that baptism may only result in condemnation if it's not correlated with faith. Speaking of Simon Magus he noted: 'What good did it to him to be baptized? Don't brag therefore that you are baptized as though that were sufficient for you to inherit the kingdom of heaven.'[36] No, *nuda* baptism does not save.

Beza offers several rebuttals to Andreae's argument that baptism saves of its own power. In essence, he argues that God is still strong to save, even if some neglect the grace offered them in baptism. In this line of argumentation Beza stresses the responsibility of persons to see and receive God's grace proffered them. Certainly salvation originates in God's will alone, but that does not alleviate persons of the responsibility to respond in faith. Baptism, then, is still powerful and a gracious symbol, even if 'some refuse the grace offered in baptism.' In

---

33. Beza, *Excellent Treatize*, p. 563.
34. Beza, *Excellent Treatize*, p. 564.
35. Beza, *Excellent Treatize*, p. 565.
36. Beza, *Excellent Treatize*, p. 565.

the same way, the gospel is the power of God for the salvation of everyone who believes. Has it been enervated of its power 'because it is to such as do not believe the savor of death to eternal death'? Of course not! The Lord's Supper functions in the same sort of way. 'May not the Supper of the Lord be a pledge of God's covenant, [even if] so many abuse these holy signs or (as is Dr Andreas' opinion) the very body and blood of our Savior, Christ?' Finally, Beza appeals to an illustration from nature: 'Can the Sun be said to be without light because those that are blind and asleep have no benefit by the light of it, nor those who shut their eyes so close that they won't enjoy the comfort of the light?'[37] Baptism is similar, then, to the gospel, the eucharist, and the Sun. Each offers tremendous benefits. Yet people must open themselves up to receive their assistance.

Next, Beza avers that Andreae's reasoning concerning the vitality of baptism, along with his Lutheran view that one can fall away from grace and be damned is flawed. Rather than supporting hurting souls who are doubting their salvation, it actually causes them to doubt more. Andreae reasons that only if baptism is efficacious for salvation could Christians in the past have flown to their baptisms when they were tempted to doubt their salvation. This doesn't follow, though, because in the same way Christians believe that the preaching of God's word and the eucharist are comfortable to doubting souls. Yet not even Andreae believes that all who hear the gospel or receive communion are regenerated and adopted as God's sons.[38] Even if we grant that Andreae is correct that baptism is powerful to save, the rest of his theology neuters baptism's efficacy. For all his assertions that baptism saves, he also believes that one can lose his salvation. Beza asks him, 'what else do you now do but lift me up with one hand to heaven and with the other cast me down into hell?' There is no comfort here. So Beza concludes, 'See now what sure consolation consciences that are grievously

---

37. Beza, *Excellent Treatize*, p. 566.
38. Beza, *Excellent Treatize*, p. 566.

afflicted may reap by this doctrine of their comforter, Dr Andreas.'³⁹ There is no comfort here. Andreae's teaching leads to despair. Beza has said enough to prove Andreae's position vacuous.

Beza now turns to those afflicted. In stark contrast to the Lutheran's pastoral reasoning, Beza offers a different model for coming to a settled conviction that one is saved. His is based on a very different theological system, one that looks not to baptism but to Jesus as the rock of our salvation. Andreae looked to baptism. Beza did not. Rather, he wanted assurance that was 'grounded upon a sure foundation', and he had often found something else 'to be true in my own experience.' That something else was the character and power of God.⁴⁰

Beza's first response was to counter Andreae's *ad hominem* attack on the Genevan's doctrine of predestination. At Montbéliard Andreae had asserted that Beza grounded assurance in God's eternal decree to save the elect. This was a common Lutheran charge, claiming that a doubting soul, therefore, had to try to read the mind of God as to whether he had been eternally elected or reprobated. Beza would have none of this faulty reasoning. Not God's decree, but God's invitation to sinners was the only true basis of certainty of salvation. Beza countered Andreae's false charge: 'We teach, contrarily to that which Dr Andreas most falsely objects against us, that the eternal decree, or as Paul speaks, "the purpose of God", [is known] in the manifestation of it, namely, in his vocation [that is, his calling], by the word and sacraments. This I speak of such as are of the years of discretion, and they have to be, whom we seek to comfort in this place.'⁴¹ So Beza asserted that God calls people to Himself through the gospel and the sacraments. This external call was for all persons generally. Andreae is at fault,

---

39. Beza, *Excellent Treatize*, p. 567.
40. Beza, *Excellent Treatize*, p. 568.
41. Beza, *Excellent Treatize*, p. 568.

though, for not distinguishing the general call of God to all people in the gospel from the internal call of God to the elect. The first one lacked power to save, but the second gave life to those God had chosen. The Lutheran not only merged the two together; he also wrongly asserted that Beza taught that one could attempt to read God's mind from eternity past. Beza had never done this. In the rest of the treatise he proceeded to apply the 'comfortable and restorative medicine which is taken from God's effectual vocation, as it were out of an apothecary's box' to believers who were suffering from doubt.[42]

The rest of the treatise, then, is filled with pastoral reasoning that surprises one who is predisposed to assume Beza is a rationalistic Protestant scholastic. Beza's reasoning is warm, comforting, and hopeful as it points doubters to Christ. Abounding in biblical principles, it is Puritan-like in being both rigorous and warm.

As a seasoned pastor, Beza begins by noting that there are only two kinds of people in the world—Christians and non-Christians. Some non-Christians, though, struggle because they wonder if they will ever be saved. It's that group of people he addresses first. The biggest struggle they have is with the lie of Satan that since they don't now believe in Jesus they will never do so. To these people Beza strongly cries out that 'Satan plays the sophister', since this is not necessarily the case. This kind of reasoning proceeds 'as if a man looking at midnight, and seeing that the sun is not then risen, should therefore affirm that it would never rise.'[43] Of course that would be an incorrect conclusion to make. Beza says this sort of unbiblical reasoning can be annulled by looking to God's external call to all persons to come to Him in the gospel. Those who hear the gospel are in a much better place than those who've not heard of Jesus. They can answer the devil's assaults by reminding themselves that they can still be saved if they respond in repentance and faith.

---

42. Beza, *Excellent Treatize*, p. 569.
43. Beza, *Excellent Treatize*, p. 569.

Struggling to Gain Assurance of Salvation

Here is Beza's counsel: 'I tell' such a troubled person, he says, 'that they who never had external nor internal calling, they, if we regard an ordinary calling must perish.' These are the ones beyond the reach of gospel preaching. But this isn't the status of the doubters Beza is answering here, for 'whoever is once called, he has set, as it were, his foot in the first entry into the kingdom of heaven. And, unless it is by his own default, he shall come afterwards into the courts of God and so by degrees into his Majesty's palace.'[44] The one who has heard the gospel and is troubled about whether or not he believes should take comfort in the fact that he can be saved.

Beza proceeds with a battery of questions to such a person, the point of which is to show him that God's mercy is readily available for him. 'For why, I say, do you doubt of his good will towards you, who in mercy has sent me, a minister, to call you to him?' The only possible rebuttal such a person might offer is that their sins are great. Beza responds to this by pointing out that the Lord's mercy is greater than any amount or degree of human sin: 'If this is all, why oppose the infinite greatness of God's mercy against your sins, who has sent me to bring you to him.' They must remember that God is greater than their rebelliousness. By sending gospel preachers to this person, 'the Lord vouchsafes to bring you into the way of the elect.' He brings preachers to those whom He desires to save. They need to stop arguing against God and listen to His summons to them: 'Why are you a stumbling block to yourself and refuse to follow him?' Especially, Beza urges them to see evidence of God's grace to them in the fact that they're even concerned about their salvation: 'If you don't feel as yet inwardly yourself to be stirred forward' to claim Christ as their own, he urges, 'pray that you may be. Know this for a most sure truth that this desire in you is a pledge of God's fatherly good will towards you.' Beza concludes his address to these as-yet-unconverted troubled souls by urging them not to conclude that since they

---

44. Beza, *Excellent Treatize*, p. 570.

have lived long lives in rebellion against God this is proof that they can't be saved: 'I show him how some are called at the eleventh hour, how the Gentiles after many thousands of years were called to be God's people, how the thief was saved upon the cross.'[45] Beza had counseled many such persons, and he found such arguments as these to be effective in answering their concerns.

Now he turns to those who have trusted in Jesus at some point in the past but who now doubt that they ever were truly saved. These people were often 'very good and godly' generally, but they had committed grievous sins or failed to attend church regularly and so concluded that they must not have ever been truly converted. They lamented their standing with God. They might, but Beza did not. He reasoned that they, like the troubled unbelievers, were chiefly at fault for neglecting to hold on to the mercy of God shown in Christ: 'They are so altogether busily conversant in reprehending and judging themselves, that they for a while forget the mercy of God.'[46]

Beza admits that there are some persons who have 'some natural infirmities' that need an expert minister's help lest they be 'most dangerously tempted'.[47] This is a small number, however. The rest, he says, should be helped in the following way, according to an order of steps that will assist them to come to full assurance of faith.

The first step of the counselor helping the doubting soul was to ascertain exactly what was troubling this person. We see Beza's pastoral sensitivity in the counsel he offered about balancing trumpeting God's mercy with pointing out the real consequences for sinful choices the individual made in the past.

> I take special care of this, that they being already overmuch cast down, that I then by the severe denunciation of the Law

---

45. Beza, *Excellent Treatize*, pp. 570-1.
46. Beza, *Excellent Treatize*, p. 571.
47. Beza, *Excellent Treatize*, p. 571.

do not quite overturn them. Yet so as that I do not altogether withdraw them either from condemning their former sins or the meditation on God's judgment. And so, as much as I can, I temper the words of consolation, so that I [in] nothing cloak God's anger against them for their sins.[48]

Aware of individuals' unique tempers and experiences, Beza tried to proceed cautiously in the first step.

His second step was a litany of questions Beza asked the troubled person, in the form of a dialogue.[49] He had obviously counseled many people who struggled with coming to certainty of salvation and knew the types of deep doubts they harbored. The point of this reasoning process was to turn their minds to the overwhelming hope they had in the gracious character of God. Sure, they doubted. But God was unwilling to let them stew in their doubt. No, they needed their minds turned towards God's goodness which in turn would move their affections to trust Him more:

'Have they ever been in this case before or not?' he asks at first. Typically, they respond negatively, averring, 'The time was when I was in great joy and peace of conscience. I served the Lord, was then a happy person, full of faith, full of hope. But now (wretch that I am) I have lost my first love, and there is nothing that vexes me more than to remember those times past.'

Their response leads Beza to have confidence that they truly are converted. Their love of the times of God's favor they formerly had indicates that they have genuine love for God. To be sure, though, Beza has one further query: 'Which consideration is more grievous to you—the apprehension of God's judgments [against their sins], or their dislike of themselves that they should offend so gracious and loving a Father?'

When they reply, 'Both, but especially the latter', Beza knows he's speaking to a believer. So he has a final question for them:

---

48. Beza, *Excellent Treatize*, p. 572.
49. This lengthy dialogue is found in Beza, *Excellent Treatize*, pp. 573-5.

'Therefore, does sin also displease you in that it is sin, namely, because it is evil, and God who is goodness itself, is offended with it?' They usually reply affirmatively, even asserting that they are 'ashamed that so vile and wicked [a person] as myself should come before so gracious and merciful a Father.'

But Beza presses home now how incongruous their view of God's mercy is with their fear that He won't be merciful to them. 'I tell them that no man is offended, but rather is glad, when he can injure one whom he hates.' Feeling the weight of Beza's logic, they agree and assert, 'God forbid that albeit the Lord hates me, I in like sort should hate him, unto whom (if it were possible) I would be reconciled again.'

Beza concludes his questioning by telling the troubled soul that his situation is not as dire as he thought. He has every reason, in fact, to believe that he's a true Christian: 'Be of good comfort, my dear brother, you are in good case. For who can love God, especially when he is wounded by him? Who can bewail the loss of his friendship? Who can desire to come again into his favor, but he whom God still loves, although for a time he is angry with him?' The fact that they desire to be reconciled to God out of love for Him—especially when what they are experiencing feels like God's displeasure towards them—is proof that they truly know God.

Beza isn't done though. He reminds the troubled soul of an answer to his questions even better than the line of reasoning Beza has gone through with him up to this point. He now tells the doubter that the highest proof of salvation is the Holy Spirit's inward testimony to his soul that assures him of his right standing before God. He asserts that 'the knowledge of our salvation comes not from flesh and blood, but from God himself, who first promised to instruct us, and from Christ Jesus, manifesting the Father unto us.' Beza's strong encouragement, then, is for the doubter now to pray to the Lord for His mercy. He is one of the Father's loved sheep and needs to act like it and call out to his Father until sensing that he truly is a Christian:

You have inwardly and, as it were, dwelling with you, evident testimonies of your future reconciliation with God; especially if you cease not to pray to him earnestly, who has laid the foundation of repentance in you, namely, a dislike of sin, and a desire to be reconciled to him. The sheep which wandered out of the fold ceased not to be a sheep, albeit it went astray for a time. You now are that sheep, to whom that faithful shepherd of all those sheep, which the Father has committed to him, leaving those ninety and nine, does not so much by my ministry, declare that he seeks you, as having already sought you—though you, not seeking him—has indeed found you. Knock, says he, and it shall be opened unto you. And have you now forgotten those promises, which were so often made to them that repent, and also which they had experience of, who in the sight of the world were in a desperate case?

Still, though, the doubter often objects, asserting that because he doesn't feel any sense of God's favor right now he cannot be a Christian. 'I feel no motions of the Comforter; I have now no sense of faith or hope. But I feel all the contrary.' Surely, the troubled soul concludes, I must be damned.

You're wrong, Beza responds. The doubter is seeking the Spirit's inward testimony in the wrong place. He's looking for feelings. The Lord, though, has already testified to him through his hatred of sin and love for God: 'No, I say, you deceive yourself, as I told you before. For it is the Comforter alone, who teaches you to hate sin, not so much for the punishment, as because it is evil and dislikes God.' The troubled soul only has dislike of sin and love for God due to the reality of the Holy Spirit's dwelling in him.

The afflicted person needs to take into account the reality that God is likely disciplining him for outright sin or at least for his spiritual laziness which has led him to this low point spiritually. God may not be showing Himself in a powerful way to be His Father right now

> because you had [in] so many ways grievously offended him, so that he seemed for a while quite to forsake you. And you

have not quite lost him, but he is yet in some secret corner of your soul, from where at your instant prayers he will show himself unto you. ... But let us grant as much as you say, yet, sure it is that your faith was not dead, but only possessed with a spiritual lethargy.

Beza presses home this point. He adamantly stresses that life often exists even where to outward appearances it seems to be lacking. Several illustrations show this. 'You lived in the womb of your mother, and there were ignorant of your life. A drunken man, although for a time he lose the use of reason, and also of his limbs, yet he never loses reason itself. You would think that in winter the trees were dead, but they spring again in the summer season. At night the Sun sets, but in the next morning it rises again. And how often do we see by experience, that he who at one time took the foil in a combat, at another did win the prize?'

So, the doubter's lack of evident fruit right now is not the final word. Beza urges him to look to his heart in order to see what he loves. He'll see that he loves God and hates sin. He must remember that the Christian life is not a leisurely stroll through the park but a bloody conflict. So Beza ends with these hope-giving, but sober, words: 'Know this, that in the spiritual combat of the flesh with the Spirit,' we will be hurt. The pain may be a result of 'the weakness of our nature, partly through sloth to resist, and partly for' not being aware of the danger. But with these reminders we should be ready for the combat ahead.

Application

This little treatise by Beza is a useful one to reflect on. We have observed Beza's unflinching commitment to be honest. Life is hard and believers will suffer in it. One result of the hardship of life is that some believers for some time may doubt the reality of their relationship with Christ. We need not be afraid of this, nor should it surprise us. Life is hard during our earthly pilgrimage to our heavenly home. So, we should be ready to help others (and maybe ourselves too) when they're struggling to gain assurance.

If we forget everything else that Beza said, let's strive to point people to the gospel of Jesus Christ as the means of attaining salvation. The gospel is *the* way that people can find hope. As we direct their gazes to the cross of Jesus, we point them to the one event in the history of the universe that can help them. There they see the righteousness of God on display as He pours out His wrath for sin on His Son. And there they see full forgiveness on display as the sinless Son of God dies for sinners. 'It is finished' is the cry of the cross. And we can tell our doubting friends that it is finished for them too. They need not seek to save themselves (indeed, we might even gently remind them that this is a bit of self-righteousness on their parts) any more. Instead, they need to look on Jesus in His suffering for sinners and find hope there. 'Leave off everything else and go to Jesus because he has accomplished everything for you,' should be our constant refrain to our friends. Let us learn from Beza to do this more and more. For Jesus is able to save them.

Uses

The text I have used is Theodore Beza, *An Excellent Treatize of Comforting Such, as are Troubled about Their Predestination. Taken Out of the Second Answer of M. Beza, to D. Andreas, in the Acte of Their Colloquie at Mompelgart*. It is in *A Golden Chaine, or, The Description of Theologie ... by that man of God, Mr William Perkins*, translated by Robert Hill, (London: John Legatt, 1621), pp. 563-75. It is available on the website, *Early English Books Online* (eebo.chadwyck.com).

1. Do you struggle with assurance of salvation or do you know Christians who do? What have been the most beneficial biblical truths for you, or them, to reflect on as a means of gaining assurance?

2. Did you find Beza's rationale of the means of gaining assurance helpful? Why or why not?

3. Compare Beza's pastoral reasoning in this treatise with John Calvin's exposition of the Christian life in the *Institutes* 3.7-9. How does Calvin's description of the Christian life as a cross-bearing life always looking forward to heaven compare to Beza's?

4. The English Puritans also dealt with questions of assurance at length. Compare Beza's treatment of assurance with that of Richard Sibbes and that of *The Westminster Confession of Faith*, chapter 18.[50] Do you think they agree with each other?

---

50. See especially Sibbes's *The Bruised Reed* (Edinburgh: Banner of Truth, 1998). Helpful modern treatments of assurance of salvation include Thomas R. Schreiner, *Run to Win the Prize: Perseverance in the New Testament* (Wheaton: Crossway, 2010), and Sam Storms, *Kept for Jesus: What the New Testament Really Teaches about Assurance of Salvation and Eternal Security* (Wheaton: Crossway, 2015).

8
YEARNING FOR GOD—
Maister Bezaes Houshold Prayers

Introduction
Just as a loved child delights to talk to his father, so a Christian delights to talk to his Heavenly Father. This has been the case from the time of the Bible until now. What did the disciples want to know? How to pray (see Luke 11:1). What did Paul model in almost all of his epistles? Fervent prayer for the church (see, for example, Ephesians 1:15-23 and Philippians 1:9-11).[1] What are Christians exhorted to do? Pray (see, among other places, Philippians 4:6-7; 1 Peter 5:6-7). Prayer is central to the vitality of biblical Christianity. It's vital since it is one of the main ways in which a child of God relates to his Father in heaven.Furthermore, prayer has played a large role in the church's historical reflection on the Christian life. From numerous treatises that have been written giving instruction on prayer, I surmise not only that pastors have regularly felt the need to write on the importance of prayer but also that they have deemed that their parishioners needed instruction on how to pray. We can see this, for example, in the writings of Augustine (d. 430) who devoted a lengthy letter to the subject

---

1. For an excellent consideration of many of Paul's prayers, see D. A. Carson, *Praying With Paul: A Call to Spiritual Reformation*, 2nd ed. (Grand Rapid: Baker, 2015).

of prayer.[2] At the time of the Reformation in the 1500s, Martin Luther was asked by his barber for help in his prayer life. Peter was struggling to pray. So Luther ripped off a treatise to his friend giving him wise instruction on how to fight through the difficulties of prayer.[3] John Calvin similarly taught on prayer. In fact, one of the longest chapters in his *Institutes* is his compendium of directions for prayer.[4] There is a wealth of help in the Christian tradition to spur us to pray more fervently.

Theodore Beza is in this stream of vibrant, heart-felt Christianity. His prayers show him to be a faithful disciple of Calvin. More importantly, though, his prayers put to rest the odd opinion that Beza was more 'scholastic' than Calvin (whatever that means!) and that his existence was mostly one of thinking rarefied, esoteric thoughts in an office away from real human beings. Beza prayed. He prayed because he loved God. He prayed because he knew he was deeply flawed and needy. He prayed because he loved people and wanted the best for them. He prayed because he knew this life was temporary and was a pilgrimage on the way to eternity. He prayed. And by listening to his prayers, we get to know Beza the man.

Fortunately we have access to some of Beza's personal prayers. He seems to have composed them for his private and family use, originally in French, probably in the 1590s. When some friends from Bohemia (including one who as a student at Geneva had

---

2. See Augustine's *Letter 130* (A.D. 412) *to Proba*, in Philip Schaff, ed., *Nicene and Post-Nicene Fathers*, first series (1887; rpt., Grand Rapids: Eerdmans, 1994), 1: 459-69; Tim Keller, '4 Principles on Prayer from Saint Augustine,' http://thegospelcoalition.org/articles/saint-augustine-on-prayer (accessed August 5, 2014).

3. Martin Luther, 'How One Should Pray, for Peter, the Master Barber,' in *Martin Luther's Basic Theological Writings*, 2nd ed., ed. Timothy F. Lull (Minneapolis: Fortress, 2005), pp. 2-17.

4. Calvin, *Institutes*, 3.20. 'The longest chapter in the 1559 *Institutes* is devoted to prayer which Calvin called "the chief exercise of faith, and the means by which we daily receive God's benefits"' (Timothy George, *Theology of the Reformers*, rev. ed. (Nashville: B&H, 2013), p. 237.

Yearning for God

lived in Beza's home for about six months and had heard Beza use these prayers in his household) asked Beza for a copy of the prayers, he translated them into Latin for them in 1597. We, however, do not have a copy of that translation. The English Protestant publisher, John Barnes, somehow came across the French copy of the prayers, translated them into English, and published them in 1603. This is a significant date, because the elderly Beza could have denied his authorship of the prayers. He did not. The prayers were subsequently republished in 1607, 1608, and 1621. The only surviving copy of these prayers is the English translation. In this chapter we will use the 1603 edition, published as *Maister Bezaes Houshold Prayers*.[5] What a nice providence that we can learn from Beza how to pray.

The book is too long to examine in detail. Instead, after briefly noting the whole contents of the work's twenty-eight prayers, we will spend a bit of time on Beza's rich introduction to the whole work. This is a meaty treasure-trove of a theology of prayer. We will conclude by examining the contents of a few of the prayers to learn how Beza prayed. It is fitting that we draw our study of Beza to a conclusion by listening to him pray. Not only do we truly know a person by listening to him pray to his Lord and Savior, but we are also challenged to more eagerly come before the throne of grace ourselves. May our heavenly Father use Beza to make us more faithful in the noble duty of praying.

The Contents

The book is filled with the fully-written-out contents of twenty-eight prayers that Beza composed for his own use on varied occasions. The titles of all the prayers demonstrate how varied the petitions were.

---

5. See Gardy and Dufour, *Bibliographie des Oeuvres*, p. 217. For details surrounding the authorship of this book of prayers, see Scott M. Manetsch, 'A Mystery Solved? *Maister Beza's Houshold Prayers*,' in *Bibliothèque d'Humanisme et Renaissance* 65.2 (2003), pp.275-88.

1. The first prayer, upon the Lord's Prayer
2. Upon the Symbol or Articles of Belief (the Apostles' Creed)
3. Upon the Decalogue, or Ten Commandments
4. To the only God in a Trinity of Persons
5. For obtaining the knowledge of God in Jesus Christ
6. For obtaining the gift of the Holy Ghost
7. To crave of God the light of his word
8. That we may not depart from the Church
9. For obtaining the efficacy of holy baptism
10. For communion in the holy eucharist
11. For thanksgiving after communion
12. To obtain the gift of faith
13. To demand the virtue of hope
14. To obtain the virtue of love
15. That we may well use afflictions
16. For obtaining the virtue of patience
17. For the good use of man's life
18. Upon temporal death
19. For heavenly life
20. Upon eternal death
21. For the morning
22. Among the family
23. Before meat, among the family
24. After meals, among the family
25. Evening prayer for the household
26. Of him which suffered much by sickness
27. At the visitation of the sick
28. For him that feels his death at hand

The fact that Beza wrote these prayers for his private use gives us insight into his passion for the Lord. They display a wide depth of piety. The early prayers are directed to the Lord in praise (prayers 1-4). Then there are a set of prayers, beseeching God to shower spiritual blessings on His people, specifically seeking His blessings to rest on His people in the fellowship of the church (5-16). Five prayers direct the person praying to eternity, asking the heavenly Father to bring him safely there through the turmoils of this life (17-20, 28). A final group of petitions are for people in different stages of life, including petitions for a Christian's family (21-27). Surely this is a varied group of prayers.

The Introduction
Beza's meandering introduction to his prayers stresses many points. He doesn't try to prioritize them in terms of a hierarchy of importance, so we won't try to force a false paradigm on them either. Attempting to whet his readers' appetites for prayer with hopeful anticipation, Beza highlights several truths. The reality of the spiritual battle that involves all Christians, the desire experientially to know God better, the awesomeness of prayer considering how sinful we are, and the twin desires to glorify God and find joy in our lives—each of these facets of prayer gains the attention of Theodore Beza in his rich introduction to his collection of prayers.

In the first place, he avers, Christians won't pray until they know that they need to pray. When all seems well and easy, what need is there for prayer? But of course all is not well. Things are not easy. Christians are especially part of a battle between God and the evil one, a battle whose stakes include their very souls. Therefore it shouldn't surprise us that Beza stresses once again the reality of his eschatological vision. When believers see that prayer is essential as a means of their safe conduct through the turmoils of life, they will pray. They will pray when they know that prayer will help them to arrive at their true home. Beza frames prayer as a necessity for the Christian given the fact that believers are strangers in this world, bound for their real inheritance in heaven. He here echoes Calvin's thought, and poignantly calls on Christians to realize the shortness of life here. Life is hard, so they should call out to their heavenly Father to empower them to reach their true home. In this sense, prayer is a powerful means the Lord has instituted to help Christians attain to that final salvation.

We see this in several places in the introduction to *Houshold Prayers*. For instance, Beza teaches that 'by prayer we bless God for his goodness, power, wisdom, justice, and mercy towards us. Because of our prayers, he blesses us in doing us good and distributing his benefits amongst us. It is unto us as the soul of our souls. For prayer quickens our affections, and lifts up our hearts unto heaven who otherwise would be dead in sins and trespasses, by following the vanities of this wicked world.'[6] In a sense prayer enables believers, while communing with God, to experience their future salvation in the present.

In another place he notes that 'in the miseries of this life, we comfort ourselves, by looking for the benefits of the kingdom of God' through prayer. It does this by refreshing 'us through the remembrance of his gracious promises, which confirm us in the same, and of the blessings already received at his hands, which move us in our necessities to hope for the like, and wait for it with all patience. It augments in us a desire to be conjoined with him through our Lord Jesus Christ in whom all our good does consist.'[7] We look to the Lord for assurance through prayer, specifically for 'the benefits of the kingdom of God' that we've already received from His hand. Prayer will fortify us for our pilgrimage.

After setting forth the necessity that we have true estimation of our need and of the Lord's willingness to help us, Beza unpacks what the purpose of prayer is. Here he notes two guiding motivations for a Christian going to his God in prayer. First of all, prayer is a means of our offering ourselves up to God and committing ourselves to the Lord in a tangible way. Following this, in the second place, prayer affords us the opportunity to seek out God's fatherly protection over us by asking Him to meet our needs. Beza is eloquent in telling us why we should pray. Prayer enables us

---

6. Beza, *Houshold Prayers*, B2v-B3r.
7. Beza, *Houshold Prayers*, B3r-B3v.

to present ourselves before God, to offer unto him our vows, and to beseech his fatherly love, or direction, for guiding us, by his good Spirit, unto the light of his truth, to increase in our hearts, faith, love, constancy, humility, and others of his heavenly gifts, to forgive us our debts, to mortify the corruptions of our nature, to clothe us with his spiritual armor, against the assaults of the devil, the world and the flesh, to provide for our necessities, to preserve us from infinite dangers, which compass us round about—in short, to grant us his Holy Spirit, to guide the whole course of our life, to the glory of his name, and the peace and salvation of our own souls.

Beza's willingness to confront the realities of life's hardships is stark, because Christians face numerous evils in their earthly pilgrimage. Whether they're attacked from outside by the world's temptations, or from within by their own indwelling sin, or by the schemes of the evil one, believers face numerous, and real, dangers. These perils could keep them from the peace and joy of heaven. That's why they pray. Confronted with the harsh realities of this life, they call out to the Lord for help. They beseech the aid of the Spirit of God who will guide them in this life. The result will be God receiving glory and believers ultimate salvation. 'Oh, how happy shall these men then be, whom the Lord shall find thus watching, and praying! For they shall depart unto him in peace, in the contemplation of his glory; which grace, may God grant unto us all. Amen.'[8]

Beza also believed that prayer is intensely relational. He pressed the importance of praying as a means of growing a Christian closer to his heavenly Father. Children love to know their fathers and to be in close relationships with them. So too, a true child of God will yearn to be in a closer relationship with his heavenly Father. Beza pressed this simple, yet profound, observation on his readers. What could inspire them to pray more than knowing it was through this activity that they grew closer experientially and relationally with their God? In

---

8. Beza, *Houshold Prayers*, B9v.

prayer we both give and receive. 'By prayer we bless God for his goodness, power, wisdom, justice, and mercy towards us; because of our prayers, he blesses us, in doing us good, and distributing his benefits among us. It is unto us as the soul of our souls, because prayer quickens our affections, and lifts up our hearts to heaven, which otherwise would be dead in sins and trespasses, by following the vanities of this wicked world.'[9] This is a remarkable statement. Not only do we bless God in prayer; we also receive His blessings due to our prayers ('because of our prayers, he blesses us'). Beza here exudes with passion and experience as one who has felt the kindness and goodness of the Lord through prayer.

Beza presses the truth that prayer is essential if we wish to have a sense that God is our good heavenly Father who cares for us. 'Prayer,' he teaches, 'is as it were the key which opens to us the treasury of our heavenly Father, as faith is the hand, laying hold upon those sure and permanent possessions of eternal life, which desire should cause us continually to pray to and fervently to love God.'[10] Again, he presses home that Christians have a responsibility to pray. They must do it. And in doing it they will experience great joy and gain assurance that God has indeed saved them.

Prayer is relational. We pour out our needs to God, and He responds by blessing us. But we must realize that prayer is not magic. We're not saying incantations forcing the spirit world to do our bidding. God hears His children's prayers, but He is sovereign over the answers to their requests. Certainly at times in the Bible miracles result from prayers (think of Joshua and the sun standing still), but we must not 'simply attribute so great and profitable effects to the work of prayer, but to the goodness, love, power, and counsel of God, who works so, and by such means as he pleases in his creatures; and who, of his free mercy, crowns

---

9. Beza, *Houshold Prayers*, B2v-B3r.

10. Beza, *Houshold Prayers*, B3r.

the prayers of his elect with rewards, and with grace for grace.'[11] In His sovereignty, our God decides how He will respond to His children's prayers: 'According to his wisdom, he knows the time and convenient means to let us fully enjoy the efficacy of our prayers.' The key, then, to receiving what we ask for in prayer is to ask those things which tend to God's glory. So Beza urges us to 'persevere in only asking those things which are to his glory, and he will not fail to help us in all our necessities.'[12]

Prayer is part of a two-way relationship that exists between God and His people. He speaks to them in His word. This word is directed to them in promise and rebuke, in comfort and in hope. They must take it to heart, receive it as God's word to them, and then in turn go to the Lord and cry out to Him. Prayer is thus the reciprocal part of our relationship with God:

> These things, therefore, being by God joined together to prayer, let us take great heed that we not separate them, considering that by the same we converse with our Father which is in heaven, and so enjoy the fullness of his blessings. For whenever we apply our eyes, or our ears, to those things which he declares unto us in the holy scriptures, he speaks to us; and calling upon his name, we speak to him.[13]

Highlighting even more starkly the awesomeness of prayer for a Christian, Beza pointed out that Christians should remember that by all rights our sin should hinder us from being allowed to pray. God can have no fellowship with sinful creatures like us. Beza—ever the Protestant—can never get far away from the salvation of Christ's cross as the ground for our praying efforts. Only the sin-bearing work of our Savior enables us to pray. We must see our desperate need, and we must know that when we call out to our Father, He hears and answers

---

11. Beza, *Houshold Prayers*, B4r-B4v.
12. Beza, *Houshold Prayers*, B5r.
13. Beza, *Houshold Prayers*, B7v.

our prayers. Beza instructs believers: 'If we are endued with the true knowledge of our estate, and condition, and also, the efficacy of holy prayers, we should not need to be advertised often, to present ourselves before God.'[14]

Finally, Beza asks what the purpose is in prayer. What should be our goal in prayer? In fact, he's already noted several purposes (a means of getting believers to heaven and knowing God more intimately, among them). In the final part of the introduction he delineates two more. Christians should pray so that God receives glory. And Christians should pray so that they might receive salvation. Far from being disjointed, these two purposes were closely connected in Beza's mind. The latter one, of course, is closely related as well to his unblushing seriousness in painting a picture of the stark realities of spiritual battle.

The ultimate reasons, then, that Christians are to pray come down to two purposes: first, they seek God's glory; and, second, they yearn for their own salvation. These twin themes bound how Christians should pray, as Beza averred when speaking of what we learn in the Lord's Prayer. In this prayer, he says, Christ 'has set down the perfect rule, by which we may rightly form our petitions and keep them within their bounds—that is, the glory of God and our salvation.'[15] So, God's glory and our salvation are the proper bounds (Beza also calls them 'limits or purposes') of prayer. These make our prayers effective and give us assurance that we will be heard. They are extremely useful to us, because Beza also teaches that if we pray outside of these bounds—for example, by praying with wrong affections—we will not be heard by God.

But how do we know what tends to God's glory? Beza sums up those things we can ask for in prayer that result in God's receiving glory:

> These therefore are the fruits and benefits we are to look for from our good God and Father, when reposing ourselves

---

14. Beza, *Houshold Prayers*, B1v.
15. Beza, *Houshold Prayers*, B6v.

upon his love in Christ, and with humble and penitent hearts, we prostrate ourselves before his face, to sanctify his name, craving his mercy, and beseeching him to bless us, teach and guide us as his children, to believe his word, even as he whom we call upon, desires our good, because he loves us, may give unto us what we ask, because he is almighty and is willing to hear us, for his Son's sake, because he has so promised.[16]

More than this, even, Beza reminds Christians that God is not impressed just with the words of their prayers. He wants their hearts. And he wants their obedience. In other words, prayer must be offered up with proper affection to the Lord:

> It is not the sound of the lips which the Lord requires of us, unless the same be also guided with the holy affections of the soul. For he hearkens rather to the heart than to the voice, and gives to us openly that which he sees us in secret to desire with our affections mortified in his sight. Therefore we must (praying carefully) lift up our hearts with a true zeal to God, banishing out all other thoughts, abandoning Satan with all his baits, opening our hearts, that our Heavenly Father may infuse it and pour down his blessings.[17]

And the Lord also seeks obedience to His will:

> Remember that those who used many times to say, 'O Lord help us,' do not, notwithstanding, thereby obtain salvation. But those who do his will. And to that end, he commands us that we have his word dwelling peaceably in our hearts, that we may be ready to perform every good work.[18]

Besides these things, Beza notes other aids to effective prayer. One is Bible reading, which is a fuel for prayer: 'Neither ought

---

16. Beza, *Houshold Prayers*, B4v-B5r.
17. Beza, *Houshold Prayers*, B5r-B5v.
18. Beza, *Houshold Prayers*, B7r-B7v.

our prayer to be bare or naked, but conjoined with reading and meditation of God's holy word.'[19] Another fuel for prayer is Jesus' model prayer which Christ gave to His disciples as an example. We especially need it because when we try to pray according to God's will we're often attacked by the evil one. The Lord's Prayer assists us to petition our heavenly Father according to His will:

> But alas, if it is most true that in all our exercises of piety we are never able to separate ourselves from ourselves, but that our corruption will still evidently appear, it is sure the same will especially befall us when we prepare ourselves to pray to God and frame our petitions according to his will. For besides that the devil at all times lies in wait to seduce us, so he, especially, at such times seeks to creep into our minds, to divert our thoughts elsewhere, that they may be polluted with many blemishes. Notwithstanding that they of themselves sufficiently go astray. Yes, our vanity, imperfection, and coldness, many ways betrays itself, that we may well say, in one word, no man prays rightly but he whose mouth and mind Christ directs with his Spirit. And therefore he has delivered unto us a sacred form for all holy prayers in that prayer which is usually termed, The Lord's Prayer, in which has set down the perfect rule by which we may rightly form our petitions and keep them within their bounds, that is, the glory of God and our salvation.

We see again that the ultimate bounds for our prayers should be the twin desire for God's glory and our own salvation.

One of the reasons that Beza composed this handbook of prayers was his realistic evaluation of how difficult it is to sustain a life of prayer in the midst of the other activities of life. Other things can swamp a believer's time and, before he knows it, he has forgotten to pray for days on end. So having set times to pray every day will aid the Christian in this aspect of his piety:

---

19. Beza, *Houshold Prayers*, B5v.

> Inasmuch as naturally we are but little inclined, or rather utterly careless, of these spiritual exercises, it will not be amiss if we restrain ourselves to prayer at certain hours of the day—not for superstition, but to withstand our sloth, slackness, and other worldly matters, which otherwise might induce us, to overslip diverse days, without any practice of this duty.[20]

The conclusion to the introduction is remarkable in what it tells us about Beza's personal life. Here we see his own estimation of the importance of prayer in his own life. And we also see how he ties prayer together with an individual's joy. Prayer leads to a joyful outlook on life. Finally, we see that Beza intended this manual to be used in church, in families, and in private devotions:

> Now therefore, gentle readers, feeling myself toward the declining evening of my days, with a taste of so many solid and permanent joys as are daily to be found in prayer. And withal being inflamed with a desire to finish the rest of my course in this sweet labor, which I find to be accompanied with so large a recompense, I have here formed for myself, and for any other that lift to read it, this small manual of holy, short, and familiar prayers, grounded upon the texts of scriptures, such as are indeed to instruct, comfort, and make us perfect in faith, love, constancy, and, to be short, in all Christian life. Be of good cheer then, all godly souls, and let us unite all our petitions in this so devout and profitable an exercise of all true faithful people. Let us pray, and meditate, if not incessantly, yet at the least daily at certain set hours, and as often as we may—as well in the congregation as in our families, morning and evening among our household, as also in our secret chambers.[21]

Since we cannot deal with all of Beza's prayers, we will look at four of them. These will provide us a window into Beza's

---

20. Beza, *Houshold Prayers*, B7v-B8r.
21. Beza, *Houshold Prayers*, B8r-B8v.

prayers in a wide variety of life's situations. We will look at his prayer 'for obtaining the knowledge of God in Jesus Christ.' After that, we will discuss his prayer 'that we may well use afflictions.' Then we will consider his prayer 'upon temporal death'. We will conclude with his prayer 'among the family'.

The Fifth Prayer: For obtaining the knowledge of God in Jesus Christ

Beza begins the prayer with four biblical references that will be the fuel for this prayer. He conflates and reflects on John 1, Colossians 1, Luke 2, and Hebrews 1 when he puts this as the heading to the prayer: 'The word was made flesh and dwelled among us, full of grace and truth, the image of the invisible God, which is Christ the Lord; who by himself having purged our sins sits at the right hand of the Majesty, in the highest places.'[22]

Beza begins the petition by acknowledging that a Christian's happiness can ultimately only come from knowing God and being convinced that He is gracious towards the believer: 'O God and Father of our Lord Christ Jesus, and of all them whom in your love you have given to him to be his brethren, it has been your good pleasure to settle our true and only happiness in the knowledge of your holy name and the effects of your grace.'[23] However, there is no way for a Christian to know this love of God except in and through the work of Jesus for him. Jesus' work and the salvation He procured for His own is the only means by which they may know God:

> But we are unable to know you or to feel the efficacy of your love towards us, except in the same Christ who is the brightness of your glory, and the engraved character of your person—God with you and man with us. By him, your eternal Word, you have created all the world, giving to us the first testimony of

---

22. Beza, *Houshold Prayers*, E3r.
23. Beza, *Houshold Prayers*, E3v.

the manifestation of your wisdom and providence. But you give to us a more singular benefit in the miraculous work of our redemption, which moreover represents to us both your great goodness and love, and your justice and infinite power. Your love—in that you have vouchsafed freely to redeem man who being proud and unthankful, withdraws himself from you his Father and benefactor to surrender himself to Satan the enemy of our salvation and of the honor of your name. Your justice—in that you have not spared the blood of your innocent Son, to the end in his sufferings to justify your goodness and mercy. Your power—in that for the accomplishing of this supernatural work, your Word, which from all eternity was resident in your bosom, of one essence and glory with you, was made flesh.[24]

Without Jesus Christ there are no Christians. He saves. And He mediates all the knowledge of God that Christians have.

There is always a tendency, though, for a believer to desire to know God apart from His chosen means, Christ. Beza eschews this, saying he won't be like Adam who coveted what was not his. Rather, God has given to Christians the gospel which allows them true access to God:

> Nevertheless I do very well know that the depth of these profound mysteries cannot be discovered to our senses, likewise that the treasures of your wisdom, of your counsel, and of your judgments, are a very bottomless gulf, and your ways impossible to be found out. Also, O Lord, I do not rashly enter into that place which is forbidden me; neither will I imitate my first father, Adam, who coveting to know too much stretched forth his hand to the forbidden tree, and desiring only one fruit, was deprived of all the rest. I do only with flexible heart embrace, and carefully in my cogitation, according to the measure of your gifts, meditate upon that secret of godliness, which I have received by the preaching of your gospel, and do in part know it. Until being delivered from

---

24. Beza, *Houshold Prayers*, E3v-E4v.

sin and corruption, I may see you face to face, and in presence behold that which now I see as it were in a very dark glass.[25]

Not only does Beza teach that true knowledge of God is mediated to believers through the gospel of Jesus alone. He also avers that God's Spirit must teach these truths to us, and he calls on the Spirit to do this work:

> I beseech you, therefore, my God, vouchsafe by the light of your Spirit to address and guide me to the faithful knowledge of this great Savior whom you, Father, have promised from the beginning and in the latter times revealed in signs and wonders surpassing all miracles. To the end that being instructed by his doctrine, I may by him and in him know you to be the eternal living God and the God of your people, so that according to his word I may worship and serve you in Spirit and truth. And in his name call upon you only in full confidence of your mercy, accounting him the only subject thereof, and the only Mediator of my salvation, who died for my sins and rose again for my righteousness.[26]

Knowing God then, according to Beza, is a work of the triune God as the Spirit works to grant the believer knowledge of Christ in the gospel which alone allows him to know God.

Next, Beza prays that the knowledge of Jesus would be his supreme treasure, as it was the treasure of the apostle Paul. A Christian may be tempted to want knowledge of any number of God's mysteries. He needs, however, to be disciplined to know God as He's chosen to reveal Himself in the gospel:

> Even, O Lord, because it pleased you in this manner to ordain of the estate of human nature, the work of your hand. For who was your counselor? And what do we have that we have

---

25. Beza, *Houshold Prayers*, E4v-E5v.
26. Beza, *Houshold Prayers*, 'The Fifth Prayer: For obtaining the knowledge of God in Jesus Christ,' n.p..

> not received? Grant me, therefore, in the study and mediation of so many mysteries, so high and so wholesome, that I may humbly condescend to your divine counsels in worshiping them with this resolution of your apostle, that I will not know anything but Christ, nor possess anything but him—because the treasures of all wisdom consist in him, and that they who lodge him in their hearts have you, O God, truly present and do enjoy you and your benefits.[27]

Significantly, here Beza broadens the benefits we have in the gospel from merely knowing God, as wonderful as that is. In the gospel, and through Jesus, Christians enjoy God and His benefits. We therefore pray that God will give us this joy of knowing Him and being satisfied by Him.

Beza concludes this prayer by meditating on the completed work of Christ on behalf of His people. Only He could free them from their sin and from Satan's power. He prays that remembrance of Christ's work for him would lead him to offer heart-felt thanks to God. And he prays that meditating on this truth would also give him assurance of God's love for him. Christ's obedience and righteousness are thus the great foundations of Beza's hope, the only things that can give him assurance of salvation and knowledge of God:

> Make me also to feel and confess this necessity common to all the children of Adam, that for the canceling of this obligation, which held us bound to eternal death—the just reward of sin—we were forced to have this great King of heaven—holy, innocent, and separate from all sinners—to be our High Priest, our sacrifice and oblation, upon the altar of the cross, to the end, O Lord, that according to your unsearchable decree—grounded on mercy and justice—your well-beloved Son having to himself united our nature the bond-slave of Satan, might lead it to the combat, directing it how to overcome this great adversary.

---

27. Beza, *Houshold Prayers*, 'The Fifth Prayer: For obtaining the knowledge of God in Jesus Christ,' n.p..

And this has he done, obtaining for us the victory, when he broke the sting of death, and the bonds of hell, and that he rose out of the tomb, carrying with him this human nature as the earnest of our hope, to your right hand into heaven. Let the remembrance of this singular benefit be always before my face, that I may offer to you, O my God, the sacrifice of thanksgiving all the days of my life. So that having my Redeemer for a perpetual object and sure foundation of my faith in the knowledge of your name, I may thoroughly learn Christ, not only to believe by his word the sacred history of his conception and birth, with his office of a sovereign King, great Prophet, and perpetual law-giver of his church, and his passion, death, resurrection, and ascension, but also that in full assurance of his promises, I may appropriate to myself the gifts and graces which he purchased for us by fulfilling that charge that he had received from you, O Father, to the end, through him to make us worthy of your salvation. So as I may comfort and wholly repose myself upon his obedience and righteousness, showing forth and sealing this my hope by good works to your glory, O eternal God and the peace of my conscience. So be it.[28]

At the outset of our study of Beza's prayers, then, we see how essential knowing Jesus is. In Him alone we have salvation. Through Him alone we know God. In knowing Him alone do we have joy.

The Fifteenth Prayer: That we may well use afflictions
This prayer reflects many of the themes Beza stressed in the introduction. Especially prominent is Beza's insistence that our earthly lives are transitory preparations for the greater and richer reality of being ushered into God's presence in heaven. Life may be difficult, but it will be short. In this prayer Beza especially reflects on the normalcy of suffering. We should

---

28. Beza, *Houshold Prayers*, 'The Fifth Prayer: For obtaining the knowledge of God in Jesus Christ,' n.p..

expect nothing less. But in Christ we can have hope that our afflictions are working for a more meaningful reality to come.

The texts Beza reflects on in this prayer are Matthew 16, Acts 14, and Hebrews 12. Putting them together, he makes the scriptural theme of this prayer 'If any man will follow me, let him forsake himself and take up his cross and follow me. By many tribulations we must enter into the Kingdom of heaven. He chastises him whom he loves and scourges every child that he receives.'[29]

He begins the prayer making the point that true followers of Jesus should expect nothing less than to suffer, especially since their Lord has called them to that vocation:

> O Lord, my God and my Father, I learn in your word that none are true disciples of Jesus Christ except those that follow his steps, whereof he has delivered us a sure mark in these two chief points—the renouncing of ourselves and the voluntary enduring of the cross. For naturally we are enticed with a disorderly love of ourselves and presume too much of our own persons. It is therefore necessary for us to renounce our own nature and reason, and to abandon our own affections, to suffer you and your love, O our God, to live and reign in us. Then must we proceed to the other point, that is, cheerfully to bear out the afflictions and miseries of this life, wherein it pleases you especially to exercise your own upon diverse good considerations, namely, to make them conformable to the image of your Son to the end that suffering with him they may also reign with him in glory.[30]

All of humanity suffers in this fallen world. But only Christians, taught by the Holy Spirit, are able to see that their sufferings have a purpose. Afflictions are meant to make them like Christ.

---

29. Beza, *Houshold Prayers*, 'The Fifteenth Prayer: That we may well use afflictions,' n.p..

30. Beza, *Houshold Prayers*, 'The Fifteenth Prayer: That we may well use afflictions,' n.p..

Specifically suffering creates holiness by purging the evil from within them:

> It is very truth that all men by sin do eat the fruits of the earth in labor and bread in the sweat of their brows; that they all live in a sea, tossed with many storms and crossed with many anguishes. But all do not have the gift of your Spirit, to learn by his doctrine that the bread of affliction nourishes and strengthens the faithful soul, that the cup of bitterness is thereunto a sweet and wholesome drink, and all tribulation a spiritual medicine to purge it from the leaven of sin and so to form every true Christian to godliness and holiness of life.[31]

Only Christians can embrace the paradox that God brings affliction in their lives in order to nourish and strengthen their souls.

Christians' great comfort lies in the knowledge that God brings about the afflictions they are undergoing. He brings hardships into their lives so their faith will increase. He especially causes difficulties to come into their experience in order to make them long for heaven, and to relish God's fatherly care for them in the midst of their trials.

> For indeed the many temptations your children endure are not properly a punishment for sin but are profitable corrections from your hand, to make the trial of their faith to redound to their commendation and profit. So that their hope may increase in the expectation of the blessedness to come, that their love may kindle through your fatherly care that you take of them, in holding them under the bridle of your discipline, and that they may be more pricked forward to pray to you fervently and more and more to reverence your power. But principally that they comfort themselves in this lesson of the apostle—that your easy afflictions, which do but pass over them, bring forth an eternal weight of most excellent glory.

---

31. Beza, *Houshold Prayers*, 'The Fifteenth Prayer: That we may well use afflictions,' n.p..

> It is true that by the miseries of this world the outward man declines; but on the other side the inward man renews himself with grace in the goods of the soul, so long until by degree he shall be accomplished and obtain his perfection. So that if our bodies languish our souls quicken; if we sustain loss of earthly things you, O Lord, present us your Kingdom of heaven; and if this affliction befalls that any man put us to death he only hastens our passage to the true eternal and blessed Being.[32]

Beza's eschatological vision is vividly portrayed here. Trials may come. But the worst thing that can come to us here—death—is actually the best. For death just quickens our passage to be with our Father in heaven.

Beza then gives us a key to enduring trials well. Christians need to beseech God to taste the fruits of His good care for them even in the afflictions. And they need to rely on God's goodness as a protection against fear when undergoing trials. God's perfect character is the answer to the struggles of this life:

> I beseech you therefore, O merciful Father, to give me grace to acknowledge and to taste well so many sweet and profitable fruits as your fatherly corrections bring with them; constantly meditating that the eyes of those who look to you in Christian hope never fail, that their experience has not confounded them, that the number of your consolations has surmounted their sorrows, and that the end of your visitation has always been profitable and happy to them. For you delight in mercy, and your compassion is on all those who call on you in their distress. Therefore let the invocation of your name be to me a strong tower, to defend me against all fear and temptation, since I am assured that having reposed my confidence in your grace which is purchased for me in Christ, I shall in my necessity find your favorable hand by your power to overcome all the enemies of my peace.[33]

---

32. Beza, *Houshold Prayers*, K1r-K2r.
33. Beza, *Houshold Prayers*, K2r-K3v.

Significantly, Beza doesn't pray that he would have understanding of all the purposes behind the disappointments and struggles of this life. Many things are, and will be, mysterious to Christians. However, there is a way forward. Believers should pray that God would give them trust in His providence, and a vibrant faith to believe that what He brings about in their lives is the design of their good Sovereign who only has their best interest at heart:

> Especially grant, O Lord, that I may attain to this reason of true wisdom, always to be content with your will, the sovereign and just cause of all things; namely, in that it pleases you, that the livery of your household should consist in carrying their cross after your Son, to the end that I should never but be seasoned to drink the wholesome myrrh which purges the soul from the lusts of the flesh and replenishes the same with the desires of eternal life. Also that I learn in whatever my estate, cheerfully to submit myself to the conduct of your providence, being well assured that whatever I suffer, all the crosses of my life shall be to me so many blessings and helps from you my Father to make me go the right way into your kingdom, and increase to me the price of glory in the same. For it is very true that everyone shall freely receive his reward according to the burden that he has borne here below. Amen.[34]

So Beza concludes his prayer for strength in the midst of afflictions where he began. Ultimately, Christians should take hope that God will bring His chosen children through the difficulties of life to a better, truer reality. Soon we will be free from the trials of this life because of Christ's work on our behalf. We will be with our Father in heaven very soon.

The Eighteenth Prayer: Upon temporal death

This prayer by Beza is remarkable in several ways. Surrounded by death the way he was, Beza does not sugar-coat the harsh

---

34. Beza, *Houshold Prayers*, K3r-K5r.

realities of life. He looks death straight on. But he doesn't blink. He's not afraid of death, and he doesn't want those who pray this prayer along with him to fear death either. Yet he does want them to use the prospect of death well. Only if they realize that temporal death presages eternal death will they use it as a Christian should. Only then will they put their trust in Jesus to be saved on the final day of judgment.

Beza's texts for reflection are Romans 6 and 1 Corinthians 15: 'Our life is but a vapor which appears but for a while and then vanishes away. For the reward of sin is death and the sting thereof is sin. But thanks be to God who has given us victory through our Lord Jesus Christ.'[35]

Beza commences the prayer by reflecting on the vast chasm that looms between us and God. He is eternal and boundless. We, by contrast, live for a short time according to the bounds God has set for us. Our stance towards the Lord should be one of humility in light of this:

> O eternal God, with whom a thousand years are as one day and one day as a thousand years, and whose diverse judgments are holy, just, and incomprehensible. Where is the man so gallant or proud, who thinking on the vanity and shortness of his life, does not easily assuage his pride and presumption, even to the end that he not extend his musings too far but keep them bounded within the limits of your law and refer them even to the good pleasure of your will?[36]

We must firmly grasp that we are limited creatures. Even the healthiest and strongest of us will live just a short time:

> The virtue of our fairest days is but affliction of mind and misery of our flesh. We fall as by a gushing of waters. We pass

---

35. Beza, *Houshold Prayers*, 'The Eighteenth Prayer: Upon temporal death,' n.p..

36. Beza, *Houshold Prayers*, 'The Eighteenth Prayer: Upon temporal death,' n.p..

away as a dream or a smoke. Our years consume like grass that withers from night to morning. And the longest time of our course—whereof sleep nibbles away a good part—is but three-score and ten years, or four-score for the strongest bodies, while in every moment of life, the nearest and smallest danger that threatens us, seems to be death, which as our shadow, follows us at the heels, and laughs at our good devices, until she has scattered them in the wind, and brought us into ashes.[37]

Once again, we see that Beza does not shrink from declaring how difficult life is. Our days on earth will be short. And those short days will be filled with hardship.

Even worse than that, though, is the reality of what awaits each of us after death. For we must each stand before God's judgment seat to receive from His hand for those things we have done in this life. A right awareness of this should lead us to fear—unless, of course, we are found in Jesus Christ, hoping in the redemption that He provides as the shield for God's wrath:

> But which is worse, where is the man, so holy and perfect, that does not tremble and quake, if there be represented unto him, O Lord, the tribunal seat of your sovereign justice, where we all, after death, must appear? Your indignation against sinners is manifest, and there is none righteous, your vengeance is ready against rebellion, whereof we be all guilty, which does also cause, that death is unto us, not only as a temporal ending as concerning the flesh, whereat nature is moved and abashed, but also an interior feeling of the curse fallen upon sin, yea even an entry into eternal death, unless there be for us with you, our Father, redemption in our Lord Jesus Christ.[38]

---

37. Beza, *Houshold Prayers*, 'The Eighteenth Prayer: Upon temporal death,' n.p..

38. Beza, *Houshold Prayers*, 'The Eighteenth Prayer: Upon temporal death,' n.p..

Yearning for God

With these realities in mind, Beza turns to the Lord, asking him to orient Beza's thinking about his life. Specifically he petitions God to give him a right perspective on the shortness of life and to use it as a means of mortifying his desires for ungodly things. Reflecting on death should allow Christians to live their lives now for God's glory:

> I beseech you therefore, my God, to give me grace to know how to meditate every day of my life upon this sentence of the Holy Ghost—that it is decreed that all men shall die once, and after that the judgment shall follow—to the end that while I creep up and down in this earthly mire, I suffer not myself to be deceived with the deceitful baits of the pleasures of this world, nor with the allurements of the devil who still seeks by his subtleties to race out of our hearts the remembrance of death in order to detain us in the thoughts of vanity and to entangle us in the snares of our lusts.[39]

Knowledge of eternal realities doesn't lead Beza to turn a blind eye to the realities of life. So he asks for the Lord to grant him some requests. He first asks God to allow him to grow in love with the life to come in heaven. The corresponding reality will be that life on earth with its sinful pleasures will seem less appealing:

> Grant me rather, O Lord, to know the villainess and bitterness of this miserable life, to the end that withdrawing my affection from mortal things I may be able to direct and stay myself in steadfast and eternal things. And also that thereby the remembrance of death may daily be to me as a trumpet to waken and call me to the pursuit of my life in the path of your truth. And to kindle in me a holy desire soon to depart out of the world, wherein the longer a man sojourns the more is he loaded with infernal merchandise—which is the filthiness of sin—and the more he cuts himself off from

---

39. Beza, *Houshold Prayers,* 'The Eighteenth Prayer: Upon temporal death,' n.p..

that portion of sovereign happiness which is in the life to come. Truly he who has most years has most iniquity, and he that crouches most in the mire of the world rots most. And therefore to the children of darkness the uncleanness of the flesh is a pleasant habitation. But to the children of light, to the immortal spirits, to the regenerate hearts, heaven is much more desirable.[40]

Secondly, Beza asks the Lord to allow him to live his life on earth in a cheerful manner, even though life is filled with difficulties. The reality of the joy of the life to come, and the certainty the Christian has that he will soon be there with his Father, should give him joy to sojourn here for a short time:

Grant therefore, my God, that as I daily grow towards my end, so I may live the more cheerfully, learning in your school, to prefer your eternal life, before the light of the Sun, the glory of heaven, before the vanity of the earth, the glorious habitation in paradise, before the painful tumults of the world, the society of angels, before the fellowship of mortal men, the only blessed and permanent life, before the passing shadow of this life, which is fruitful in anguishes, riots, and labors, the triumph before the combat, the present possession of sovereign good before the hope of enjoying.[41]

Specifically, Beza reflects on the reality of facing one's own death. We are struck again with his unflinching realism about the hardships all Christians must face. Knowing that the prospect of taking one's last breath can be ominous even for the strongest believer, Beza asks the Lord to uphold him with the knowledge that this is merely a transitory passing to a better life that is unending:

---

40. Beza, *Houshold Prayers*, 'The Eighteenth Prayer: Upon temporal death,' n.p..
41. Beza, *Houshold Prayers*, 'The Eighteenth Prayer: Upon temporal death,' n.p..

And that attending this haven of health I may know how to prepare myself by continual meditation in these excellent Christian consolations, that happy are they that die in the Lord for they rest from their labors. That death is to them no death, but a sleep in regard of their bodies. Then they are freed from the miseries of life. And that, as for the soul, which finds itself delivered from the tyranny of sin, it is to her a change to a better life. That this death is to all the faithful the time of receiving the garlands for their race and the crowns of their labors. That to them she is an acceptable issue of a laborious travail, their delivery from all terror and fear, and the steadfast accomplishment of their calling to happiness. Which made the apostle to say, 'Alas! wretched man that I am. Who shall deliver me from this body of death? I desire to be dissolved and to be with Christ.'[42]

Rather than filling Christians with anguish, the prospect of death may have the salutary effect of allowing them to realize they are going to be with the Lord. Seeing this, they can yearn for it.

Beza concludes the prayer reflecting again on how extremely difficult the prospect of death is for a Christian. The only remedy really is for the Holy Spirit to move in the believer's mind and heart and protect them from the onslaughts of the evil one who desires to paralyze God's people by the fear of death. Although Satan's wiles are great, Beza knows that the Spirit is more powerful than the evil one. So he asks God for the Spirit's work to be evident in the believer's life at the point of his death. Specifically, rather than allowing the accuser to mesmerize him with fear of the judgment due for his sin, Beza prays that God's Spirit will cause him to look to Christ in the hour of his death. Christ's righteousness alone will give believers the assurance of God's favor through this last fiery trial of life:

> Howbeit if not withstanding in the infirmity of my flesh the fearful image of death trouble me in the straits of my

---

42. Beza, *Houshold Prayers*, M1r-M1v.

departure, if the world always too much bewitches us, makes my thoughts then bow to his will. If Satan pitches his assaults and snares, and upon the remembrance of my sins sets hell before my face; moreover, if my own anxieties keep me from apprehending your eternal consolations in such most necessary extremities, vouchsafe, my good God and Father, in these anguishes to approach to me, to save me from the running and swift stream of such brooks, that they may not carry me away to perdition. Illuminate my thoughts with your Spirit, waken my soul out of the sleep of death, renew my heart by the virtue of your Spirit, and put into my hands the staff of your assured conduct, to bring me out from the labyrinth of this sorrowful passage, causing me, with the eyes of faith to behold my righteousness upon the cross of my Savior, the discharge of my debts in his sacrifice, my victory in his combats, my life in his death, my glory and joy in his resurrection. That so replenished with peace, I may cheerfully resign my body to the earth as assured that it shall rise again, and my soul to heaven with these last words of Christ ('Into your hands, O Father, I commit my spirit.') So be it.[43]

Theodore Beza was realistic about life's hardships and shortness. He was intransigent, however, in insisting that these realities could have the positive effect of moving Christians both to seek the Lord in the midst of their struggles and to yearn for heaven when all hardships would be removed. And in praying they would experience joy as the Lord met their needs.

The Twenty-second Prayer: Among the family
The final prayer we will note seems much less flashy than the previous one. After all, what could be more adrenalin-pumping than death? And what more benign than family relationships? Yet Beza's prayer for the family shows us his vision of the importance of praying for the eternal realities we've seen in his other petitions to be lodged deeply into the hearts of his family members.

---

43. Beza, *Houshold Prayers*, M1v-M3r.

Beza's texts for meditation are Psalm 18, Psalm 55, and Daniel 6: 'At noon, at night, and in the morning I will cry to God, and the Eternal shall deliver me. I will make a noise and he shall hear my voice, said David, and Daniel kneeled down three times a day in his house, prayed to, and magnified his God.'

Beza begins his prayer by magnifying God's goodness and glory. What an incredible honor it is for poor, depraved sinners to be able to enter into the presence of God:

> O Lord, our God and our Father, only great in glory and of infinite power. It has pleased you so far forth to honor men (poor worms of the earth) that they may in full confidence, in your love and bounty, present themselves before your face, to magnify your name. To talk of your beneficence, and to crave your mercy. We humbly beseech you therefore by your Spirit to dispose of our souls, our hearts, and our lips to glorify you, and so to call upon you, that our vows may be acceptable to you, and our prayers heard.[44]

Once again, Beza calls out to the Holy Spirit to aid believers. Their hearts and lips must be moved by God's Spirit to be able to offer up prayers pleasing to the Lord.

Not only are we sluggish in prayer, in need of the Spirit, but we are also deeply sinful, in need of forgiveness. So Beza next confesses the depths of his sin and rebellion to the Lord:

> We confess ourselves, in your presence, to be so great sinners that our unworthiness will not suffer us to look up unto heaven without fear that you should, in your just wrath, thunder upon us. Neither can we cast our eyes upon the earth, but we shall see as it were hell open for the reward of our wickedness. For we are, not only as the children of Adam, conceived and born in sin, worthy of your curse, but also, by our own faults, lusts, uncleanness, bad thoughts, and wicked works, whereunto through our corruption and frailty we do daily fall, which also

---

44. Beza, *Houshold Prayers*, 'The Twenty-second Prayer: Among the family,' n.p..

in consciences are so many witnesses to condemn us, and as it were heralds that do denounce unto us death and hell.[45]

God would be infinitely just to pour out His wrath on us for our rebellion in Adam, our continued rebellion, and the depravity of our lusts by which our consciences remind us of our deserved punishment.

But like Paul's miraculous adversative conjunctions in Romans 3:21 ('but now') and Ephesians 2:4 ('but God'), Beza introduces an adversative that leads to the glorious truth of the gospel. So having recounted his sin, he now turns to God's grace which exceeds our sin and allows us, through Christ, to come into His presence. Our hope is in Christ, whom God has given to us and for us:

> But, O Lord, your mercies do infinitely exceed our malice, and your eternal compassions, are upon sinners that convert and turn to you. You are that pitiful Father who gladly received his prodigal and unthrifty son, that loving shepherd who carefully seeks the lost sheep, that charitable physician who freely comes to the sick to cure them. We therefore—the children of your love, the sheep of your fold, and the poor in spirit—do most humbly beseech you in the name of your well-beloved Son, our Mediator Jesus Christ, to vouchsafe to take away all our calamities in pardoning our sins because you have given us this great Savior in the world, to the end that whosoever believes in him should not perish but have life everlasting. We are baptized in his name; we have received his gospel; and he gives us his body in your church for spiritual food, that we may live in him, and of him be forever blessed.[46]

It's the gospel of Jesus Christ, then, that grounds the believer's confidence that he can turn to the Lord—even in his sin—

---

45. Beza, *Houshold Prayers*, 'The Twenty-second Prayer: Among the family,' n.p..

46. Beza, *Houshold Prayers*, O1r-O2r.

and find a gracious God. Jesus is the Savior of the world and His death is of such merit, according to Beza as he quotes John 3:16, that whoever believes in Him will not perish but have everlasting life.

With this gospel foundation secure, Beza now turns to the Lord with requests. He asks, first of all, that God would graciously allow us to understand the tremendous benefits Christ has given us through His cross work: 'Give us grace, therefore, O our God, with a true and lively faith upheld by hope and doing every good work, to apprehend to the glory of your name, and the peace of our souls, these great benefits that are purchased for us in the death and passion of our same redeemer, that we may incessantly yield praise to you, and live in holiness according to your word.'[47]

Our problem is that we continue to struggle with our own sin, and we are also plagued by the assaults of the evil one. So Beza turns now to these twin ideas, asking our Father to strengthen us against the assaults of both our own flesh and Satan's schemes:

> For the performance hereof vouchsafe to increase the gifts of your Spirit in our hearts whereby the desires of the flesh, and vanities of the world, may be mortified and the pure fire of your love so kindled, that we may love, honor, and serve you with all our souls, with all our strengths, and with all our minds, and loving our neighbors as ourselves, to pleasure them in all duties of love to your power.
>
> Strengthen us likewise with your power, O almighty God, against the temptations and assaults of Satan, delivering us victoriously, preserving us also from such dangers and miseries, as everywhere follow us at the heels in this life. And above all, giving us grace in whatsoever estate we be, still to be content with your will, which can never be other than good and just and profitable to us, because we are of the number of your children.[48]

---

47. Beza, *Houshold Prayers*, O2r-O2v.
48. Beza, *Houshold Prayers*, O2v-O3v.

Once again, it's the power of God made manifest through the Spirit's presence and work that Beza counts on to mediate the peace purchased by Christ on the cross.

This is very significant for Beza. He is now going to turn to prayer for the family and its different members. But several times he will come back to the gospel as the only hope he has in praying and as the only hope any family members have, for in the gospel God's righteousness meets God's love. Because of Christ's death for sinners God is able to be both the just and the one who justifies those who believe in Jesus.

Beza's first request for the family is that all its members will be content with the calling the Lord has for their lives. Even though these callings may be hard, and since life will certainly be filled with trials, Beza asks the Lord to remind all the family members of the shortness of this pilgrimage and the reality of the life to come. Indeed, this is the principal calling of all Christians:

> So let your peace be in us and upon all the works of our hands that we may happily pass the rest of our days, every one of us walking in his family, in the duty of our vocation, in a good conscience, as before your face, to whom nothing is hid. And meditating diligently on the shortness and afflictions of this our life, that we may so advance you and finally end in the wisdom of true Christians. Whereby we may principally learn to desire heaven, and patiently to take all human crosses, and whatever may seem to us most grievous to the flesh, knowing that all things shall turn to our good, always provided that constantly we persevere in your service, for so shall we live and die with Christ, that we may enter into his joys in heaven, there to behold his glory.[49]

Next Beza prays for God's spiritual blessings to be on all people. He first of all asks the Lord to be good to those who don't yet know Jesus. His desire is that those outside of the kingdom would hear the gospel and come to embrace Christ.

---

49. Beza, *Houshold Prayers*, O3v-O4v.

And he prays for Christians, that they would grow in the grace and knowledge of Christ:

> Furthermore, howsoever unworthy sinners we are, yet O Lord, inasmuch as you have commanded us to pray one for another, to the advancement of your Kingdom, we pray to you for all men, that it may please you so to work that those who as yet do not have the knowledge of your holy gospel may, by its preaching and by the illumination of your Holy Spirit, be brought to know you, the only and true God, and him whom you have sent, Jesus Christ, to save the world. Also that those whom you have already visited with this grace, as ourselves, may daily increase in your spiritual blessings. So that all together we may worship you with heart and mouth in one Spirit, one faith, and one baptism.[50]

Then Beza turns to different types of people, asking the Lord's blessing on them. Specifically he asks the Lord to bless them for the sake of the family, so that family members may receive the blessings God intends them to receive from them. First, then, he asks God's blessing on magistrates:

> And since you have also ordained governments and callings, so that all people may be governed in the fear of your name and to common commodity we beseech you to inspire, guide, and bless our Queen and all princes, magistrates, and superiors, that have the government of your sword on earth, that every of them reigning in godliness and righteousness, may employ your power which they hold from you, to cause you to be served and honored, and to the tranquility, peace, and relief of their subjects, wholly submitting themselves and their people to your holy word.[51]

Then, he prays for the pastors of the church, that God would strengthen and use them for the good of all the members of the church:

---

50. Beza, *Houshold Prayers*, O4v-O5r.
51. Beza, *Houshold Prayers*, O5r-O5v.

> Likewise, for the publishing of your word in all places, vouchsafe more and more with your gifts to enrich the pastors and doctors of your church, and daily to raise up more to execute in a good conscience their charge, to the edification and perfection of your holy temple, whereof in general, O Lord, and of every faithful, vouchsafe to show yourself the Almighty protector, to the confusion of all the adversaries of the name of Christ and of his holy church.[52]

Having prayed for the church's leaders, Beza then thinks of those within the family who are undergoing hardship, either physical or spiritual. He concludes by praying the Lord's Prayer on their behalf:

> We also pray you for all those whom you visit with tribulation, whether it be sickness of body, or anguish of soul, that you, O merciful Father, vouchsafe to give them comfort and patience, to the bearing of their calamities, and deliverance from their afflictions. Asking all these things of you in the name of your Son, our Mediator, and as he has taught us to pray, *Our Father which art in heaven, etc.*[53]

Beza concludes this prayer by praying that those within the family may be conformed in mind and heart to the faith of the church. He desires that they understand the faith the church teaches. In this regard, Beza prays through the Apostles' Creed ('I believe in God, the Father Almighty'), desiring that all family members understand the historic faith of the church. Flowing from that, he prays through the ten commandments, asking the Father to conform the family's members to the Lord's faith, asking that they may be obedient to do what the Lord requires of them:

---

52. Beza, *Houshold Prayers*, 'The Twenty-second Prayer: Among the family,' n.p..

53. Beza, *Houshold Prayers*, 'The Twenty-second Prayer: Among the family,' n.p..

Yearning for God

We also beseech you, O Lord, to increase and confirm us in the catholic faith of your church, to the end that it may take lively root in our souls to fructify to all righteousness and good works. And that even to our last gasp we may make like confession thereof, as we do now both with heart and mouth. (*I believe in God, the Father Almighty, etc.*) And because the faith of your children, O Lord, is inseparable from the obedience due to your word, especially in the ten commandments of the law, and that you ordain that we should have them perpetually in our hearts and mouths, to keep them and to teach them to our families, give us grace to our powers, to conform ourselves to the same, even as we understand that they were delivered from your mouth, saying…

[Here he lists the Ten Commandments]

And the sum of all these commandments is this: that we love you, O Lord, with all our hearts and with all our minds and our neighbors as ourselves. Your blessing therefore, O our God and Father, with the peace of our Lord Jesus, and the comfort of the Holy Ghost, be thus given to us by your grace, and remain with us forever. Amen.[54]

Application

At least four uses flow from this survey of Theodore Beza's prayers. We see, in the first place, that Beza was much more than just an academic, philosophically-oriented logician. Even though this is a common picture of the man, it just doesn't cohere with reality, in this case the reality of Beza's varied prayers. Scott Manetsch is surely correct in his assessment of one of the values of these prayers. This book of prayers, he avers,

> suggests the need to reassess the common portrayal of the reformer's theology and theological method as unduly speculative and rationalistic. At least in these prayers, we discover a profoundly experiential and pastoral side to his

---

54. Beza, *Houshold Prayers*, 'The Twenty-second Prayer: Among the family,' n.p..

theology, a concern to bring the truth of God's Word to people beginning a new day, eating at table, suffering illness, preparing to die. Here we find theology that is intended not only to instruct, but also to comfort and edify. The practical devotional quality of the *Houshold Prayers* should cause scholars to pause before they dismiss Theodore Beza's theology as being merely 'metaphysical' or 'scholastic'.[55]

In the second place, we see how varied Beza's prayers were. For his own personal and family's uses, he wrote out twenty-eight prayers for different occasions. This should challenge us in our relative prayerlessness. How often do we pray? How similar are all our prayers? Do we really see our need for prayer? Beza was convinced that on several normal occasions of the Christian's life, he should pray. May we be spurred on to do likewise.

And may we, in the third place, especially have our visions expanded to look beyond just the immediate needs of life. Of course, these matter. And so we should bring them to our heavenly Father. But don't they often dominate our prayers? In the process, don't we often lose sight of eternal reality as we pray? May Beza's emphasis on the dawning day of eternity fill our prayers more and more. In the process, may the Lord help us to filter the trials of life through the lens of eternity. We would be firmer and more mature if we did. We would be better able to withstand the pressures of life and the attacks of the evil one. May the Lord grant us a biblical perspective while we pray.

Finally, we can follow a biblical injunction by seeking to emulate Beza in his praying. On many occasions, the Apostle Paul called on the churches to imitate him in how he lived the Christian life (for example, 1 Cor. 4:15-16; 11:1; Phil. 3:17). We need guides to show us what it means to be Christians. Of course, we are to follow the apostles. And we are to follow those who are more mature in Christ in our churches. As a

---

55. Manetsch, 'A Mystery Solved?,' p. 288.

baby learns to talk by imitating his parents' words, and as a new Christian often learns to pray by listening to more mature believers, so may we listen to our elder brother, Theodore Beza. By listening in on his prayers, may we imitate his praying, to the glory of our God.

Uses

I have used Theodore Beza, *Maister Bezaes Houshold Prayers*, translated by John Barnes (London: John Barnes, 1603). It is available at *Early English Books Online* (eebo.chadwyck.com).

1. What do you think are your greatest hindrances to praying more fervently and effectively? What in this chapter has helped your situation the most?

2. Do you ever write out your prayers? How could Beza's written prayers serve as a model for you? With this in mind, spend time writing out a prayer you might use on one of the occasions Beza mentions.

3. Reflect on the way in which your reliance upon the finished work of Jesus Christ on the cross for you should influence your praying. How can Beza help you in this regard?

4. Do you know that your life is short and that you will soon face the judgment seat of Christ (2 Cor. 5:10)? Are you prepared for this? Use Beza's prayers as helps to meditate on the life to come.

9

Conclusion

On the grounds of the University of Geneva stands an interesting wall. Usually known as 'the Reformation Wall', it's famous for its statuary. Stretching over a hundred meters it includes several key figures of Protestantism. Right at the middle of the wall, set apart by their fifteen-foot height are four figures—William Farel, John Calvin, Theodore Beza, and John Knox. Below them is Geneva's motto, *post tenebras lux*, 'after darkness, light'. What this wall represents is appropriate for us to reflect on as we conclude this study.

Calvin and Beza are side by side in this exhibit. This is just as it should be, since they considered themselves co-laborers in the cause of Protestantism, as we have seen. Calvin is a bit taller than Beza (perhaps not as in real life), appropriately, I think, portraying that Calvin was the more senior, the groundbreaker, the founder of the movement that spread out from Geneva. Beza was his supporter, his understudy, the one who took over when Calvin's labors were ended. Beza saw himself as Calvin's successor, not deviating from his mentor. We have seen indications of that too.

Two other facets of the wall interest us. We notice, first, that it's appropriately on the grounds of the University, the very sight of the Academy which Calvin founded and which Beza served as its first rector. The two were united in their labors, teaching students preparing for pastoral ministry. Beza, of course, did so longer than Calvin. But it had always been

Calvin's desire. So Beza, again, was his protégé and heir. Second, reflecting on Geneva's motto (*post tenebras lux*) reminds us that Beza and Calvin were united in their Protestantism. As we have seen, this means that they were united in their belief in, their holding for dear life on to, and their proclamation of the gospel. The gospel was central in all Calvin's labors. The survey of Beza's works that we've just completed has crystallized the reality that the gospel was also central to all of his labors. The two were united in proclaiming the gospel.

Theodore Beza loved the gospel. He loved it because he believed that it was God's chosen means of saving lost, hopeless sinners like him. He loved it because it vividly portrayed both the justice and the mercy of God. He loved it because in receiving the Christ of the gospel Beza both had life and had a vibrant relationship with the living God. He loved it because it was God's ordained means of keeping Beza in the faith through the turmoils of life and of bringing him to be with his heavenly Father for all of eternity. May his love for the gospel—and the God of the gospel—result in our having greater love for our God too.

So, Theodore Beza? Who is he?

Well, now you know a good bit about him. As you reflect on his life and thought, remember that he was a frail man like you and I are. He was wrong at times. (I, for one, don't always agree with him.) He struggled and doubted the Lord's goodness at other times. But his goal was to know God and serve God's people on the path to eternity. You now know quite a bit that separates Theodore Beza the man from Theodore Beza the myth. May the Lord give you strength, joy, and perseverance as you walk through this life as a pilgrim on your way to be with Him forever. Hopefully, Beza will inspire you on the way.